Cities and Plans

Cities and Plans

The shaping of urban Britain in the nineteenth and twentieth centuries

Gordon E. Cherry

Professor of Urban and
Regional Planning
Head of Department of Geography,
University of Birmingham

Edward Arnold
A division of Hodder & Stoughton
LONDON   NEW YORK   MELBOURNE   AUCKLAND

© 1988 Gordon E Cherry

First published in Great Britain 1988

Distributed in the USA by Routledge, Chapman and Hall, Inc
29 West 35th Street, New York, NY10001

British Library Cataloguing Publication Data

Cherry, Gordon E. (Gordon Emanuel), 1931–
   Cities and plans : the shaping of urban
   Britain in the nineteenth and twentieth centuries
   1. Great Britain, urban development,
   1800–1985
   I. Title
   307'14'0941

   ISBN 0–7131–6562–6

Typeset in 10/11 pt Mallard Compugraphic by Colset Private
Limited, Singapore
Printed and bound in Great Britain for Edward Arnold, the
educational, academic and medical publishing division of
Hodder and Stoughton Limited, 41 Bedford Square,
London WC1B 3DQ by Richard Clay plc, Bungay, Suffolk

To
the
memory
of
E.C.,   N.C.,   T.L.C.,   L.V.R.C.

Contents

Acknowledgements

This book is not based on original work. It is synoptic, and as an overview it is heavily dependent on a range of secondary sources. It presents a story in a particular way and has a perspective and interpretation of its own, but a good deal of hard work has been done elsewhere; it is to a large number of earlier workers, therefore, that I am so much indebted. It has been a pleasure to draw on the writings of so many people, not all of whom are listed in the Bibliography; after a while one's own work and theirs become fused, but that is no reason to fail to acknowledge the individual product of so much endeavour in the field of cities and plans over the last two centuries.

For the last fifteen years or so it has been a particular privilege to have rubbed academic shoulders with large numbers of people working in planning history. The Planning History Group has put me in touch with an international network. With my co-editor, Professor Anthony Sutcliffe, first with Mansell's series, Studies in History, Planning and the Environment, and then with the journal *Planning Perspectives*, I have been agreeably exposed to the work of other scholars who have contributed so much new understanding to the interlocking processes of planning and urban change. To them all, I acknowledge a debt of gratitude for their own insights which I have unashamedly used to reassemble for a viewpoint of my own.

When it came to the task of producing a manuscript, cheerful and willing helpers were at hand. I am grateful to all those who have typed for me: Gretchel Coldicott, Janice Rawlinson and Irma Schweggler, but especially Claire Fothergill, who bore the brunt of it all. I thank Geoffrey Dowling for expert help with the illustrations, and my wife for the index.

One's home life is disrupted in a task of this kind, but, as ever, Margaret has been tolerance personified. If I say 'never again', I don't suppose she will believe me, and I am grateful to her for that.

Gordon E. Cherry
Department of Geography
University of Birmingham
January 1988

List of Illustrations

The author and Publishers wish to thank the copyright holders mentioned above for permission to reproduce material. Every effort has been made to trace copyright holders of material published in this book and any rights not acknowledged here will be acknowledged in subsequent printings if notice is given to the publisher.

1 Ideal Cities and Social Utopias

One feature of the British industrial city is the way in which it has been progressively shaped and regulated, and the various component parts controlled by public authorities, over the last two centuries. The ensuing chapters chart the story over a 150-year span from the 1830s to the 1980s. The relationship between city form and structure on the one hand, and the plans or regulations prepared for the urban environment on the other, is the principal theme to be explored.

In the twentieth century, town planning has constituted the main activity through which the State, both local and central, has sought to exercise its plan-making role and impose its control function. In the previous century public officials had already begun to take steps to regulate the urban environment, first of all with regard to health and housing. The measures characteristic of the two centuries are very different, but they are bound by common threads of continuity; one of them at least was local government, as, strengthened by ever-additional powers, it became a key agent of change in regulating the location and character of urban growth.

The chapters which follow, then, describe the steps taken in the public regulation of the industrial and (recently) the post-industrial city: from by-laws to town planning in its many changing forms over a century and a half. The story aims to be synoptic and wide ranging; each particular phase could be amplified in detail, such is the volume of material available, but a comprehensive overview is the primary objective, and makes a contribution to planning history in those terms. The dynamics of urban change in the nineteenth and twentieth centuries are reviewed and placed against the set of measures taken to deal with the various environmental and related problems, which from time to time assumed importance as issues to be addressed. The account is therefore set in the context of societal change (values, politics, governance, economics, demography and technology), and offers explanations as to how and why the direction of urban regulation has taken its particular course.

But the context can be drawn even more widely, because we should regard the events of the last two centuries as a period of 'town building', in a process which has extended over a considerable time-span. I have noted elsewhere that recent developments in town planning have rested on two main antecedents: 'One is a concern for urban form and the search for the ideal city in architectural terms; the other is the search for the ideal community' (Cherry, 1970).)The same point, this time suggesting an inner tension, has been made by Barnett (1987) who notes 'a long struggle in western civilization between attempts to design cities and the relatively intractable social and economic forces that make city design so difficult to achieve'.

There is a rich literature from urban and architectural history and from historical geography to demonstrate not only that throughout history have cities been important in the rise of civilizations, but also that they have been consciously regulated and designed (Haverfield, 1913; Smailes, 1953; Hiorns, 1956; Rosenau, 1959; Mumford, 1961; Morris, 1972; Carter, 1983; Barnett, 1987). The etymological relationship between 'cities' and 'civilization' is significant: in world history all major civilizations have been urban based, with cities housing their cultural and artistic splendours. In the founding and development of these cities we see two repetitive themes: the designers' promise of the ideal city and the social reformers' drive to establish the ideal community. In nineteenth- and twentieth-century Britain both these imperatives have been met in a variety of different ways. Taking the long view it is remarkable that forms of environmental regulation in our recent past have shared so many of the characteristics from two millennia, particularly from a common set of European traditions. This chapter highlights this wider context and serves as an introduction to the main story which follows.

Ideal cities

Across time and across cultures, city building has been treated as an art form, with conscious layout and applied design. Twentieth-century town planning, at least, shares that one aspect of an urban past: design and purposive layout for artistic merit. A generation of civic designers in post-war Britain has been engaged in an activity as old as towns themselves. The environmental limitations of British towns and cities in the nineteenth century prompted a corrective, expressed by successive designers keen to give to the society of their day the quality of urban conditions they considered necessary. British twentieth-century town planning from this point of view fits into a world model; it is not exceptional, rather it conforms to a historical pattern in which, from time to time, creative design 'explosions' have punctuated the chronology.

We can begin with the first urban revolution along the fertile riverine lands of the Nile, Euphrates and Indus, where the early towns had a particular form, often in a rectangluar shape, showing a conscious concern for orderly layout. The underlying pattern was a square where buildings and spaces perhaps suggested some expression of an unchanging cosmic order. The Ancient Greek tradition embraced both the square and the circle, though the chequer-board type of layout was the most common, as in the cities laid out by Hippodamus of Miletus, about 450 BC. Athens itself was untouched by town planning, though its port Piraeus was, and we have to turn to the later Macedonian period to see one of the best examples in

Priene, on the east coast of the Aegean. Rectilinear layouts were also very much the hallmark of the Roman towns, the gridiron pattern characteristic of *coloniae* throughout the Mediterranean world and beyond. The architect Vitruvius emphasized formal layouts in town building. Meanwhile the Jewish tradition emphasized the importance of the temple in any city representation. It all meant, however, that Greek, Roman and Jewish influences were felt in Europe during the Middle Ages in the figurative representation of cities.

Urban layout, both formal and symbolic, therefore possessed these unifying features in the Christendom of Europe. Remarkably, however, one can also look at other urban civilizations elsewhere in the world over these centuries and detect ample evidence of conscious regulation, with formal street systems and the design of space. In Central America the Mayas colonized Yucatan after the fourth century AD and have left the remains of well-organized towns, as too did the civilization of the Incas in South America. China, substantially free from extraneous influences, still produced Peking with its formal composition. In Japan, Kyoto, capital for 1100 years after AD 793, was laid out on rectangular lines. Returning to Europe, the genius of Moorish planning laid out Granada in Spain.

The survival and continuity of traditions in layout and design is striking. In Christian Europe the monastic centres of early medieval learning maintained the classical forms; monasteries replaced cities and at St Gall, preserved in the monastery, there is an outstanding example (c. 818) of an ideal site-plan with a basic rectangularity. But the New Towns (*bastides*) of the thirteenth century in France and England form the clearest examples of the continuity in the coordinated street pattern, regular building plots, market squares and planned enclosures.

The European Renaissance gave the practice of town design a considerable fillip, first through the work of Alberti and Averlino (who adopted the Greek name of Filarete, 'lover of virtue', and was responsible for the design of the fictitious city Sforzinda) in the fifteenth century, and later, in the sixteenth century by Scamozzi, who himself laid down rules for the planning of the ideal city. Palmanova, the fortress city for Venice begun in 1593, was inspired by both Filarete and Scamozzi. But it is in the Rome of Pope Sixtus V that we see the first comprehensive replanning of a city; between 1585 and 1590 his architect Fontana imposed a succession of long, straight streets, with changes of directions marked by piazzas punctuated by central obelisks.

The Mannerist phase of the Renaissance led to the Baroque age and the monumental cities of grand-manner style of dignified order and symmetry. Wren's plan for London would have created a complete Renaissance city with straight avenues and plazas, but it involved such a complex exchange of property that it was never carried out. But the city square gradually replaced the emphasis on the street pattern, as witnessed in Covent Garden and the planned western extension of London, a feature later exported to America, where it made its appearance in Philadelphia and the tidewater settlements along the eastern seaboard.

Regular geometry reappeared in another guise in the fortified European cities of the mid-seventeenth century. The star-shaped fortifications closely resembled the star-figured diagrams of the early theorists of ideal cities. The design for Karlsruhe in the eighteenth century is one of the best examples of a mercantile city clashing in its layout with the dictates of an autocrat's avenues radiating from a central palace. A rather similar feature is shown in L'Enfant's plan for Washington. Major Pierre Charles L'Enfant had come from France to enlist in Washington's army in 1777 and after the war was selected by Washington to prepare plans for the new capital; subsequently dismissed and in conflict with Jefferson and his grid plan, nonetheless L'Enfant's basic plan was successful, drawing on all the traditions from Sixtus V and Wren.

Britain at this time, and into the nineteenth century, provided ample evidence of a strong urban design tradition. John Wood's work at Bath at first followed the pattern already established in London, namely the street and square, but the Circus begun in 1754, was a novel architectural concept. John Wood the younger completed the innovation with the Royal Crescent. Indeed the circus and crescent proved highly influential in fashionable development over the next century, as for example in James Craig's designs for Edinburgh New Town.

By comparison, nineteenth-century urban design in Britain had few major developments to record. John Nash's design for Regent Street, London, successfully linked a number of points between Carlton House (the Prince Regent's residence) and Regent's Park to provide an irregular line of new streets on the western edge of the capital. In Newcastle 20 years later John Dobson fashioned a basic plan for a new centre, but beyond that there was remarkably little by way of coordinated urban development or surgery, merely piecemeal new thoroughfares, here and there. How different it was in Paris, where Napoleon III's Préfect of the Seine, the energetic administrator Georges-Eugène Haussmann, over a period of 17 years transformed the French capital with new streets and building, utilizing again the concept of the long, straight city street as the main instrument.

From Haussmann and monumentalism we pass to the American city-beautiful movement at the end of the nineteenth century, first coming to prominence at the World's Columbian Exposition in Chicago, 1893. The coordinating architect, Daniel Burnham, became a national figure and his Chicago Plan, published in 1909, became the critical document of the city-beautiful movement, so influential in America up to the depression years of the 1930s. The combination of a monumental centre, placed in essentially a garden city, had echoes in the design for Canberra (Walter Burley Griffin, 1912) and New Delhi (Edwin Lutyens, 1913).

The tradition swung to a preference for picturesque architectural compositions, first led by Camillo Sitte in *City building according to artistic principles* (1889), a critique of Haussmannesque planning. The British garden city and garden suburb proved a powerful influence of international significance, combining two features: a strategic model for metropolitan growth (Howard's Social City), and residential architecture and informal layout for neighbourhoods which broke away from the more usual conventions of the industrial city. Picturesque suburban villadom had certainly been an aspect of nineteenth-century towns, but Raymond Unwin and others introduced it as a mass feature, setting in motion a century-long trend.

By comparison, the modern movement in architecture made very different statements about the modern city, its function and appearance. Tony Garnier, an architect from Lyons, presented designs between 1901 and 1917 for the *Cité Industrielle*, but it was Le Corbusier's drawings of a contemporary city for 3 million people, shown at the Paris Salon d'Automne in 1922, which effectively broke from the past. He went on to apply his ideas to central Paris in the Voisin Plan, exhibited in 1925; the old fabric of the city was obliterated by a scheme containing skyscrapers and a highway driven through the heart; just Notre Dame and the Louvre survived. Meanwhile German architecture emphasized the use of industrial material, particularly steel and concrete; and new styles of mass housing development appeared at, for example, Stuttgart (the Weissenhof Housing Settlement), Frankfurt (Ernst May) and, under the influence of the Bauhaus and Walter Gropius, Dessau. Internationally the Congrès Internationaux d'Architecture Moderne (CIAM) brought together leading modernist architects, and principles of city planning were laid down. In Britain these flowered briefly under the Modern Architectural Research Group (MARS); its revolutionary plan for London centred on massive highway corridors with linear residential districts separated by green spaces.

The modernist city remained broadly in the ascendant and it maintained its strength until about the 1960s, but uncertainly thereafter. The post-war city, and particularly the redeveloped city in Europe, displayed all the familiar features, though variously country by country. In Sweden the new business centre for Stockholm and the new planned suburbs (Vällingby was to become famous) set early models in the early 1950s. Le Corbusier's Marseilles apartment house, the Unité d'Habitation, as a prototype, proved influential. In Britain the rebuilding of East London, the reconstruction of Coventry (particularly, of all bombed cities) and residential design in New Towns and elsewhere reflected a dominant pattern. World-wide, influences radiated from particular projects: the plans for Chandigarh and Brasilia are but examples.

A reaction against aspects of these developments appeared in the 1960s and gathered force in the 1970s. A renewed interest in preservation of the historic past and a combination of the environmental movement and community architecture has since created a demand for small-scale projects. The mega-structures of the modern movements, as reflected in Newcastle's Byker Wall or Sheffield's Park Hill, or in individual tower blocks and complexes throughout Britain, did not fit the resurgence of individualism and the search for community involvement in the creation of an environment of more personal appeal.

All this is highly selective and over-condensed, but its purpose is to be illustrative of two important points. One is that cities have been subject throughout man's history, in all cultures, to the hand of conscious design. Britain in the nineteenth and twentieth centuries is no exception; through processes ranging from piecemeal urban management and comprehensive town design, attempts have been made to impart a style, a form and an appearance. (This century we have called that process town planning; plans have been prepared and schemes implemented for cities of convenience, beauty and health. The second point is that architectural and design phases change over time because of fluctuations in fashion, taste, patronage and power, and adjustments to economics and technology. Again, the British experience has been no exception, though during this century Britain itself became a dominant influence for forms of residential architecture and suburban layout and design, which it exported to the rest of the world. By comparison, Britain for long remained largely untouched by the modern movement, though post-war development has featured all the main characteristics.

Social utopias

The second repetitive theme in town building is a capacity to incorporate a concern for social purpose and community organization. Throughout history town builders have founded settlements, or given purpose to existing settlements, according to particular assumptions: economic (trading), military, religious, and also social. In our present century, for example, the British New Town has had an explicit social role, being conceived as a small, balanced community in a setting designed for cohesive, interactive living. Human history is studded with examples of this idealism expressed as ideal communities. British town planning fell heir to this tradition in the twentieth century.

In past centuries, just as in the present, communities have been founded to proclaim a particular religious, moral or social purpose. These include monastic settlements, Jewish *kibbutzim*, and hippy communities in California. Sometimes urban features have been changed with the introduction of a new religious order: for example, up to the fifteenth century Constantinople was a Byzantine city, a polyglot of ethnic neighbourhoods, but after 1453 the Muslim city developed under Islamic social and religious codes.

Perhaps the most sustained settlement pattern which declared a religious purpose is that given by Mormon-founded towns in the USA. During the first half of the nineteenth century the Mormons established well over 500 towns throughout the Great Central Basin after the Church of Christ (later the Church of Jesus Christ of Latter-Day Saints) was founded by Joseph Smith and others in 1830. Missionaries spread west and founded settlements, all carefully laid out with rectilinear plans, wide streets and central positions for churches. Brigham Young led the pilgrimage of Mormons westward, assuming Church leadership in 1844. At that time Nauvoo had a population of 11,000, but the great migration continued to Utah, where the location of the Mormon Kingdom was decided upon. The settlement pattern for the State of Utah was then laid out, with Salt Lake City the most impressive of all the communities in a strip of semi-arid land converted to productive farming and grazing.

Britain has no such large-scale example, though the Protestant Plantations in Ireland in the seventeenth century offer a parallel. Neither does Britain exemplify the political idealism expressed in ideal communities seen in other countries, with life structured according to political tenets, which usually imply explicit central organization. In this experience particular communities are tightly controlled by State bureaucracies. In the twentieth century, settlements founded in China or Cambodia exemplify these characteristics. In a more modest way the rigid planning of socialist cities, particularly in the Soviet Union has followed scientific principles based on the dominant party ideology. The critical features include explicit control over city size (an internal passport system ostensibly determining where people might live); state control over new housing – its location, size and standards; a system of spatial equality in the allocation of consumer and cultural services; and the design of the central city, to provide massive open spaces necessary for public displays and demonstrations.

Settlements founded and subsequently designed in such a way that their communities reflect the apparatus of State power, have not been a feature of British urban history. But other communities dictated by 'ideal' principles have been widely represented in Britain, with considerable significance for twentieth-century perspectives on urban development.

The keyword is 'utopia' from the book of that title by Thomas More, published in 1518. In using an imaginary narrator to discover the island of Utopia and describe its appearance and social organization, he offered a satire on the world of his day – a typical literary device to draw attention to contemporary shortcomings, in keeping subsequently with Swift's *Gulliver's Travels*, or some works of science fiction. Utopia was described:

> There are fifty-four splendid big towns on the island, all with the same language, laws, customs, and institutions. They're all built on the same plan, and, so far as sites will allow, they all look exactly alike. The minimum distance is twenty-four miles, and the maximum, no more than a day's walk . . .
>
> At regular intervals all over the countryside there are houses supplied with agricultural equipment, and town dwellers take it in turns to go and live in them. Each house accommodates at least forty adults, plus two slaves who are permanently attached to it, and is run by a reliable, elderly married couple, under the supervision of a District Controller, who's responsible for thirty such houses. Each year twenty people from each house go back to town, having done two years in the country, and are replaced by twenty others. This system reduces the risk of food shortages, which might occur if the whole agricultural population were equally inexperienced.
>
> (More, 1518; 1965 edn, p. 70)

A communistic order of life is suggested: groups of families, a hierarchical system of organization, centrally directed economic and social systems and strict limitations on individualism. This in fact was the characteristic of all the Renaissance literary utopias which followed. They were homocentric (as opposed to theocentric). They emphasized central economic control, aiming for equality and the regulation of disparities between individual fortunes. Socially the focus was on the group, rather than the individual. There was environmental control because it would help to determine social objectives. Finally we should observe that they were scarcely democratic in our sense: benevolent despotism was the explicit form of governance.

These particular features were all part of the set of imaginary concepts which made up the various utopian myths which appeared in European literature between the sixteenth and eighteenth centuries. Their significance was that they took practical root in the nineteenth century in Britain, the USA and elsewhere in a vigorous flowering of various ideal communities.

The trend was set with Robert Owen's experiment at New Lanark. A mill built around 1785 by a Scottish merchant David Dale, and the cotton-spinning pioneer Richard Arkwright, at a site where water power could be obtained from the Falls at the River Clyde, ultimately became one of the world's largest cotton mills, employing 2,500 people. Dales's son-in-law Robert Owen became manager in 1800, and embarked on his social experiment. His philosophy was broadly that of the perfectibility of man, through education. In his book *A new view of society* (1813) we read:

> the governing powers of all countries should establish rational plans for the education and general formation of the characters of their subjects. These plans must be devised to train children from their earliest infancy in good habits of every description (which will of course prevent them from acquiring those of falsehood and deception). They must afterwards be rationally educated, and their labour be usefully directed. Such habits and education will impress them with an active and ardent desire to promote the happiness of every individual   (Owen, 1813; 1969 a edn, p. 106)

Owen, then, was a social reformer with an outlook which stressed the influence of environment upon character – a view with which many were to sympathize. Further, his belief in a harmonious, organic community inspired a variety of successors. At New Lanark he undertook housing improvement, provided health and education facilities and ensured that the village store became a cooperative. His Institute for the Formation of Character was both a meeting place and a point where hot meals could be obtained. In his *Report to the County of Lanark* (1820) he advocated a series of agricultural and manufacturing villages, built up on the principles of 'unity and mutual cooperation', in order to tackle the problems of social distress, pauperism and unemployment. In these villages:

> As it will afterwards appear that the food for the whole population can be provided better and cheaper under one general arrangement of cooking, and that the children can be better trained and educated together under the eye of their parents than under any other circumstances, a large square, or rather parallelogram, will be found to combine the greatest advantages in its form for the domestic arrangements of the association.
> (Owen, 1820; 1969b edn, p. 230)

Owen went on to compare this 'superior mode of living' with the 'cellars and garrets of the most unhealthy courts, alleys, and lanes, in London, Dublin, and Edinburgh, or Glasgow, Manchester, Leeds, and Birmingham' (p. 240).

A beacon had been lit, a signal to the utopian reformers of the nineteenth century. Many of their experiments took place in the USA, but Britain's share was a significant one, with a range of 'alternative communities'

(Hardy, 1979). Small groups of people experimented in alternative forms of social and economic organization, rejecting established patterns of nineteenth-century society and its basis, capitalism. The origins of these communities were located within the processes of historical change (though the groups were sustained by the utopian idealism of many centuries' duration). They were forms of protest, therefore, and have to be seen in the context of other movements: Chartism, Trades Unions, revolutionary socialism and cooperativism (In this context Hardy suggests that four types of alternative communities were established, broadly in the following sequence. The 1820s to 1840s produced communities of utopian socialism. From the 1840s onwards communities of agrarian socialism were associated with a 'back to the land' movement. In the middle of the century communities of sectarianism, particularly religious groups, were typical. Finally at the very end of the century communities of anarchism were more common.)

None of these lasted very long and many disintegrated in bitterness. But their overall effect was to keep alive the idea of alternatives to prevalent economic, social and community arrangements, and in a century-long adjustment to changing environmental conditions, new urban models as alternatives to the nineteenth-century city were increasingly put forward by reformers and visionaries of one persuasion or another. James Silk Buckingham was one example, with his book *National Evils and practical remedies* (1849) in which he proposed a Model Town Association for the building of a new town, Victoria. It was never built, but its carefully detailed physical plan and provisions for social regulation nurtured efforts by later idealists and practitioners. The design for Victoria was in the form of a series of concentric squares extending up to a mile square, with eight main radial avenues; it would accommodate a maximum of 10,000 people.

We see the first attempt here, on any large scale, to marry the two themes: the ideal city in physical terms as architecture and urban form, and the ideal community as a social utopia with communities of health and happiness. It was significant that the eight radial avenues segmenting the box-like town structure of Victoria were named Peace, Concord, Fortitude, Charity, Hope, Faith, Justice and Unity. For the first time, by mid-century, town building projected a comprehensive model, clearly an alternative to the towns and urban societies of the time. Fifty years later, after further experiments, the new practice of town planning would translate into action the combination of the two themes which Victoria articulated.

That step was reached through a process marked by the establishment of model villages, one of the best early examples of which was Saltaire. Probably the most complete model industrial village in Britain, it was built between 1851 and 1876 by Sir Titus Salt, a wealthy Bradford mill owner who had amassed a considerable fortune from pioneering the processing of alpaca wool. By 1850 he was the owner of five mills in the city, employing more than 2,000 people; his personal wealth allowed him to build a new establishment on a green-field site to the north of Bradford close to the Aire, by the Leeds–Liverpool canal. His new mill (six storeys) was known as the Palace of Industry, around which the practical effect of his philanthropy was laid out in compact village form. Eight hundred and fifty houses

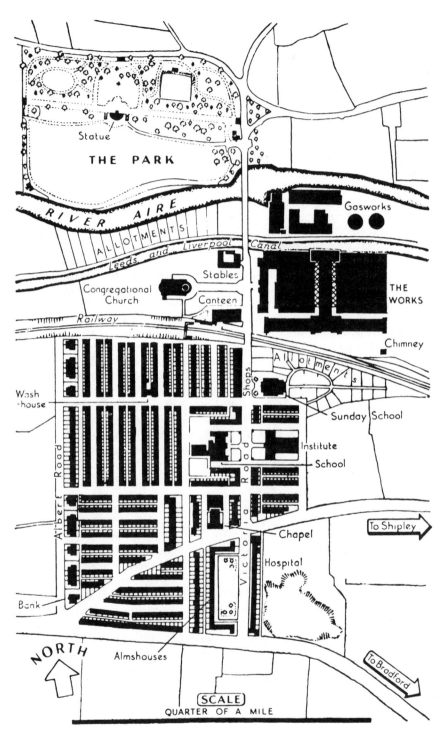

1.1 Completed development at Saltaire, 1851–76

and 45 alms houses were built. Three-storey houses with front gardens were provided for overseers and managers; those with two storeys but no gardens were for the mill hands; and other workers had a rare provision of backyards. The village had a hospital, school, boating park, baths, and public washhouse, an institute, shops and a church, but no public house or pawnshop: overall a dramatic combination by industrial philanthropy of better housing, improved environment and crude social engineering. Healthy town life and urban morals went together.

Other model communities followed as the century progressed. Port Sunlight, William Lever's village, was begun in 1888; Bournville, George and Richard Cadbury's estate to the south-west of Birmingham was begun earlier with the factory, but the village proper was developed later. There were in fact a very large number of model settlements and their representation extended into the twentieth century, not only in Britain, but also in Germany, Italy, France, Holland and the USA. By the end of the century a powerful tradition had been established in community and housing experiments, which in terms of urban form and appearance, provided sharp contrasts with the prevailing features of the late-Victorian city. In one instance at least, Bournville, the opportunity was taken to provide environmental conditions of low density, housing with gardens, tree-lined streets and a layout of informality, with parkland and generous open space. New residential architecture in a setting of openness, sunlight and fresh air was a vivid departure from the norms of the by-law streets adjoining, and certainly the courts and alleys of inner Birmingham. It was at Bournville that the tradition of the model village, as a corrective to the urban forms of the past and as a signal to how future development should be, embraced the new dictates of environmental design, with social purpose. The conditions conducive to the new twentieth-century town planning were in place.

The scene is set

We have argued that town building, throughout history, has been featured by two main considerations. One is that cities may be designed and structured in ways whereby their streets, buildings and spaces reflect a dominant art form in which social, economic, technological and ideological influences compete for primacy. The other is that cities house and shelter people, and the urban environment provides a setting for social organization; in this context community aspirations around ideal forms of living and interaction are the overriding considerations. From time to time the two themes have come together, notably late in the second half of the nineteenth century when the perceived relationship between environment, behaviour and social organization was particularly strong. This was in the context of the set of adjustments then being made to the unsatisfactory nature of the late-Victorian city, particularly its health and housing conditions. In the twentieth century the two themes have continued to surface, the town-planning tradition reflecting them.

This historical background helps towards an understanding of the

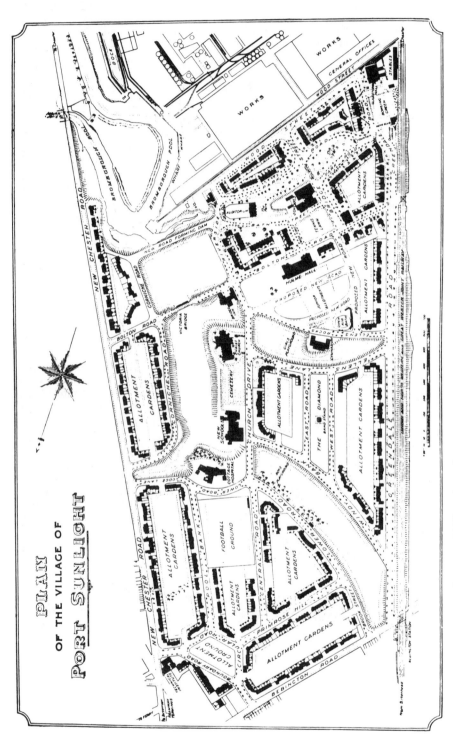

1.2 Model estates: Port Sunlight (William Lever)

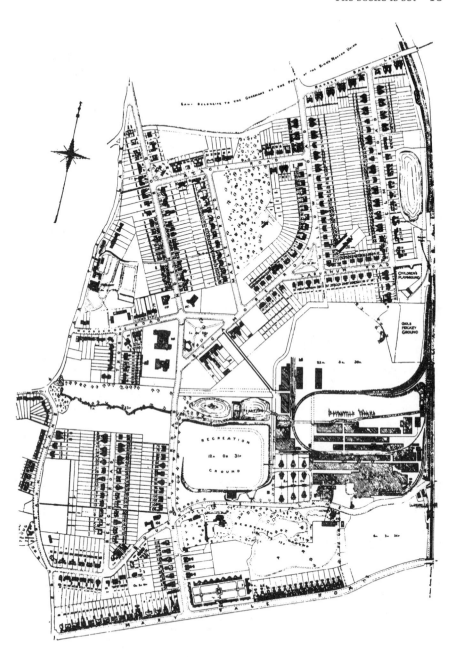

1.3   Model estates: Bournville (George Cadbury)

evolving story of the regulation of the urban environment in Britain over the last two centuries. For a variety of reasons the State has come to intervene massively in the management of cities: drains and sewers, urban health, environmental pollution, housing, land use, roads and traffic, open space, the design and construction of buildings; the provision of facilities and services of various kinds. It has done this to improve their economy, to ensure social acceptability, to house people in better conditions and surroundings and to enhance the quality of life. The activity of regulation has been, from time to time, a conscious act of design (comprehensively, as with New Towns, or with large improvement schemes); equally it has explicitly embraced the objectives of social welfare (as with public housing or the equitable provision of parks and open space). At all times the activity of regulation has drawn on past objectives in human history: to create and maintain cities of dignity commensurate with man's status and to foster social groups and organizations of harmony.

The processes of conscious regulation over the last two centuries have to be set against this background: the interplay of explicit objectives confronting the processes of historical change. Industrial capitalism produced a particular set of circumstances in the creation of cities of a size, and urban environments of a nature, which were unique. By the early nineteenth century, it was clear that new forms of control and management would be necessary to deal more effectively with the emergent problems: first of all, health and sanitation. Just how, and in what form, and with what consequences, forms the story in the chapters which follow.

We should always remember of course that cities, both in their form and structure, reflect the nature of their society at any particular time. A medieval city had a skyline of Church, fortification and burghers' houses around a market place, reflecting the triple sharing of power between religion, the military and commerce. In the nineteenth century the industrial city was punctuated by chimney and mill, representing the dominance of manufacture. Today, a city profile of office blocks highlights the transference from the primary sector to the tertiary. Alternatively, consider the residential features of cities at various times and reflect how they mirror the society of their age. In the eighteenth century the elegant town houses around squares, circuses and broad streets, contrasted markedly with the hovels beyond, pointing to the gap in society between the powerful and the powerless. In the nineteenth century the aspiring middle-class suburb articulated the acquisitive urge of a growing middle class based on commerce, rather than landed property. In the twentieth century the much broader uniformity in residential style mirrors a more equal society and a greater spread of mass consumption.

Likewise, the conscious forms of intervention in, and regulation of the built environment also reflect the nature of the society that conceives them. Politics, institutions of the State, the development of representative democracy, the strength of the civil service, the rise of the professions, the flux of societal preferences, the force of reform movements, the rise and fall of special interest groups, and throughout, the interplay of people in their search for power and influence: all these factors provide the drive behind the story of the public regulation of the urban environment.

We identify a period of 150 years or thereabouts, say from the 1830s to the 1980s, during which the saga unfolds. On the one hand there are economic, social, technological and geographical transformations of the British city; on the other there is the regulatory response of the State – central and local – influenced by myriad pressures – political and social. Our account proceeds to describe and account for the processes whereby the ever-increasing extent of public-sector regulation engages with the processes of city formation and growth.

2 The Years of Improvement

In the half century between the 1830s and the 1880s the growing problem of British towns evoked a set of responses which provided the basic features of Victorian urban management. The State, in the form of government and local councils, was increasingly drawn into arrangements for tackling a set of insistent urban questions: health, sanitation, housing, the provision of open space and the general safeguard of environmental conditions. These were the years of improvement, when faltering steps were taken to provide for the regulation of the growth and development of British towns.

No great city plans were drawn up and no city was subject to long-term urban surgery, in great contrast to Paris for example, during the second half of the century. But by the 1880s a rudimentary system for the control of building development was in place in most of the larger built-up areas, and some of the basic features, not only of the public regulation of the environment but also the public provision of amenities, had been established. The system emphasized the dual relationship between government and local councils, and admitted a pragmatic adjustment to ongoing change in response to lobbies, pressures and special-interest groups of all kinds. It established a 'culture' of public regulation, which has been preserved in a tradition robust enough to assume different forms in the twentieth century, when the whole field of environmental control has taken on new dimensions.

The background

The change in forms of regulation which took place have to be seen against a particular background: the growth of towns and their general features; the development of municipal institutions; and shifts in political philosophy.

During the nineteenth century, Britain both industrialized and urbanized earlier than any country in the western world. At the time of the first census in 1801, 20 per cent of the population of England and Wales lived in towns of more than 5000 people; at mid-century the proportion was 54 per cent; in Scotland the proportion was rather less, but the proportion for Great Britain as a whole was still just above half. At the beginning of the century only London had a population of more than 100,000 (many more, in fact exceeding 900,000); but in 1851 there were 10 towns of more than this size. London grew as a world giant; elsewhere the great manufacturing towns of the North and Midlands multiplied; Bristol retained its importance; and in Scotland Glasgow easily overtook Edinburgh. The metropolitan area of London had a population of 2,363,000 in 1851, more than six times as populous as Liverpool, which topped the list of other cities in England and Wales with more than 100,000 people: Liverpool 375,000; Manchester–Salford 367,00; Birmingham 232,000; Leeds 172,000; Bristol 137,000; Sheffield 135,000; and Bradford 103,000.

A striking aspect of the urban geography of mid-century was the existence of an inland group of giant provincial towns (Harley, 1973). Around Manchester the coalescence of nearby towns had begun, with a continuous line of houses to Oldham and ribbon development elsewhere. In Birmingham urban extension had also taken place across the borough boundary. The inner parts of all these cities was a tangle of narrow, irregular streets where a medley of industrial premises was interspersed with the dwellings of the working classes. Jerry-built districts had sprung up piecemeal, with cheap properties built without order. High building densities prevailed; new houses and workshops were built in the gardens and yards of old premises. Through a process of subdivision, large total floor areas were squeezed into the pre-existing framework of many towns (Powell, 1980). Sunless alleys, culs-de-sac and courts proved a sharp contrast to the favoured residential districts of the outer suburbs: Chapel Allerton and Headingley for Leeds; Fallowfield, Withington and Didsbury for Manchester; and Edgbaston for Birmingham.

Beyond these centres there was a straggle of manufacturing towns in Lancashire and Yorkshire, and elsewhere in the Potteries and the Black Country. In the East Midlands, on the coalfields, and in more isolated locations as at Norwich, towns were also growing. Another urban group was represented by the sea ports, of which (excluding London) Liverpool was pre-eminent, with its vigorous programme of dock development between 1848 and 1852, though with examples of overcrowding in courts and cellars as bad as anywhere in the country. Seaside resorts were also expanding and Brighton boasted a population of more than 65,000 in 1851.

But London was outstanding; its sheer size and congestion was often overwhelming to observers of the day:

> The first thing which strikes a person on his visiting London, for the first time, is its amazing extent. In walking through its streets he fancies himself in a vast world, of houses, out of which there is no escaping.

Hyde Park Corner to Poplar was a distance of nearly eight miles and:

> To walk over such an extent of ground amidst the everlasting jostling and interruptions which one has to encounter in the crowded throughfares of London, is no easy task. (Grant, 1837; 1985 edn, Vol. I pp. 1 and 2).

On the north bank there was already in mid-century a solid mass of development from the West End to the City and the East End; extensive development on the south bank gave the capital a breadth of four miles from north to south. It was a city of many parts, embracing both the squalid rookeries of inner London and the growing suburbs beyond such as Kilburn, Tottenham, West Ham, Lewisham and Balham – districts accessible now by improved public transport.

In essence, a new metropolitan urban system was created in Britain, which strengthened its hold on the country throughout the nineteenth century (Morris, 1986). It was dominated by its primate city: in 1811 London was twelve times its nearest rival in population terms, in 1861 it was five-and-a-half times, but it recovered to six times by 1911. The urban map of the country in fact showed some interesting changes according to different periods in the century. In the first half, growth was dominated by the resource-based textile and metal goods towns of Lancashire, Yorkshire and the West Midlands, typically St Helens, Burnley, Bradford and the Black Country settlements. The second half witnessed growth in the capital goods and coal exporting areas of South Wales, North-east England and West Scotland, represented by Clydebank, Jarrow, Middlesbrough and Cardiff. Throughout, London's outer ring of towns was growing apace to create by far the largest single, contiguous urban centre.

This broad picture of urban growth is one for which there is a wealth of detailed documentation by geographers and by economic, social and urban historians. Synoptic texts abound, as in Waller (1983), Dennis (1984) and Mingay (1986); more directed to the design and layout of towns are Bell (1969) and Cherry (1972); for Scotland there is Adams (1978); and for aspects of Irish urban history, see Bannon (1985). For London, Rasmussen (1934) offers a comprehensive study, while Olsen (1976) focuses on the Victorian period. Overall, the nature of the Victorian city is captured in two volumes by Dyos and Wolff (1973), while in addition Briggs (1963) highlights particular Victorian cities for detailed examination.

As the urban areas expanded in size, and grew in internal complexity, the problems of urban administration were soon confronted. The historical geographers' re-creation of the urban and industrial landscapes of nineteenth century Britain (see for example Coones and Patten, 1986) amply demonstrate the colossal environmental problems that had arisen. An altogether new situation quickly emerged, highlighted by the fact that during the early years of the nineteenth century neither government nor local bodies had displayed much concern for environmental matters, nor (with the exception of the poor laws) for conditions of life (Checkland, 1983). Intervention in respect of public health was largely confined to the general law of nuisance, a principal anxiety being the disposal of human waste along the length of watercourses. The burgeoning growth of the new manufacturing towns, and of course London, brought major problems for health and environmental regulation, for which the imperfect machinery of local administration was quite unsuited.

Forms of urban regulation rested on the chartered boroughs, with their privileges and rights, dating from the early Middle Ages (West, 1983). Originally they were the designation of a fortified town, or burgh. The term 'borough' came to mean a town which returned burgesses to Parliament. By virtue of their charters the towns obtained the right to own property and exercise their corporate identity in the name of Mayor and Council. With the passage of time the incorporated boroughs formed a 'commonalty' of burgesses, aldermen or freemen; they were privileged groups, acting as the incorporation of vested interests, rather than as representative bodies. By the eighteenth century the position of any corporation might have been modified by the creation of other independent bodies which had assumed certain functions: for example, responsibility for law and order, the poor, maintenance of local courts of justice, the regulation of trade, and street or bridge repair, for which rates were taken and overseers appointed. Outside this system, education and health were a matter for Church or charity.

As towns grew, most corporate boroughs established a body of Town (or Improvement) Commissioners to regulate their affairs; these discharged their functions over and above the Mayor and Corporation. Local Acts were widely sought by interested bodies of town residents, prepared to act as commissioners, perhaps for a limited period, in order to attain certain objectives. In time, the scope of the Improvement Commissioners' work was considerable, particularly after 1760. The growing Birmingham, for example, was improved by eight Acts between 1768 and 1828. Perhaps as many as 300 Improvement Commissions were appointed throughout the country, charged with undertaking certain tasks: demolitions, opening up new streets, building bridges, paving, lighting, or drainage.

The State therefore had an uncertain experience of environmental regulation. Inevitably problems developed in severity before much action was taken; undoubtedly in a period of delayed response there were many social casualties. Towns were growing virtually without conscious regulation, managed only by the sporadic action of a variety of independent bodies. The example of a planned layout at Ashton under Lyne for the landowner, the Earl of Stamford, was a rarity. As we have seen, it is true that local institutions were granted powers to meet certain urban needs, one precedent being that of the Turnpike Trust in the eighteenth century, authorized to charge tolls on public roads in return for marks of improvement and modernization. But these bodies were *ad hoc* and non-elective, and overall the pattern of local government was a patchwork quilt of overlapping bodies responsible for critical environmental matters from street improvements to drainage as well as the maintenance of ancient rights and privileges (markets, port dues and so on). The institutions of local administration were haphazard and ill-equipped to meet the new problems of the day.

An improved set of local government arrangements was almost a precursor for the attack on ill-health and the necessary improvements to sanitation that followed. The opportunity came with a national change in political power. With the resignation of Wellington in November 1830, Grey (Charles, the second earl) was invited by William IV to form a ministry, and his coalition under Whig leadership revitalized English politics (Briggs, 1959). The return of the Whigs implied reform and within five years three major initiatives had been taken: parliamentary, poor law and municipal reform. After tense debate, marked by rioting in the country and organization of political unions, Grey's Reform Bill was finally passed in 1832, ushering in a new electoral system; the New Poor Law of 1834 abolished independent parish control of relief and introduced the forms of administration which made English local government so efficient later in the century; and the Municipal Corporations Act, 1835 constituted a comprehensive reform of local government. It is with this third measure of the trilogy that we are most concerned.

In July 1833 a Commission was appointed to enquire into the state of municipal government in England, Wales and Ireland. Twenty-two Commissioners investigated conditions in the old corporations, producing their report in 1835, highly condemnatory of the existing system of oligarchic corporate organization. The resultant Municipal Corporations Act, 1835 swept away at a stroke all previous charters, usages and rights inconsistent with itself and placed the constitution and powers of the municipal corporations named in its schedules upon a simple uniform and popular basis. It reformed existing corporations and created boroughs; they were given powers previously held by Improvement Commissioners. They were elected bodies, though the franchise, albeit extended, was restricted to those with significant property qualifications.

As the century unfolded, the motors for change were allowed new scope. The evangelical-humanitarian movement, dating from the eighteenth century, encouraged some to seek to establish a new moral order in the emergent industrial society. The work of Lord Ashley (Lord Shaftesbury from 1851) in respect of the working conditions of the labouring classes is an illustration of that, and the same concern of the social reformers spilled over into matters of health and sanitation, and the search for an environment more fitted for human dignity. With philanthropy came the powerful contribution of the new professions and the cadre of civil servants and practitioners. Data were assembled, reports were published, inspectors demanded action, and administrators drafted legislation. However, against these forces of reform was the very powerful body of political philosophy, united under *laissez-faire*, which held to the sanctity of private property and a deep reluctance to extend any State powers. The arguments reverberated throughout the century, and into the twentieth, and form a backcloth to the assumption of powers of environmental control, a battle which was so hard fought during this period.

The Act of 1835, though far-reaching, was only a cautious introduction to municipal government. Just 178 reformed cities and boroughs came into existence on 1 November 1835 (Vine, 1879). Calculated on the census of 1831, within their new boundaries they had a population of 2,193,000. London was excluded, and the largest cities were Liverpool (185,000 population), Leeds (123,300), Bristol (104,300), Norwich (61,000), Newcastle (53,600), Bath (50,800), Portsmouth (50,300) and Nottingham (50,200). In the size range 40,000 to 50,000 population, there was Hull, Leicester, Stockport and Sunderland; between 30,000 and 40,000 came Macclesfield, Plymouth and Preston; and between 20,000 and 30,000 Cambridge, Chester, Coventry, Exeter, Ipswich, Oxford, Shrewsbury and Wigan. Excluded from this list, however, were some of the largest and fastest growing towns in the country.

Section 75 of the Municipal Corporations Act enacted that the 'Trustees appointed under sundry Acts of Parliament for paving, lighting, cleansing, watching, regulating, supplying with water and improving' the whole or certain parts of the boroughs named in its schedules, which possessed Local Acts for sanitary purposes *may* 'if it shall be seen to be expedient' transfer their power to the remodelled corporations. In fact, for a long time after the passing of the Act few transfers took place, and by 1871 only a further 46 municipal corporations had been created. The census of that year lists 938 places in England and Wales to be classed as 'towns'; these were the municipal boroughs, places under Improvement Acts for sanitary purposes, and places of more than 2,000 inhabitants. Of this total only 224 had true municipal organization in that they were governed under the 1835 Act. Cities and boroughs incorporated after 1835 included Manchester (population 351,100 at 1871), Birmingham (343,700), Sheffield (239,900), Bradford (145,800), Salford (124,800), Brighton (90,000), Bolton (82,800), Oldham (82,600), Blackburn (76,300), Huddersfield (70,200), Wolverhampton (68,200), Birkenhead (65,900) and Halifax (65,500).

Very slowly, then, a new pattern of government was established, and a hesitant relationship evolved between local and central powers and responsibilities. Certain functions were imposed upon the corporations by parliament but many more functions were made permissible, with freedom of local choice. Thereafter the corporations could seek powers through private Acts of Parliament, and in due time borrowing powers became important for capital-intensive projects.

A second Reform Act, in 1867, radically changed the structure of political power, with the working classes first entering the constitution in an increase in the male electorate of Britain from about 717,000 in 1832 to 2,226,000 after 1867. The political parties inevitably had to adjust their presentation to a tripling of the electorate. After the 1860s we see the emergence of popular politics and party machines, and some key cities threw up new political leaders. But the response to environmental and social problems remained slow and cautious. There was powerful resistance to taxes and extensions to public regulation, except where circumstances permitted alliances between the middle classes and organized labour. Nationally and locally the political preferences were sharply demarcated: Gladstonian Liberalism, believing in minimal state action and seeking the lowest levels of taxation and expenditure, versus Disraeli's 'two nations' and Tory paternalism.

The next change for local administration came with the Public Health Act 1875, which formed a complete code of sanitary, self-government law for local administration by 'Urban' Authorities. Meanwhile applications for, and grants of, municipal charters of incorporation continued and in fact the New Charters Act, 1877, made it financially easier to seek charters, in that costs of application were met. The new local-government map of England and Wales now contained over 700 Urban Sanitary Authorities; London with its own Metropolitan Board of Works had its Metropolitan Sanitary Authorities; and there were the cities and boroughs governed under the 1835 Act. Scotland was governed by Police Authorities.

These then were the political and institutional contexts in which Britain, during the middle years of the century, lurched uncertainly into taking public steps with regard to environmental issues: sanitation and water supply, health and surroundings, housing, and investment for engineering works on a new scale. The emergent structure of central – local relations is part of a fascinating process of historical change over the last 150 years, as Hennock (1982) has indicated. With growing interference with property rights, collectivism strengthened as a political philosophy while the limitations of voluntaryism became apparent. Units of local government increased in size and power: the bureaucracy expanded. A state role was established in new fields and assumed a pattern that proved to be irreversible for well over a century. As the historian G.M. Trevelyan observed:

> No one in 1835 foresaw the day when the 'new municipalities' would not only light and pave the streets, but control the building of houses, and the sanitation and health of the borough; convey the workmen to and from their work; provide public libraries; carry on great municipal trades and industries; and finally educate the people.   (Trevelyan, 1942; 1944 edn, p. 526)

Health and sanitation

To all intents and purposes the story begins with the outbreaks of cholera between 1831 and 1833. Most European countries underwent the epidemic as it spread from Asia. In the first attack roughly 32,000 people died; it struck again in 1848/9, with 62,000 deaths. With diminishing virulence 20,000 died in the epidemic of 1853/4, and a further 14,000 in 1866/7 (Wohl, 1983, p. 118). It was a shock disease because it caused alarm, fear and even occasioned disturbances, as when there were alleged instances of body-snatching by medical students, premature burial or burial in unconsecrated ground; the fatality itself was accompanied by distressing physical symptoms.

For many years medical opinion was divided on the causes of cholera, but in time it was recognized as a water-borne disease. The research of Dr John Snow in 1854 conclusively demonstrated that cholera deaths in a street in Soho were linked to the suspect water of the local Southwark and Vauxhall water company. The cholera bacillus is transmitted between animal tissues where it thrives and multiplies; more precisely it travels from the intestine of one person to another – perhaps by flies carrying contaminated matter, but more usually through drinking polluted water. Accordingly, until remedial action could be taken on effective sanitation, all classes of society were exposed to its ravages.

Of the other major diseases of the time, typhoid was also spread by the intake of contaminated food and drink. By comparison typhus, another great killer of the nineteenth century until at least the 1870s, was spread by the faeces of the body louse, and was therefore prevalent in conditions of overcrowding. Tuberculosis, the other great lethal disease, thrived in circumstances of undernourishment, squalor and lack of ventilation. The incidence of these ravages was a set-back, nationally, for Britain had experienced no bubonic plague since the seventeenth century and national death rates had been falling. By the beginning of the nineteenth century, however, the downward trend was first halted and then reversed. The association with a higher rate of urban living in general, and the poor quality of urban living in particular, led medical opinion by the 1830s to attribute the resurgence of disease to a combination of increased over-crowding and poor, or absent sanitation.

A dramatic growth in the number of British physicians was recorded from the later years of the eighteenth century, as illustrated first in the number of medical graduates trained at the University of Edinburgh, then the centre of medical education in Britain, and subsequently at the newly established University College, London. It was from the ranks of the medi-cal profession that an early concern over urban health was to emerge. C. Turner Thackrah, for example, published a treatise on urban conditions in Leeds in the early 1830s, followed by James Phillips Kay in 1832 with a more influential work on the working classes in Manchester.

Associated with an increasing anxiety about national health matters came the collection of data as part of the 'statistical movement' of the time. Local statistical societies came into existence and in one at least, Manchester, Kay was prominent. Events were moving quickly, for in 1837 under the influence of William Farr (who himself had trained as a doctor but had moved into the field of population statistics) a General Register Office began to record data concerning births, deaths and marriages in respect of England and Wales; Farr was appointed Compiler of Abstracts in the new office.

The public health movement gathered pace, with reliable data on the causes of death available for the first time. In 1838 the Poor Law Commis-sion secured the services of three doctors to help them enquire into the prevalence and causation of preventable sickness in London. They were Kay, Neill Arnott and Thomas Southwood Smith, and the influence of the latter was to prove the greatest in the developing struggle for sanitary reform. Their enquiries were soon extended throughout England and Wales and later to Scotland. It was this work that formed the basis of the Commission's Report of 1842 on the Sanitary Condition of the Labouring Population of Great Britain. There were three Reports, two being Local Reports and one a General Report (this latter being entirely the work of Edwin Chadwick, to whom we must now turn), but suffice to say that the principles on which sanitary reform were to be based over the next half century were established in this pioneering investigation.

[handwritten margin note: Sanitary reform in London. Doctors Investigate for]

Edwin Chadwick was born in Manchester, in 1800 (Frazer, 1950). As a young man however he lived in London, training as a lawyer and working with Jeremy Bentham, the Utilitarian philosopher; he was called to the Bar in 1830. He was appointed Assistant Commissioner of the Inquiry into the State of the Poor Laws in 1832, becoming a full Commissioner the next year and Secretary in 1834. During the 1830s the work of the triumvirate of doctors (Kay, Arnott and Southwood Smith) was underway and their report, probably drafted by Chadwick, on conditions affecting public health in certain districts of London was published as an appendix to the Fourth Annual Report of the Poor Law Commissioners in 1838. A further report on the health of London by Southwood Smith followed in the Fifth Report in 1839. When the Bishop of London moved, in the House of Lords, that an enquiry be set up into the sanitary condition of the labouring class, the task was given to the Poor Law Commissioners. Chadwick, as secretary, was at this time in fractious dispute with the three central Commissioners and it was convenient for him to be released from his secretarial duties to be engaged full time on the enquiry. Meanwhile an MP, R.A. Slaney secured the appointment of a House of Commons Select Committee to investigate the health of towns; it reported in 1840.

In Chadwick the public health movement, so far unorganized and relatively aimless, gained the leadership it required and the spark for effective action. It was he who lent direction to the necessary drive for inquiry and who mobilized the weight of the various sections of protagonist opinion. But Chadwick was not alone. The doctors assumed a new authority and the professional administrators were now armed with statistics for the first time. Politically the Whig Administration of 1830 to 1841 was reformist in matters of local government, parliament, factories and poor law, and was not hostile to public health reform. An equally favourable moral reception was presumably present amongst the humanitarians and philanthropists whose contribution to human welfare had already been seen in the abolition of slavery and in factory reform.

It was in this encouraging context that Chadwick set to work, though his own position was at risk during the politically turbulent years at the end of the Whig Government when the New Poor Law was attracting hostility. He worked through a considerable labour force mobilized from Poor Law Assistant Commissioners, medical officers, clerks, factory inspectors, doctors and various experts, extending the original metropolitan surveys first to England and Wales, and then to Scotland. The flood of evidence was finally brought together as a House of Lords paper and published as the *Sanitary report* in February 1842; it appeared under Chadwick's own name, the other three Commissioners disassociating themselves from it. The first half of the Report established the basic facts of correlation between insanitation, overcrowding and disease; the economic costs of ill-health and the social costs of squalor and bad housing were asserted; and the inefficiency of existing legal and administrative machinery was exposed. The voluminous Report is impossible to summarize, but two sections from 'Recapitulation of conclusions' illustrate the main findings:

That the various forms of epidemic, endemic, and other disease caused, or aggravated, or propagated chiefly amongst the labouring classes by atmospheric impurities produced by decomposing animal and vegetable substances, by damp and filth, and close and overcrowded dwellings prevail amongst the population in every part of the kingdom.

That such disease, wherever its attacks are frequent, is always found in connection with the physical circumstances above specified, and that where those circumstances are removed by drainage, proper cleansing, better ventilation, and other means of diminishing atmospheric impurity, the frequency and intensity of such disease is abated.   (Chadwick, in Flinn, 1965, p. 422)

What emerged from the Report was that health and bodily fitness depended very much on what part of the country a person lived in (the cruel distinction being between the country, and London and the industrial towns of the North) and on occupational group and social class. Table 2.1

shows the average age at which death occurred among different classes of the community in rural and manufacturing districts:

Table 2.1

Place	Gentry	Tradesmen	Labourers
Rutlandshire	52	41	38
Truro	40	33	28
Derby	49	38	21
Manchester	38	20	17
Bolton	34	23	18
Bethnal Green	45	26	16
Leeds	44	27	19
Liverpool	35	22	15

Source: General Report on the Sanitary Condition of the Labouring Classes of Great Britain, 1842, p. 153.

As to the means of improvement the Report was unequivocal:

> The primary and most important measures, and at the same time the most practicable, and within the recognized province of public administration, are drainage, the removal of all refuse of habitations, streets and roads, and the improvement of the supplies of water.   (Chadwick, in Flinn, 1965, p. 423)

The battle lines were drawn. Although Chadwick made no specific recommendations for legislation, it was clear that improved health was dependent on improved sanitation and related measures; that the removal of sewage could be effected economically not by hand labour from privies, but through suspension in water conveyed in glazed circular drains (not brick-built tunnels); and that existing administrative arrangements were inadequate to implement these objectives.

There was no immediate response to the Report but the public health movement was advanced in 1843 when a Royal Commission was appointed under the chairmanship of the Duke of Buccleuch to investigate the health of towns (often known as the Health of Towns Commission, its full title was the Commission of Inquiry into the State of Large Towns and Populous Districts). Chadwick was not a member of the Commission, but Arnott and Southwood Smith were, together with others sympathetic to the sanitary cause. Two reports followed, in 1844 and 1845, the first largely the work of Chadwick. But there was no Government enthusiasm for any kind of public health measure. Neither Peel's Administration, nor Russell's which succeeded it in 1846, saw it as a priority in view of the Irish Famine and the question of the Corn Laws which then took precedence of concern.

In the meantime the banner of reform was also being carried by the Health of Towns Association, a propaganda body established in 1844, first in London and then with branches in towns and cities elsewhere. Publications and public meetings advanced the lobby, spearheaded by Southwood Smith but also involving Lords Ashley and Normanby. But their influence was limited – certainly in relation to the much more powerful Anti-Corn Law League.

Pressure for legislation, however, could not be denied, but there were many tortured steps before a successful measure was enacted. A Sewerage, Drainage etc. of Towns Bill, designed to effect improvements in public health was introduced into the Commons by Lord Lincoln in the parliamentary session of 1845. It was heavily attacked by the Health of Towns Association, but in any case the Bill fell with the resignation of Peel in 1846 over the question of the repeal of the Corn Laws. Meanwhile the cause could always be advanced by local enactments: notably, the Liverpool Sanitary Act, 1846 had the reputation of being the first comprehensive Sanitary Act in the country, making the Town Council the highways authority, solely responsible for drainage, paving and cleansing; giving the authority the power to appoint a Medical Officer of Health (the celebrated Dr William Henry Duncan was appointed in 1847), a Borough Engineer and an Inspector of Nuisances. In 1847 the Towns Improvement Clauses Act set out the provisions usually contained in Local Acts for paving, drainage, cleansing, lighting and improving towns.

But in the Parliamentary session of 1847 attention was focused on Viscount Morpeth's Health of Towns Bill, based on the recommendations of the Royal Commission and differing from Lincoln's earlier Bill; it ran into opposition and was withdrawn. But a new cholera epidemic was already spreading west from Asia, the outbreak having been first observed in Afghanistan in the hot season of 1845. A strenuous campaign was mounted by Southwood Smith and several (particularly the Metropolitan) of the Health of Towns Associations. The key issue still was that high death rates showed a distinctive geographical pattern: towns had higher rates than country districts, some towns were more unfavoured than others, and some parts of the same town had excessive mortality over other parts.

There could be no false security in believing that urban sanitary conditions were improving; there was ample evidence as to inadequate water supply, an insufficiency or even an absence of sewerage over many areas, the existence of open drains and a general lack of street cleansing. Moreover the congested towns were grossly affected by the presence of pig sties, cow sheds, knackers' yards, slaughter houses and a range of offensive trades. As Hector Gavin, a lecturer on forensic medicine and public health at Charing Cross Hospital, concluded in a lecture in 1847 on behalf of the Health of Towns, and of London Associations:

> The causes of the high mortality of towns are traceable to the density of population, to the want of ventilation and consequent impurity of the air; to the defective state of the paving, drainage and sewage; to the filthy state of the dwellings of the poor and of their immediate neighbourhood; to the con-centration of unhealthy and putrescent emanations from narrow streets, courts and alleys; to the crowded and unhealthy state of the workshops and to the injurious occupations which are carried on in them.
>
> (Gavin, 1847, p. 20)

The Bill was redrafted and reintroduced as a Public Health Bill by Lord Morpeth in 1848; this time it was successful and the Public Health Act, 1848 became the first in a long line of measures of similar title. Inevitably the legislation was a compromise and so failed to meet some of Chadwick's hopes, as expressed in the *Sanitary Report*, for example; there was no comprehensive national system of public health commissions. But the lobby had done its work and the various Health of Towns Associations faded away. It was the first real measure, nationally, designed to secure sanitary control over the growing towns by public regulation; a set of principles had been established and there was no going back. It applied to all parts of England and Wales, except the Metropolis, which had its own Metropolitan Commission of Sewers (1847). It was permissive legislation and did not come into force without adoption in individual areas. Hence for the sanitary movement it was but just an early victory and more had to follow, though it did have the effect of establishing a Public Central Board of Health and it led to the creation of local bodies of skilled administrators, which in due time created their own momentum for extending sanitary reform within the ranks of public bodies, particularly local authorities.

The Act provided for the setting up of Local Boards of Health, and in incorporated towns they were to be the Town Councils. (The immediate significance of this is that from the mid-nineteenth century onwards we see a whole succession of measures extending powers and duties related to environmental management to local councils. It was to be a feature of public regulation that provided a particular stamp to the British scene.) The Boards were compulsory only where the death rate exceeded the figure of 23 per 1,000, well above the national average, but quite arbitrary because it took no account of the varying age composition of local populations. They were permitted to appoint key officers including a Surveyor, Inspector of Nuisances, Treasurer, Clerk and an Officer of Health. There were numerous sanitary clauses. For example, all sewers were to be vested in the Local Board, and their duty was to ensure that they were cleared, cleansed and emptied. An important breakthrough was that it became unlawful for new houses built within the jurisdiction of the Board to lack drains or provision for sewage disposal. Ownership of streets was vested in the Local Boards and they had powers to undertake levelling, paving, flagging and repair.

The Act created a new Central Board, with three members: Chadwick, Southwood Smith and Lord Ashley. It had few powers of central direction and its powers were largely limited to consideration of appointments or dismissal of officials, except of course for initiating public health work, where neither municipal government nor an existing improvement, police or sewage commission existed, and where death rates exceeded the statutory norm. In the event the Board had a short life, effectively terminating in 1854, thereby bringing to an end Chadwick's own official career. In 1858 the central supervision of public health was transferred to the Privy Council where it remained until 1871, responsibility passing to the highly influential figure of John Simon.

The 1848 Act was tentative, but it established principles of sanitary improvement; it also instituted a new pattern of central–local relationships and gave encouragement to the emergence of effective regulation at the local level. It established a bridgehead from which there was to be no retreat, and this was to be significant not just for public health but for environmental regulation in wider fields.

In the meantime it is important to note that the 1848 Act did not apply to

Scotland. One explanation was that the Act of 1837 had not extended the civil registration of births and deaths to Scotland, and as a consequence it was impossible to know officially whether the death rate of 23 per 1,000 had been exceeded. But there was also professional objection: the Scots, objecting to supervision by a non-medical bureaucracy in London, considered that the Poor Law Board of Supervision in Edinburgh (the equivalent of the London Poor Law Commission) was a preferable central authority. It was not until 1867 that a Public Health (Scotland) Act gave the Board of Supervision the required powers. The systematic registration of deaths was introduced to Scotland in 1854 and this provided the data for local action.

In this respect sanitary reform in Glasgow proved to be of wider influence, as well as of great local significance. Parliamentary powers for the municipalization of the city's water supply were obtained in 1855 and the new supplies from Loch Katrine were inaugurated four years later. A fresh political impetus to sanitary reform came through the person of John Ure as Chairman of the Committee on Nuisances; subsequently becoming Lord Provost 1880–83, his local impact mirrors that of Joseph Chamberlain in Birmingham at roughly the same time. A Medical Officer of Health for the city was appointed in 1862 and a corps of Sanitary Inspectors established. Measures of urban renewal were also undertaken, as we shall see later (p. 43).

Except for local instances of this kind, for 20 years and more after 1848 the Public Health Service and the movement for sanitary reform experienced considerable difficulties. It faced uncertainties and political weakness at both central and local levels. It was subject to the exposure of parliamentary criticism with no protecting ministerial arm, and, even though located in the Privy Council, medical affairs were only one of a large number for which that body was responsible. In local government the parsimony of elected councils ensured that expenditure on unnecessary work was not incurred and appointments not made. From 1855 Medical Officers of Health were compulsory throughout London, but elsewhere in the country few authorities chose to make the appointment; Leicester and Liverpool had set an early pattern, but Leeds did not appoint a Medical Officer of Health until 1866, Manchester following in 1868 and Birmingham in 1873.

The logic of the movement, however, could not be denied in the face of the unrelenting problems faced by the growing towns. The Sanitary Act, 1866 ensured that it became the duty of all local authorities to inspect their districts and to suppress nuisances; vestries were enabled to form special drainage districts. A Royal Commission, set up in 1869 to survey the sanitary administration of the country, reported in 1871, and with the Government accepting its recommendations events proceeded quickly. The Local Government Board Act, 1871 established a new Government Department (of that name) taking over all the powers and duties of the Poor Law Board, and those of the Privy Council and the Home Office concerning public health and sanitary legislation. The Public Health Act, 1872 provided a new map of local government for England, outside London, placing all sanitary authorities under one defined district. The Public Health Act,

1875 was a comprehensive measure, covering the entire field of sanitation. It provided a Public Health Service administration for the whole country, with authorities empowered to regulate the construction of new streets and buildings under the supervision of the Local Government Board. Model building codes were embodied in local by-laws – to which we shall return later (pp. 40–1).

There followed a period during which the provision of improved sanitary environments in towns and cities was significantly accelerated. During the last quarter of the nineteenth century the basic aims of the public health movement were largely realized in the larger settlements, though of course inherited problems remained and death rates kept high. Abundant water supplies were brought to the towns, largely through municipal concerns; sewers and drains were installed; streets, space and buildings were all regulated. The Local Government Board established a reputation for efficiency, and the authority, power and self-importance of local government was enhanced, confirming an administrative structure which would ably regulate more and more features of the environment over the next century. The professional prestige of local government officers grew apace: the Associations of Municipal and Sanitary Engineers and Surveyors were formed in the 1880s and a national Association of Medical Officers (with various names) was active.

In addition to sanitation there were two further particular areas of health improvement of environmental significance, in which government felt drawn to intervene: one was the question of clean air, the other related to river pollution.

2 other concerns along w/ sanitation

With regard to atmospheric pollution, nineteenth-century literature is full of references to foul air, smoke and fog, while the legacy of respiratory diseases speaks for itself. Not only industrial and mining areas, but the cities themselves polluted the atmosphere from a variety of factory and domestic chimneys. The open coal fire released vast quantities of fine soot, and dense fogs became lethal. The great fog of 1886 gave rise to mortality rates as high as the worst cholera years. A major problem was the domestic hearth and any attempts to control coal-burning implied domestic inspection. The inspection of drains and other features of dwellings had been a hard enough battle and it would have been unreasonable to expect speedy action on this particular problem. Smoke, after all, was associated with industrial production, full employment and continuity of wages. But a health lobby maintained an attack on smoke, and local societies for smoke control were founded under the umbrella of the National Smoke Abatement Society.

In the first instance local by-laws and nuisances acts gave possibilities at least of securing clean air. London had two early acts: the Smoke Nuisance Abatement (Metropolis) Act, 1852 and its amendment in 1856, but the legislation extended only to certain factories and not domestic fires. Elsewhere it was a question of local acts, but it was rare for neighbouring towns with similar industries to take the same action. Improved national legislation was the only way forward. The Public Health Act, 1875 consolidated the existing nuisances acts but fell far short of giving them effective teeth. In one industry, however, considerable improvements were made:

the alkali industry, where fumes were particularly noxious and damaging to property. The Alkali Act, 1863 was instrumental in establishing an inspectorate, and central measures proved successful.

With regard to river pollution, the fouling of the country's rivers during the nineteenth century increased apace with industrialization and the growth of towns. Major watercourses became used as open sewers and the link with health hazards was obvious. Reports and commissions of inquiry spoke of inky black rivers, offensive smells, deep concern over health and concern over proper supplies of pure water. Effective legislation was slow in coming, public opinion buffeted as usual by the varying opinions expressed: health and human welfare versus costs to both government and private industry. Local interests largely prevailed and the River Pollution Prevention Act, 1876, which enabled the Local Government Board to direct local authorities to take action against polluters, achieved very little. It was not until the 1880s that the 1876 Act could be enforced, allowing the Local Government Board to establish joint committees to coordinate action along the length of any river. Before the end of the century the Mersey and Irwell Joint Committee, the Ribble Joint Committee and the West Riding Rivers Board had been established – many years after the Thames and Lee Conservancy Boards (1857 and 1864) for the London area.

As the sanitary idea became established in local government the reform movement as such, which had played a notable part in impelling legislative change over nearly half a century, fell into the background. The idealism of healthy cities however remained a powerful motor. Sir Benjamin Ward Richardson's Presidential Address to the Health Department of the Social Science Congress in 1875 is a case in point: suitably dedicated to Edwin Chadwick it was published in 1876 as *Hygeia: a city of health*, a utopia of 100,000 people living at a maximum density of 25 to the acre, an environment of cleanliness and health, a 'model city where certain forms of disease would find no possible home'. Richardson's utopia remained the spur to further public action.

Housing

A critical feature of British housing throughout the century was the poverty of the dwelling stock for significant numbers of people and the squalor of their surrounding environment. Countless reporters described the conditions, especially in London and the new manufacturing towns. Consider Frederick Engels in his survey of 'The great towns' in *The condition of the working class in England*:

> Every great city has one or more slums, where the working class is crowded together . . . These slums are pretty equally arranged in all the great towns of England, the worst houses in the worst quarters of the towns; usually one or two-storied cottages in long rows, perhaps with cellars used as dwellings, almost always irregularly built. These houses of three or four rooms and a kitchen form, throughout England, some parts of London excepted, the general dwellings of the working class. The streets are generally unpaved, rough, dirty, filled with vegetable and animal refuse, without sewers or

gutters, but supplied with foul, stagnant pools instead. Moreover, ventilation is impeded by the bad, confused method of building of the whole quarter, and since many human beings here live crowded into small space, the atmosphere that prevails in these working-men's quarters may readily be imagined. Further, the streets serve as drying grounds in fine weather; lines are stretched across from house to house, and hung with wet clothing.

(Engels, 1845; 1969 edn, p. 60)

There followed descriptions of the London rookery of St Giles, Whitechapel and Bethnal Green in East London, Dublin, Edinburgh, Liverpool and elsewhere, including the manufacturing districts of Yorkshire and Lancashire, where finally he depicted the urban squalor of Manchester. His summary was that:

The dwellings of the workers are everywhere badly planned, badly built, and kept in the worst condition, badly ventilated, damp and unwholesome. The inhabitants are confined to the smallest possible space, and at least one family usually sleeps in each room. The interior arrangement of the dwellings is poverty-stricken in various degrees, down to the utter absence of even the most necessary furniture.   (Engels, 1845; 1969 edn. p. 106)

This was Engels's description in 1845 'from personal observation and authentic sources' and there is little reason to doubt the accuracy of his representation. Journalists and similar observers pointed to the degradation in housing and living conditions for great masses of the people. Henry Mayhew, for example, a writer with a varied literary background, published a number of articles in the *Morning Chronicle* beginning in 1849; later (1851–52) published as *London labour and the London poor*, they amply confirm the lot of various occupational groups. The setting was the metropolis: 'a vast bricken multitude', where looking east from St Paul's one could 'see only narrow lanes and musty country-houses, with tall chimneys vomiting black clouds, and huge masses of warehouses with doors and cranes ranged one above another' (Thompson and Yeo, 1973, p. 113).

The evidence was also compounded through the reports of the health investigations, to which we have already made reference. We have too the novelists' contributions to our understanding of the time, though sometimes we have to infer the actual nature of housing and environmental conditions from the wider social issues they were exploring. But Charles Kingsley's *Alton Locke* (1850) is instructive on the distress of the working classes in London, while Elizabeth Gaskell's *Mary Barton* (1848), a story of poverty and class conflict, was set in Manchester. Thereafter we might look no further than Charles Dickens, who has left an indelible stamp on our perceptions of mid-Victorian British cities: *Bleak House* (1853), *Little Dorrit* (1857) and *Our mutual friend* (1865) all invoke an image of an alien environment of London, while *Hard times* (1854) was set in the fictitious Coketown, portraying a setting of ugliness and inhumanity in the northern cities:

It was a town of red brick, or of brick that would have been red if the smoke and ashes had allowed it; but, as matters stood it was a town of unnatural red and black like the painted face of a savage. It was a town of machinery and tall chimneys, out of which interminable serpents of smoke trailed themselves for ever and ever, and never got uncoiled. It had a black canal in it, and a river that ran purple with ill-smelling dye, and vast piles of building full of windows where there was a rattling and a trembling all day long, and where the piston of the steam-engine worked monotonously up and down, like the head of an elephant in a state of melancholy madness. It contained several large streets, all very like one another, and many small streets still more like one another, inhabited by people equally like one another, who all went in and out at the same hours, with the same sound on the same pavements, to do the same work, and to whom every day was the same as yesterday and tomorrow.   (Dickens, 1854, p. 65)

There was a particularly hostile view of cities by American intellectuals at this time, and indeed later. Morton and Lucia White (1962) commented that 'commerce, crime, crowds, and conventionalism were linked with the city in a horrible alliterative dream by our most important writers of fiction before the Civil War' (p. 53). But Henry Adams at least could report of London in 1858 that 'a certain style dignified its grime; heavy, clumsy, arrogant, purse-proud, but not cheap; insular but large; barely tolerant of an outside world, and absolutely self confident' (quoted in White and White, 1962, p. 65).

In this country, a reaction to the philistinism of the age was powerfully represented by John Ruskin. Ugliness offended him and he roundly condemned the culture of his day, with its deeply rooted economic and social failures. At the same time, hugely influential on others of his generation, the views of William Morris, in particular, as expressed in his lectures on art and socialism, are a repetition and expansion of Ruskin's central thesis. Morris's Prologue to *The Earthly Paradise* (1868) offered an alternative vision:

> Forget six counties overhung with smoke,
> Forget the snorting steam and piston stroke,
> Forget the spreading of the hideous town;
> Think rather of the pack-horse on the down,
> And dream of London, small, and white, and clean,
> The clean Thames bordered by its gardens green.
>   (Morris, in Henderson, 1967, p. 89)

Forgetting the town houses of the gentry, including those inherited from Georgian times, the principal house types comprised the following. The vernacular tradition was represented by the two-storey terrace, often arranged in narrow streets and courts, giving high density conditions in addition to the actual overcrowding of the dwellings themselves. The back-to-back dwelling was heavily stigmatized for the absence of ventilation and fresh air, but the worst form of dwelling was the cellar, encased almost inevitably by polluted subsoil. In Scotland the four-storey tenement centred on a common stairway was predominant, while on Tyneside the regional variation of the flatted 'two up and two down' was characteristic. In short, there was variety, and it would be quite wrong to consider that the quality of dwellings built to house the needs of the fast-growing urban population was uniformly bad – 'a testimony to the avarice of builders and landlords alike' (Hopkins, 1986, p. 80). Perhaps we have been too much swayed by Engels's work and that by the Hammonds (J.L. and B.), such as *The town labourer* (1917) and *The bleak age* (1934).

As the century wore on, the net quality of the dwelling stock improved, and geographically the location of the environmentally impoverished districts became residual to the older parts. As cities moved outwards into the suburbs the newer stock adopted higher construction standards and the provision of space around dwellings, in accordance with the measures locally adopted in by-laws. Piecemeal development and infilling took place alongside the rather more methodical enterprises of estate building; thus were the Victorian suburbs created, the speculative developer assisted by a variety of people who fashioned the resource of land ownership and capital. As Dyos graphically described the process: 'Acres of ploughland and meadow and orchard were pricked out in unending terraces with almost superhuman speed' (Dyos, 1961, p. 85).

Dyos's study was that of a south London suburb, Camberwell, and in the metropolis the last three decades of the century were marked by an overall easing of overcrowding (and therefore density levels) in the central parts of the city, as relative shifts in population distribution took place between inner and outer areas. Newer, better forms of housing, with improved space standards in the growing suburbs significantly improved over time the net quality of the dwelling stock. Outside London, the industrial cities of the north had smaller suburban rings and overcrowding levels in the central districts tended to remain for longer.

The horror of the worst conditions remained however. The rapid growth of the northern cities had been associated with the worst of the early housing development, and population densities were historically and abnormally high. In Liverpool residential pressures were particularly inflated during the 1840s by Irish immigration consequent upon harvest failures and the potato famine. But every major city had its notorious blackspots where decaying properties were jumbled together: the Wynds in Edinburgh, the Shambles in Nottingham, Gibraltar in Manchester, and in London, Agar Town, Seven Dials and Jacobs Island. Here the environments were marked typically by an absence of light (and especially sunlight), fresh air and ventilation.

Back-to-back dwellings seriously violated the objective of effective ventilation, though the honeycomb building structure (back-to-back and side-to-side) constituted cheap accommodation and was popular with both the poorer of the working classes that inhabited them and the speculators who invested in them. For reasons which are not all that obvious Leeds had a massive concentration (70 per cent of the town's dwellings were back-to-backs in the 1880s, a proportion which continued until 1920), though Manchester, Bradford, Huddersfield and Sheffield also had high proportions. In spite of continuous attempts to prohibit the construction of this form of dwelling, loopholes were exploited to ensure that they were still built; Leeds indeed continued to build them until 1937.

But it was the occupation of cellars that attracted the most adverse criticism. They were inevitably dark and unventilated, and they were grossly insanitary and perpetually damp; in addition to their small size, perhaps only 10 ft by 12 ft in dimension, their characteristics represented the worst features of the housing stock. Liverpool was the worst city in Britain from this point of view with an estimated 22 per cent of the city's population living in cellar accommodation at the height of the Irish immigration, but Manchester recorded 12 per cent in the same period. These figures did not remain at those levels for long, both cities making strenuous efforts to close the cellars and eject their inhabitants (only to increase the incidence of overcrowding elsewhere) from mid-century onwards. By the 1870s the unwelcome notoriety had largely passed.

However, it was the sheer size of the housing problem in London which inevitably focused attention on the metropolis as opposed to the provincial cities. Investigative journalism proved a popular way to expose London's social and environmental degradation. John Hollingshead in 1861 followed in the Henry Mayhew tradition, with a book originating in 10 letters published in the *Morning Post* in January of that year: 'Let us go out into the ragged streets, and ragged houses, and see what the ragged people are doing.' His conclusions made compelling reading and struck a chord for the housing debate over the rest of the century:

> Setting aside the criminal population of London, and that small number of the London industrious poor who struggle against the degrading influences of the neighbourhood in which they are mostly compelled to live, we shall find at least one third of our three millions of human beings in the metropolis housed in filthy, ill-constructed courts and alleys, or crowding in unwholesome layers, one over the other, in old houses and confined rooms. The life they lead daily and hourly is full of debasing lessons. Decency is lost where large families of all ages and of both sexes are accustomed to live in one apartment, and habits are engendered which last for generations. This carelessness about comforts and conveniences acts upon Landlords. There is a little demand for pure, wholesome, well-constructed dwellings, and they are not supplied. The court and alley property in and about London, which is a disgrace to a city of enterprise and civilisation, is in most cases up to the level of its consumers. (Hollingshead, 1861; 1985 edn, pp. 234–5)

The housing history of this period is amply documented (Ashworth, 1954; Tarn, 1973; Gauldie, 1974; Wohl, 1974; Burnett, 1978; Daunton, 1983) and we can readily discern the background against which movement for housing reform gathered pace. It progressed from essentially three directions. Whereas health reform had rested on statistics and data, impressively presented by doctors and professional administrators, housing reform depended on rather different contributions. First there was the demonstration of practical achievements in the form of model dwellings; then there was the wider appeal of the creators of model towns – in practice and in literary imagination; and finally there was the propagation of moral outrage at the reality of environmental squalor by a miscellany of housing reformers, who by a combination of voluminous writing and 'good works' brought the problems of the needy to a wider and increasingly receptive audience. Political possibilities took off from that point.

In the wider context of model housing (Gaskell, 1986) philanthropic housing associations from the 1840s onwards, largely in London, but occasionally in some of the provincial cities, pointed the way to new possibilities with their objectives of raising minimum standards of accommodation while keeping rents below that which the market would allow. 'Five per cent philanthropy', a term which describes this activity, suggests the finely balanced nature of the financial support. But the argument was not only about finance, rather it raised a whole set of ethical questions. Just as sanitary reform had been dismissed as meddling legislation which would do as much harm as good, model housing was resisted on the grounds that the quality of buildings would be dragged down to the level of the feckless tenant.

The earliest of the societies founded for the purpose of building houses was the Metropolitan Association for Improving the Dwellings of the Industrious Classes, set up in Spitalfields in 1841, though inactive for a number of years while capital was accumulated. Another was the Society for the Improvement of the Condition of the Labouring Classes, founded in 1844; one early scheme was a block of model houses for families in Bloomsbury. A number of other bodies to undertake similar work followed, the most prominent being the Improved Industrial Dwellings Co., founded by Sir Sydney Waterlow, which was building houses from 1863, and the Peabody Trust founded in 1862 on a major charitable donation by George Peabody, a wealthy American banker who had settled in this country. One of the largest associations, in terms of dwellings provided, was the Artizans', Labourers' and General Dwelling Co. Ltd, opening its first building in 1868. The model dwellings movement was helped along by a contribution at the Great Exhibition of 1851, in particular the construction of the Prince Consort's Model Cottages, which assisted in the build-up of a propaganda profile. During the middle and later years of the century an important practical pointer had been established in matters of housing improvement: although the societies did not house the very poor, and the process of dwelling stock accumulation may have been slow, higher standards could be attained, without direct subsidy. In the mid-1880s 28 associations were estimated to be housing upwards of 32,000 persons – a figure to be much increased over the next quarter of a century.

The second influence, model-town building, had a much longer pedigree (Cherry, 1970). For centuries there had been the visionary ideal of the perfect settlement, Sir Thomas More's *Utopia* (1517) establishing the literary precedent. The fictive model followed in succeeding centuries, but in response to the economic and social upheavals of the Industrial Revolution the actual building of model towns now accompanied the literary presentations (see pp. 8–11). In practice, Robert Owen's experiment at New Lanark in the very early years of the nineteenth century was one to establish his social principles of community building, but the construction of the village for 3,000 people (ultimately) laid emphasis on higher accommodation standards, as too did his later plan for Villages of Cooperation after the Napoleonic Wars. In the 1840s a scheme by an Anglican clergyman, Minter Morgan for a 'Christian Commonwealth' – a series of Institutions where people would be housed in four-roomed cottages – kept the model-village idea alive. It was given wider expression in a huge treatise published in 1849, *National evils and practical remedies*, which was in fact a proposal by James Silk Buckingham to build a new town, Victoria, for 10,000 people; in his design, built-up in a series of concentric squares, careful attention was given both to the location of the dwellings and their sanitary arrangements. The model-town concept was even transferred to a Pacific island by Robert Pemberton in his book *The happy colony* (1854), this time Queen Victoria Town.

But perhaps the model-town advocacy became more persuasive through the success of actual undertakings. Once again there were many precedents. John Grubb Richardson built a small settlement round a mill at Bessbrook, Newry, Northern Ireland. The Halifax area of West Yorkshire produced a crop of model villages and those by Edward Ackroyd at Akroyden in the 1840s were good examples of the work of the industrialist benefactor having paternalist regard for workforce and accommodation. On Merseyside, Bromborough Pool was the location for a model village of Price's Patent Candle Co. Examples are many and widespread; they included Swindon's railway cottages, and company housing for various industrial concerns, but perhaps the most influential example was at Saltaire where Sir Titus Salt, having amassed a sizeable personal fortune from pioneering the processing of alpaca wool in his five mills in Bradford, built the most complete model industrial village in Britain at that time (and probably since) during the quarter century 1851–76.

With this sort of model of what was possible, certain influential figures could turn to the problems of the existing stock of dwellings. It is in this connection that the singular contribution of Octavia Hill was made. The granddaughter of Southwood Smith, helped financially and through encouragement by John Ruskin, she added to the housing reform movement by demonstrating the efficacy of personal management. She and a band of women workers from 1865 onwards followed a policy of disciplined self-help for slum dwellers: rents paid on time, and cleanliness of common stairways, in return for which modest property improvements were made. The leases of slum properties were bought and poor residents 'upgraded' through a revival of self-respect. Effectively a housing manageress, she was soon appointed by the Ecclesiastical Commissioners to manage the greater part of their properties in Southwark. Supported by influential and wealthy friends, her work was singularly devoted to improving the dwellings of the London poor; it attracted considerable attention and she was active in the propaganda for the Artizans' Dwellings Bill of 1875 (see p. 42), as was made clear in her book *Homes of the London poor* (1875), compiled from a number of magazine articles at the time.

Housing reform was a particularly dispersed movement and its spokesmen or representatives covered many aspects, from the residents themselves to housing construction, layout and design; it overlapped with health concerns and extended over the interests of a number of the new professional groupings. It inevitably touched on aspects of social reform where focus was even more difficult to establish. It occasioned concern to be expressed in certain quarters about the *causes* of poor housing (low wages and high rents), but in fact attention was placed more on the *consequences* of deprived conditions (fecklessness, drink, crime and prostitution). Cooperative housekeeping was just one interesting initiative (Pearson, 1988).

Both a strength and a weakness therefore of housing reform as a move-ment was its sheer breadth of canvas, but it was helped along by some voluble and persistent exponents. George Godwin, for example, architect, and editor for 40 years of *The Builder*, founded in 1842, made his weekly publication a forum for an authoritative comment on housing matters. The journal was a major source of information and a great influence in opinion shaping in a variety of professional and propagandist bodies. When he retired in 1883 he had successfully diffused advice, comment and techni-cal knowledge to a wide readership in the professional associations in architecture and engineering. A collection of his writings appeared as *London Shadows: a glance at the homes of the thousands* as early as 1854; *Town swamps and social bridges* was published in 1859, both books deal-ing with the problems of slum housing.

There was in fact no shortage of essays, conference addresses, pam-phlets and treatises on matters of housing and housing reform. One of the most lively publications was that by James Hole. In 1864 the Society of Arts held a conference on the subject of the Dwellings of the Working Classes, to which representatives of the institutes in union with it were invited. The Committee of the Leeds Mechanics Institution offered a prize for an essay on this subject. Hole won and read his essay in January 1865. The essay was subsequently enlarged and was published as *The homes of the working classes with suggestions for their improvement* (1866). He emphasized the need for legal controls over space around buildings, street widths and the prevention of certain forms of dwellings, for example the back-to-back so predominant in Leeds. His concern, naturally enough, was for improve-ments to working-class housing and he was quick to see the relationship between environmental deprivation and social improvement. Today we would call this environmental determinism and dutifully call the causal relationship into question, but to the mid-Victorian reformer the message was clear enough:

> In a dark, dirty, crowded, ill-ventilated court or back street, commonsense perceives what is confirmed by the longest experience, that it as difficult for health or virtue to exist as for the vegetation of the tropics to thrive amid the snows of Iceland. The improvement of the material circumstances of the working classes is the condition precedent for all other efforts for raising their moral character. (Hole, 1866; 1985 edn, p. 1)

Hole's prescriptions for the future extended beyond the question of hous-ing to a view about the urban environment in general: from the laying-out of streets to open space and the provision of amenities. He applied his analy-sis and concern to his city of Leeds:

> There exists no power to control the laying out of streets, except the often neglected one, that the levels must be satisfactory, and that the street must not be less than 10 yards wide. In other respects they may be laid out in every

imaginable way, of any length, at any angle. The result is the greatest confusion and ugliness. There have not been a dozen straight streets of any great length laid out within the last 30 years, though the population has increased 67 per cent in that period. The town is a maze, without plan, order, or management; here a *cul de sac*, there a house projected far beyond the general line of building, spoiling what would else have been a decent street . . . In Leeds every man who lays out land, or builds does simply what is right *in his own eyes*; if it suits his neighbours, well, if not, so much the worse for his neighbour, and frequently for himself. Opportunities still exist, but are rapidly passing away, for securing *open spaces* for the health and recreation of the inhabitants . . . The water supply of Leeds requires to be freed from the existing pollutions . . . Neither ought the Aire to be longer permitted to become merely a large open sewer for receiving all the abominations of Bradford and Leeds.   (Hole, 1866; 1985 edn, pp. 142-4)

From all these sources, then, there was a groundswell of opinion, moral concern, technical information, visionary perspectives, and practical experiments. Unorganized, disparate and lacking an immediately recognizable focus, there was nonetheless a kind of coherence sufficient over time to impress political figures, both locally and centrally, whose allegiance and support were necessary if advocacy was to be translated into innovation and practical exposition, legally enforced by public intervention. Pleas were increasingly entered for the regulation of the arrangement and construction of dwellings in order to ensure light and ventilation. It was argued that Parliament had provided for the safety of the public in many ways: on the highway, on the railway, at sea, in the mine and in the factory, in the construction of sewers, walls and chimneys, and against the extension of fire. Why then should a man be permitted to let property which would injure the health of the public by virtue of its cramped design and layout?

We do well then to look at sources of influence and directions of pressure. The obstacles of public apathy, resistance to state initiative, objection to new building on the rates, and a preference to rely on voluntaryism and private philanthropy, kept housing effectively off the national political agenda for many years; but as we shall see, once some inevitable first steps had been taken there was an apparent irreversibility about it all. We look with interest therefore at the influence of such bodies as the Charity Organization Society founded in 1869, of which Octavia Hill was a member, designed to attack the root causes of need and pauperism; in 1873 a Special Dwellings Committee was set up to inquire specifically into the whole housing problem: an investigation which led them to advocate more public-sector intervention in the form of compulsory powers to acquire land for housing purposes and an expansion of loan facilities from the Public Works Loan Commissioners. With the remorselessness of the constant drip on stone, housing established itself as a subject of legitimate public concern.

In the event, progress was made on three fronts: building control and by-laws; action against insanitary housing; and local improvement schemes.

✗ **Building Control.** During the nineteenth century important steps were taken to extend the powers of the state through Parliamentary Building Acts and local by-laws, in relation to housing and a wide range of environmental matters including burial grounds, pleasure grounds, offensive trades, rubbish disposal and street construction (Gaskell, 1983). Eighteenth-century London was the subject of various building regulations drawn up following the Great Fire, and codified in the London Building Act, 1774. These regulations were to provide a model for provincial towns in later years, where for a long period the situation was plainly chaotic. Overlapping bodies (Commissioners and the Town Council) had similar powers in respect of certain functions, while in some newly developing areas building regulations did not apply at all. Consequently many authorities sought their own local Building Acts for similar purposes, and between 1800 and 1845 nearly 400 Improvements Acts were obtained for various local government purposes in 208 towns in England and Wales.

Administrative reform was clearly necessary and in a very complex period in the 1840s a measure of rationalization was introduced, parliamentarians balancing throughout the influence of central and local interests, with on the one hand the traditional respect for the sanctity of private property, and on the other the objections on financial grounds to anything that implied an increase in the cost of working-class housing. Following the second reading of Lord Normanby's Bill in 1842 (Home Secretary in Lord Melbourne's second Adminstration) the Bill was divided and a separate Building Regulations Bill was drawn up to deal with matters related to the London Building Act. Eventually it was withdrawn but the debate surrounding its passage (it was sent to a Select Committee of the House of Lords) helped future consideration of the issues.

In 1844 the Metropolitan Building Act greatly extended the range of London building regulations. It followed Lord Normanby's Bill and introduced for the first time controls relating to street widths and spaces at the rear of buildings, drainage, heights of buildings and structural safeguards.

In the provinces meanwhile each locality needed its separate Act to control buildings, streets, nuisances and drainage. This procedure was slow and expensive, and there was no great consistency in the local Bills as presented. A measure of coordination came with the Town Improvement Clauses Act, 1847: in particular, standard street widths were laid down and certain matters of building construction were standardized. Local Bills were considerably reduced in length through the practice of making reference to appropriate clauses in the Consolidating Act. Local difficulties were two-edged: on the one hand detailed local Acts cost time and money but they preserved local independence; on the other, it was feared that reliance on a national Building Act would circumscribe that independence at a time of considerable mistrust of central control.

In the event the Public Health Act, 1848 broke new ground, establishing national standards to be observed by local authorities in matters of public health. Primarily concerned with drains and water supply and paving and street cleansing, as we have seen (p. 27), it was only marginally concerned with building control, but it did stipulate the handing in of plans, not only for streets and drainage, but also for buildings before operational work began. The Act was of course permissive and by 1854 only 182 Boards of Health had been established – and not many of these were concerned with building control.

We have to look then to the Local Government Act, 1858 for the next effective extension of public regulation. With only a minority Tory Government in office Parliament in fact proceeded to significantly amend the 1848 Act by considerably extending building-control powers to include regulations for the structure and stability of buildings and the space around them. It also extended the 1848 powers for local authorities to make by-laws, for example with regard to new streets and drainage. Under the Act, town-improvement matters were placed in a sub-department of the Home Office called the Local Government Act Office, from whence came a so-called 'Form of By-Laws' which attempted to draw up a set of nationwide guidelines covering such matters as street widths (a recommended width of 36 ft for a carriage way) and space around buildings (a minimum of 150 sq. ft at the rear). The days of the future Local Government Board and Model By-Laws were clearly foreshadowed, but the balance of local and national concern and the resolution of suspicion and conflict of interests had not yet been decided.

A pattern, however, had been established. Almost all major towns proceeded to issue by-laws according to the 1848 and 1858 Acts. The need to make provision for fresh air, light and space in the urban environment gradually established primacy of concern. Increasing attention was given to the layout of land and housing development to achieve these objectives, and by-laws proved to be a welcome addition to local powers. George Godwin's pamphlet in 1864, *Another blow for life* pressed for more legal interference and Building Act application, his journal *The Builder* also taking up the cause; evasion of local controls was castigated. But against this, some local authorities were running into legal difficulties regarding the enforcement of their by-laws and the limitations of the 'Form of By-Laws' were becoming evident.

The way out of the problems encountered came with the Royal Commission established in 1869 to enquire into the sanitary administration of the country. Its Report (1871) significantly endorsed the by-law system as the appropriate means for controlling all sanitary matters, and consequently building development. Improvements were advocated and events proceeded rapidly. Again, as we have seen (p. 28), the Local Government Board was established in 1871 as a new department of state. The Public Health Act, 1872 established sanitary authorities across the whole country, with obligatory powers. The Public Health Act, 1875 consolidated and codified all previous sanitary legislation. In 1877 the Board, after due consultations with local authorities and the Royal Institute of British Architects, published its Model by-laws. By the mid-1880s virtually all municipalities had issued new by-laws and the very terms 'by-law house' and 'by-law street' came to suggest an environmental uniformity, a regulated order and a mechanistic rationing of space in the new suburbs of the late-Victorian city. For a while London remained outside the national legislation, but caught up with the Building Act, 1894. To all intents and purposes, however, we can say that public control over built form had reached new levels in a careful blend of central and local powers.

The Model by-laws were permissive, but in the event they were speedily established as standard local authority practices. By 1882 nearly 1,000 urban authorities (and 600 rural authorities) had local building by-laws approved. The categories conferred lasting features on the late Victorian urban townscape. Streets exceeding 100 ft in length were to be at least 36 ft wide. For house construction a complete scale of specifications was prescribed. In front of every domestic building there was to be an open space of 24 ft between the frontage and the opposite lands and premises. In the rear 150 sq. ft of open space was required. Every habitable room of a dwelling was to have one window of a regulatory size in proportion to the floor area of the room, opening externally. Detailed sanitary arrangements were also listed. Local problems of supervision and inspection frustrated the operation of the building by-laws for some time, as did certain vested interests (such as those concerning back-to-back houses in West Yorkshire), but the first really effective set of national building regulations had been produced. The new situation created seemed irreversible; with power shared between central and local government, the package neatly balanced the advantages of local flexibility and national authority.

The progressive adoption of the regulations, the increased administrative efficiency and commitment of local councils, and the growing competence of local officials, certainly had the effect of securing improvements in public health and upgrading the level of building construction by the later years of the nineteenth century. One problem emerged however: minimum standards tended to be regarded as the maximum by the speculative developer. But for the moment an interesting phase had run its course, illustrating particularly well how lobbies, special interests and the articulation of public attitudes impinged on government, all affecting the nature and timing of legislation. A critical background was provided by the growth of local government and the antagonism between local councils and central government, the waters being further muddied by virtue of the suspicion and jealousy with which London was regarded by the more powerful of the provincial cities. Then there was always the retarding hand not only of the builders, with generally small practices and a slowness to innovate, but also of individuals in general keen to protect property rights and their traditional independence. Amongst the professions, there was legal caution, but the doctors and, latterly, the architects lent powerful support to change. So there was no great, inevitable surge towards effective building control either nationally or locally; it was slow, piecemeal, marked by periodic surges and governed by political expediences.

Insanitary housing. While attention was being given to the improved construction of new dwellings there remained the problem of those numbers of the older stock which were clearly insanitary and of faulty construction to the point of them being unsafe as well as unfit. From the 1860s central government progressively invaded the sanctity of property rights by giving local authorities power to undertake clearance schemes through the compulsory purchase of dwellings and land. The barrier, first breached by national legislation in 1868 was widened in 1875; later the floodgates were opened further and swept aside in the twentieth century. There had, of course, been precedents: compulsory acquisition for canal building, for the enclosure movement and for railway construction, but private property in housing seemed a different matter and intervention was long resisted.

The setting was provided by the strength of the sanitary movement and the insistence that the eradication of the slums would remove the sources of pestilence and disease. There were of course related factors operating in particular cities, such as the easing of overcrowding and the sweeping away of ugly eyesores, embarrassing to civic dignity, but, as we shall see, these were matters for Local Acts. In 1866 William Torrens, a back-bencher, introduced a Bill dealing with slum clearance; it provided for compulsory powers of demolition or repair and also for the building of replacement dwellings. Fierce opposition was encountered and when the Bill was reintroduced the following year the clause relating to replacement was ultimately dropped. When the Bill reached the statute book in 1868 as the Artizans' and Labourers' Dwellings Act it was much emasculated, providing only for the local authority to secure improvement by repair or demolition. Importantly however, it was now established that an owner was responsible for the condition of his property. In effect though, the Act was without teeth because there were no provisions for compensation in the event of property being demolished, consequent upon representation by the Medical Officer and the local council.

The logic of the principle of enforced housing fitness, once having been established, could not be further denied and against a background of pressure from the Charity Organization Society, the Social Science Association and the Royal College of Physicians, the Home Secretary (R.A. Cross) introduced his Artizans' Dwellings Bill in 1875. Local vestries disapproved of its provisions but compared with the years 1866 to 1868 parliamentary opposition was much weaker. The Bill reached the statute book as the Artizans' and Labourers' Dwellings Improvement Act, 1875. Whereas the Torrens Act had dealt with single *properties*, the Cross Act was concerned with larger *areas* and introduced the idea of dealing comprehensively with the unfit-housing problems of a whole district. It was still only permissive legislation and the Act was shackled by its compensation clauses which significantly benefited propertied interests, yet it provided a model to be followed in various measures of urban renewal, guided by public action, over the next 100 years. As has been neatly summarized, the Act

> aimed to remove slums and put new working class dwellings in their place. The midwife for this operation was to be the local authority, which would designate the site, compensate the owners, clear the land and sell it to private developers. One geography would be replaced by another.
>
> (Yelling, 1986, p. 10)

The Act made the demolition of extensive slum and unhealthy areas possible, and also provided for rehousing. The land acquired could be sold to other bodies to carry out the rehousing provisions, and in this respect the large model dwelling companies in London, which had an urgent need of housing land, were seen as obvious beneficiaries. The local authorities themselves could only be the rehousing agency with the approval of central government – and then any houses built had to be sold within 10 years. National resistance to the idea of housing provided by local authorities was powerful, but an important step forward had been taken in furthering the various practices of urban renewal. Experience over the next decade and beyond would prove invaluable for the course of future developments.

In the event it was soon clear that Cross's Act had failed. Negotiations over sites quickly showed that fundamental shifts in attitudes were required to both compensation over property and public expenditure, and public opinion was not ready for this. The notion remained that the poor still had some untapped ability to pay for their own housing improvement, and hence any imposition on the public purse remained largely unjustified. Four years after the Act, of the 80 towns in which the provisions could be adopted (the Act was applicable to provincial towns above a certain population size), only in 20 had any action been taken; 11 were still at the discussion stage and none had erected replacement dwellings after demolition. Arguments about rate burdens and the difficulties of disposing of cleared sites were unbridgeable. Liverpool had begun a policy of clearance under the City's Sanitary Amendment Act, 1864, but the Corporation resolved to apply the 1875 Act to the Nash Grove district of the city. Slow progress was made because no builder would take on the prospect of rehousing the same number of people as had been displaced; ultimately, after 10 years the city itself developed its own scheme in Victoria Buildings.

In two cities, however, successful renewal schemes could be reported, though the reasons for their success lay with local situations. In Glasgow the question of sanitary reform was high on the political agenda in the 1860s. Public health regulations were strengthened in the Glasgow Police Act, 1862 and a sanitary bureaucracy was formed with the appointment of a Medical Officer of Health and an inspectorate with powers over the cleansing of housing and the reduction of overcrowding. More relevant to our story however is that provision was made for the clearance of the overcongested city. Demolition work financed by the City Union Railway made way for the new St Enoch terminus, while the City Improvement Act tackled the areas untouched by the railway works.

In Birmingham, civic improvement became a major local political issue. In the 1860s the city centre acquired a central reference library and a museum and art gallery; in the early 1870s a new plan for sewage disposal was carried through; during 1873 and 1874 Joseph Chamberlain as mayor municipalized local gas companies and, in 1875, took over the Water Works Company; meanwhile a new Council House was under construction. Cross's Act in the same year provided the opportunity for the full flowering of the civic gospel: the City Council approved an Improvement Scheme covering 93 acres of slum land in the city centre, the city actually acquiring 43 acres. New building started in 1878 based on the showpiece of an imposing new commercial boulevard, Corporation Street. The new undertaking progressed slowly, the street being completed section by section, thereby releasing land gradually on to the market. It was essentially a commercial scheme and no working-class housing was provided, but Birmingham Liberals gained Cross's Conservative blessing.

Elsewhere slum clearance was taking place in London, where the Metropolitan Board of Works and the City Commissioners of Sewers were the executive authorities. In all, 16 schemes were prepared and completed by the Metropolitan Board of Works before its demise in 1888; a further six were started and completed by its successor the London County Council. Many more representations were made but were not proceeded with. All in all the experience of implementing the Cross Act was not a happy one. Progress was slow; the various statutory procedures were unwieldly and cumbersome; and negotiations over the sale of land were protracted. Nonetheless in the completed schemes 42 acres of slum property were cleared and nearly 23,000 people were displaced (note the staggering density of about 540 persons per acre). Much of the land sold went to the Peabody Trust who replaced the old rookeries with their typical block development.

The mid-1880s came to a close. The question of urban health and the sanitary arrangements had been progressively tackled. The state had been drawn into the vortex of collective action against the interests of the individual, but we see in the knotty issue of slum clearance those Victorian political dilemmas that bedevilled speedy solutions to the nineteenth-century housing problem. In spite of its many limitations, Cross's Act had produced a political compromise which finally broke through deeply rooted objections. The major cities were on the threshold of effective arrangements which reconciled the removal of the slums for community benefit with the agreement, dependent on adequate compensation, of the property owner, redevelopment to be carried out by voluntary agencies. It remained to be seen whether the ambitions of philanthropic and municipal enterprise could be effectively harnessed.

Other urban schemes

There were other occasions, when quite apart from the immediate imperative of housing clearance, environmental works were carried out by local authorities. More often than not it was connected with the cutting of new streets or street widening.

Newcastle offered the largest single example of a local-authority-driven, central area development scheme when John Clayton (town clerk) joined forces with John Dobson (architect) and Richard Grainger (builder), and formed a triumvirate to create a pattern of central streets of elegance and style in the years during the 1830s (Wilkes and Dodds, 1964). The opportunity to build on open land in the heart of the city was seized avidly. Following a plan seemingly prepared by Thomas Oliver, the Common Council of Newcastle acquired a vast number of properties for a radical improvement of the city, the key to which was the purchase of the undeveloped Anderson Place in 1834. The new markets were opened in 1835 and Grey Street completed in 1837, with the Grey Monument erected the following year.

The regional capital was given its stamp of architectural quality which it retains to this day (for the particular contribution of the architect John Dobson, see Faulkner and Greg, 1987).

In London there was no equivalent to the schemes of Baron Haussmann for Paris. The Metropolitan Board of Works (1855–1888) was an executive authority but it had no such concentration of arbitrary power, no access to huge funds and certainly no powers for the assault on property as took place in the French capital. Instead, London had to be content with piecemeal street improvements, often at relatively low cost as they passed through congested and insanitary districts and with the bonus of removing slums at the same time. Most of the principal thoroughfares in central London owe their origin to Victorian improvements: Charing Cross Road, Shaftesbury Avenue, Queen Victoria Street, Northumberland Avenue, Holborn Viaduct and the Embankment to name but a few.

In other cities it was a question of local improvement schemes under Private Acts of Parliament. In Dundee for example a Private Act of 1871 enabled the clearance of unhealthy, overcrowded dwellings and the construction of new wide streets. In Edinburgh a City Improvement Trust with private powers began operations to remove the worst of the city's dwellings in 1867. In Liverpool work was undertaken under the Sanitary Amendment Act, 1864. Leeds had its Improvement and Gas Act, 1870. Bristol's sanitary improvements were impressive, and the city too aimed at a 'civic gospel' like Birmingham.

Municipal parks

Concern over health left an indelible mark on urban Britain by virtue of the various ways in which government, both local and central, was forced to respond to particular situations which public opinion found unacceptable. The response to housing has been examined in some detail, in which the search for fresh air and space proved so important. Exactly the same imperative underpinned the creation of municipal parks. The flavour is immediately recognizable in the Report of the Select Committee on Public Walks, published in 1833:

> With a rapidly increasing Population, lodged, for the most part in narrow courts and confined streets, the means of occasional exercise and recreation in the fresh air are every day lessened, as enclosures take place and buildings spread themselves on every side. A few Towns have been fortunate in this respect from having some open space in their immediate vicinity . . . yet even at these places . . . the accommodation is inadequate to the wants of the increasing number of the people.   (cited in Chadwick, 1966, p. 50)

The Committee reported in favour of the provision of Public Walks and Open Spaces and suggested legislation by which land could be exchanged or dedicated for the purpose. This was but an opening shot and it was not until the 1840s that a number of Acts included powers for the provision of public parks. The health lobby maintained its pressure, but meanwhile private park development showed the benefits to be obtained. In London,

Regent's Park was laid out from 1811, though the public were not freely admitted until 1838; St James's Park was begun in 1828; and there were pleasure gardens in London and various centres of fashion.

The parks movement owed much to developments in garden design and the presence of gardeners of great technical skill and artistic flair. J.C. Loudon, for example, the landscape architect, first a designer of gardens for great houses (as at Alton Towers, Staffordshire for instance) became the creator of one of the first parks designed for and owned by the public. This was at Derby where Joseph Strutt, a local manufacturer, presented an 11-acre site to the Corporation for a public park; Loudon's Arboretum was the result (1839–40), a feature found to be popular and adopted elsewhere in the Midlands in later years. Joseph Paxton was even more influential. His Prince's Park, Liverpool (1844) was a speculative development to provide a setting for the building of some handsome villas, but Birkenhead Park was a very different enterprise. The new settlement of Birkenhead was being developed by Improvement Commissioners as a rival to Liverpool; the third Improvement Act, 1843 provided for a major public park as part of the town's expansion, and the park was opened in 1847.

The municipal park movement developed rapidly with a number of urban parks laid out in the 1840s and 1850s. In London the Select Committee had noted the virtual absence of park facilities in the east of the city. Pushed by public demand, the Government promoted an Act in 1840 which enabled York House to be sold to the Duke of Sutherland, and from the proceeds land in Hackney, Bethnal Green and Bow was purchased and laid out as a park. James Pennethorne, Surveyor and Architect to the Commissioners of Woods and Forests, began the design of Victoria Park in 1844. After many delays, Battersea Park, south of the Thames, followed in the 1860s, also from his office, but a third scheme, for an Albert Park in north London came to nought. Meanwhile, the setting-up of the Metropolitan Board of Works (MBW) in 1855 meant that the question of provision of parks for the metropolis could be transferred to the new body. The opening of both Finsbury Park and Southwark Park followed in 1869. Park provision in London was therefore rather slow and piecemeal, comprising both the royal parks of Victoria, Battersea and Kennington, and the MBW parks of Finsbury and Southwark, complemented by the older Regent's Park and St James's and other open spaces and heaths.

Elsewhere in the country the situation developed rather differently. The Towns Improvement Clauses Act, 1847 gave permissive powers for the acquisition of land and subsequent maintenance of parks by local authorities. But the movement had developed its own pace with the new fashion of botanic gardens and the particular drive that Paxton and others had established, and with the powers of Local Acts where necessary. For example Glasgow Town Council bought the Kelvingrove and Woodlands Estates in 1852; Paxton's Kelvingrove Park followed the next year as a setting for well-to-do residences in Park Terrace, Park Gardens, Park Circus and Park Quadrant. In 1857 Glasgow Green, originally common land, was taken over as a public park and Queen's Park, also by Paxton, was laid out on the site of a farm. Paxton's influence continued in Halifax (the People's Park) Dundee (Baxter Park) and Dunfermline (Public Park).

The new manufacturing towns responded enthusiastically to the parks movement. There was a good deal of local kudos to be gained from association with public works that attracted praise from worthy notables and political support from an electorate, particularly if the costs involved were not all that great. Three early parks in Manchester established a 'northern' tradition and characteristically two 'key actors' appeared: a local business man, Mark Phillips, enthusiastic about parks (he had given evidence to the Select Committee), who with others contributed generously to a local fund; and the successful winners of a competition, Joshua and his son Henry Major, landscape gardeners of Leeds. The parks of about 30 acres each were opened in 1846: two in Manchester (Philips and Queen's) and one in Salford (Peel); Alexandra Park followed, the first in the south of Manchester, in 1868.

Liverpool followed Manchester a little later, but perhaps achieved more in terms of environmental impact because a veritable ring of parks was created towards the periphery of the built-up area and as wedges into the city itself. After the opening of Wavertree Park in 1856 and Shiel Park in 1862 a flurry of park development continued throughout the 1860s and under the Liverpool Improvement Act a loan of half a million pounds was raised to create three more parks (Newsham, Stanley and Sefton), financed out of the rates – a capital sum many times that of the Manchester parks.

As we have seen, in many cities municipal parks came from local gifts either as donations or the lease of land. In Birmingham, Adderley Park (1857) and Calthorpe Park (1858) owe their origins to this. In Sheffield the first public park was presented by the Duke of Norfolk in 1847. In Hull the People's Park (1863) was also a gesture of local philanthropy. Bradford's Peel Park, acquired by public subscription, was given to the corporation in 1863. Middlesbrough's Albert Park was presented to the town in 1868 by the steel magnate Henry Bolckow. For a variety of reasons, during the early years of the second half of the nineteenth century local councils had taken action to acquire or receive land for the laying-out and maintenance of public parks. A consequence was that a major feature of the urban environment fell into municipal hands for public benefit; inspired by a concern for health, but with overtones of propriety and morality for the masses and with implications for the fostering of outdoor community recreation. The movement flourished and with the strengthening of powers in the Public Health Act, 1875, park development was suitably stimulated.

Municipal parks represented just one strand in the search for urban open space. In London the founding of the Commons Preservation Society in 1865 was in response to the threat to the city's common land by building development. Lord Eversley, a barrister, liberal MP and son of a former Speaker of the House of Commons, was as chairman very well placed to obtain parliamentary sympathy for his cause. Eversley's Society fought for the continuation of common rights – not, as the Metropolitan Board of Works had suggested, by buying up of the interests of the lords of the manors concerned, selling some of the land for building purposes and improving the rest of the common land for public use. The result of the Committee's work was that a number of commons around London were saved to varying extents by means of court proceedings or otherwise under pressure by the Society. Hampstead Heath, Wimbledon Common and Wandsworth Common were saved from further encroachment and were fixed in the open-space pattern of the growing London.

At the other end of the scale there was a widespread interest, both in London and other cities, in finding small pockets of land for recreation purposes in the heart of the built-up areas. In London the reformist pressure groups included the Kyrle Society set up in 1875, and the Metropolitan Public Garden, Boulevard and Playground Association founded in 1882. One focus was on the possible use of disused burial grounds, and the Open Spaces Acts of 1881 and 1883 enabled local authorities to acquire these and other sites so that they may be used as public gardens.

The influence of two important figures should be noted: Octavia Hill and Lord Brabazon. The indefatigable zeal of the former has already been noted (pp. 36) and it is no coincidence that her concern for housing was matched by that for open space, because the two are linked through the common route of health. The Kyrle Society, which she helped to found, set up an Open Spaces Committee through which she exerted pressure for new legislative measures, the 1881 and 1883 Acts (above) being cases in point.

Lord Brabazon inspired the founding of the Metropolitan Public Gardens Association (for short). It too was involved in the re-use of old churchyards and provided influential support towards the end of the 1880s in encouraging private benefactors to give land to London for parks, major examples being in Dulwich (by the college), in Camberwell (by a local builder) and in Highgate (by Sir Sydney Waterlow).

3 The Turn of the Century

So far, the account of the development of steps taken to extend the nature and scale of the public regulation of the environment during the middle and later years of the nineteenth century has established that by the 1880s the practice of public-sector control, and the intervention in private interests concerning land and property by collective, public interests had become a recognized feature of British life. Steps had been hesitant and slow, and attended on occasion by considerable hostility, but they were progressive and seemingly irreversible in the movement towards greater public control of community and environmental affairs. In matters of the regulation of street widths, new highway construction, public health and sanitation, fire control, building construction and space around buildings, important developments had taken place, and an established local government system would jealously preserve hard-won powers. During this time, while the poor continued to live in bad, old houses, for many there had been a considerable levelling up and the solidly-built English terraced house (Muthesius, 1982) offered very satisfactory accommodation.

During a period of approximately a quarter of a century, let us say, 1885 to 1910, a bedrock of basic environmental regulation, fashioned over the previous 50 years, was considerably extended. What had been a matter of Victorian urban management, dictated by public health and expressed through by-laws, became transformed into other concepts and practices in which the idea of town planning took root and flourished. In this period it has been fashionable to see a continuum from the nineteenth to the twentieth century in terms of the planned regulation of the environment; Ashworth (1954) developed his thesis on these lines. But it was not as simple as that. Certainly we can see that local government practices were maintained, and for many years housing and town planning were regarded as so connected that the terms appeared together in the same legislation: Housing, Town Planning etc. Act, 1909, Housing and Town Planning Act, 1919. But there was in fact an important change in outlook and application from one century to the next; there was a distinct shift from nineteenth-century control, characterized by mechanistic regulation of standards and by-law control of development, to a twentieth-century regulation based on a more fluid interpretation of norms and a more pragmatic search for qualitative improvements in the environment.

The dissatisfaction with an old-established way of looking at problems and defining solutions came to a head at the end of the century in the crisis years of the late Victorian city. A new model of analysis and prescription took shape, transforming precepts of sanitarianism, by-law control and public works into those of the application of new design standards, land-use control and urban management on a comprehensive canvas. The immediate target was a solution to the problem of working-class housing; the motor was a belief in 'social progress', harnessed to the proven virtues of rational government; one particular lubricant was the emergence of a powerful garden-city movement; and the ultimate beneficiary was the new profession, with its adhesive ideology, town planning.

We should not be deluded by any fanciful idea that there was any kind of inevitable progression from looking at urban problems one way, to regarding them in another, through some notion of 'enlightenment'. Town planning was no more enlightened than by-law control though it was associated with a progressive social outlook and utopian idealism; the fact was that by the 1890s conditions conducive to the emergence of a new outlook had become established. It is necessary to look a lot closer to see how and why new practices then superseded the old; and to examine the role of key actors in the translation, and the formative influences that made it all possible. Four stages are apparent in the process, not entirely separated chronologically. First we look at the nature of the housing crisis: why after half a century of effort, did the problem seem as intractable as, or even worse than ever? Second we note the critical emergence of new design criteria for working-class dwellings. Third we acknowledge the new spatial strategies for urban growth in which, via garden cities, another solution to working-class housing was available. Fourth we see how in the new field of town planning, housing and related problems were to be resolved.

The crisis in housing

The Royal Commission on the Housing of the Working Classes (1884-5), chaired by Sir Charles Dilke and with the Prince of Wales a member, inevitably attracted a good deal of publicity. From the copious evidence supplied to it, we can see that the set of housing problems was unlikely to be alleviated by forms of State action then being pursued; indeed certain measures may have been exacerbating the problem. Overcrowding in inner London for example had worsened as a result of street improvements and the removal of bad housing, which reduced the number of dwelling houses – a contraction also made worse through commercial expansion. In areas where the poor were chiefly concentrated, the supply of accommodation was fixed or declining, with the inevitable consequence of high and increasing rents. But while this pressure was being exerted wages were static, with the poor living near the range of casual work around the city centre, adjoining the warehouses and the markets. Rack renting, whereby houses would be broken up for subletting, also led to overcrowding and high rents. The problem was at its worst in inner London, where there seemed an unbreakable chain of cause and effect in which housing was a crucial link.

Of poverty and squalor there was abundant information which was seized on in a remarkable period of sustained comment about the housing situation. Much of it spilled over into protest against social conditions and the need for social reform; some was emotive and dictated by evangelical and humanitarian ideals; some was less impassioned and as objective as the new field of social science permitted; and some was deliberately 'popular' for the widening readership of the daily press.

In 1883 'an inquiry into the condition of the abject poor' was published under the title *The bitter city of outcast London*. This short, but vivid pamphlet was written by Revd W.C. Preston, a Congregational minister who had been a newspaper editor and had experience in Wigan at the height of the Lancashire cotton famine. Revd Andrew Mearns, to whom authorship has wrongly been ascribed, was secretary of the Congregational Union; he had undertaken the field work on which the pamphlet was based. In just 20 pages the message was laid bare:

> seething in the very centre of our great cities, concealed by the thinnest crust of civilisation and decency, is a vast mass of moral corruption, of heart-breaking misery and absolute godlessness.   (Preston, 1883, p. 1)
> Few who will read these pages have any conception of what these pestilential human rookeries are, where tens of thousands are crowded together amidst horrors which call to mind what we have heard of the middle passage of the slave ship.   (Preston, 1883, p. 4)
> The State must ... secure for the poorest ... the right to live in something better than fever dens; the right to live as something better than the uncleanest of brute beasts.   (Preston, 1883, p. 15)

A familiar target was the evil of drink – not only for Preston but for many others, none more explicit than General William Booth, founder of the Salvation Army. His book *In darkest England and the way out* (1890) sold 200,000 copies in its first year and went to five editions by the end of 1891. For Booth, drink, was the common denominator of the country's social ills: poverty, homelessness, vice and crime.

> A population sodden with drink, steeped in vice, eaten up by every social and physical malady, these are the denizens of Darkest England amidst whom my life has been spent, and to whose rescue I would now summon all that is best in the manhood and womanhood of our land.   (Booth, 1890; 1970 edn, p. 15)

His strategic solution was to leave the city in planned emigration to colonies, both home (farm colonies in the countryside) and overseas.

Another, and growing concern was the plight of the poor. In 1885, that left-of-centre popular London newspaper, the *Pall Mall Gazette* took up the cause of working-class poverty by serializing the results of a survey undertaken by the Marxist Social Democratic Foundation. Its findings suggested that one quarter of Londoners lived in conditions of abject poverty.

There was some scepticism about this, not least by one given to less impassioned observation, namely Charles Booth. Born in 1840 in Liverpool to a well-to-do Unitarian family, he entered the shipping business. A long-standing interest in social issues resurfaced in the 1880s, when he became particularly concerned about the problems of poverty and unemployment in London where he was then living. Early in 1886 he repudiated the claim of F.D. Hyndman, leader of the Social Democratic Foundation, that the scale of poverty in London was that which he had claimed; he promised to conduct his own survey by means of scientific inquiry, employing the latest statistical techniques rather than relying on impressionistic missionaries, radicals and journalists. Over the next 17 years an equal number of volumes, commencing in 1889, reported his findings, patiently collected with his cousin-in-law Beatrice Potter (later Webb), under the title *Life and labour of the people in London.*

This is not the occasion to review Booth's work in full; suffice to say he told a great deal, first about East London, and subsequently about the rest of the city from the point of view of the living conditions of the people, their homes, their environments, work and conditions of work. Concerning poverty, he found that the *Pall Mall Gazette* of 1885 had been wrong, but only to the point of underestimation: (he estimated that nearly 35 per cent of the working-class population of East London could be classified as 'poor' as opposed to the earlier claim of 25 per cent). His second volume took in the rest of London (central, south and outlying), this time avoiding enquiry into the personal lives, the incomes and expenditure patterns of the poor, but rather concentrating on a description of neighbourhoods, their streets and districts. Remarkably, he found that poverty, far from being sharply concentrated in the 900,000 population of East London, was in fact broadly distributed amongst the further 3 million people of the rest of the city, with 30.7 per cent living on or below his defined poverty line. From then on, Booth, now without Beatrice Potter, worked on rather different investigations, with five volumes on the industrial life of the poor, published by 1897, and then seven volumes published in 1902 and 1903 showing how the poor came into contact with social and political institutions, philanthropic organizations, government agencies and, primarily, with the religious bodies. A 17-year study of the life and labour of the people of London came to an end, bequeathing a quite remarkable social portrait. Paradoxically, his work reaffirmed his own faith in individualism and he had only limited time for socialism and the precepts of further state intervention in redeeming the lot of the disadvantaged; however, others were to take his findings and promote their own measures of reform.

To appreciate the flavour of Booth's work and to recognize the depths of environmental deprivation in the worst areas, his street by street analysis is revealing. Take Shelton Street for example, in East London, described in vol. II:

> just wide enough for a vehicle to pass either way, with room between curbstone and houses for one foot passenger to walk; but vehicles would pass seldom, and foot passengers would prefer the roadway to the risk of tearing their clothes against projecting nails. The houses, about forty in number, contained cellars, parlours, and first, second and third floors, mostly two rooms on a floor, and few of the 200 families who lived here occupied more than one room. In little rooms no more than eight ft square, would be found living father, mother and several children.
>
> (Booth, cited in Fried and Elman, 1969, p. 108)

But a wider picture emerged of the social and environmental geography of London from which we might note the tightly packed conditions of the inner ring of East London: Shoreditch, Bethnal Green, Whitechapel and St George's, Wapping, Shadwell, and Ratcliff, with inner portions of Mile End. Space and air were everywhere at a premium with only a few church-yards and burial grounds as open areas. Booth found that nearly all available space was used for building and almost every house was filled with families. Workshops also occupied the ground, obstructing even more light and shutting out air. The target of the housing reformers for space, air and sunlight was amply justified.

It is easy, and in some ways proper, to concentrate on the harshness of life for those at the worst extremities of social polarization in London; after all, the greatest numbers were there. But we should acknowledge that deprivations of a similar scale – and perhaps worse – afflicted other urban centres. Seebohm Rowntree's study of poverty in York, published in 1901, showed that very nearly the same proportion of York's population was living in poverty, as in London (27.8 per cent compared with 30.7 per cent). Many urban histories will point to scenes of distress at the end of the century. It was calculated, for example, that in Manchester and Salford upwards of 212,000 people were in a state of poverty in 1904, more than 75,000 of whom were in severe poverty (Harrison, 1981). Glasgow had 700,000 people living in three square miles, making it the most heavily populated central area in Europe at the outbreak of the Great War; the 'wee bauchle', a man of little more than five feet in height, often with legs bowed by rickets, was the 'underweight, undersized inhabitant of the grimmest slums in Western Europe' (Checkland, 1981, p. 24). On the other hand, Aalen (1987) claims Dublin as the worst housed and unhealthiest in the British isles, with one-third of its 382,000 population (at the end of the century) living in one-room tenements, where death rates were extremely high by the standards of most European cities.

The revelations of investigative journalism, both in London and in provincial cities, reached a more immediate readership than Booth's works of scholarship. One journalist, George R. Sims had as his title *How the poor live and horrible London* (1889). Another such illustration was provided by the novelist Jack London, perhaps the first industrial worker to describe his world in writing. Born in San Francisco in 1876, his early years of hardship were spent in a succession of jobs and experiences of tramping; he was drawn to firm socialist views. Establishing his career as a writer, he was commissioned in 1902 by the American Press Association to go to South Africa and write on the situation there after the Boer War. While he was in England, the project was cancelled and he turned his attention instead to an account of the London slums. For seven weeks he lived amongst the people of East London. Later his story was placed with an American socialist periodical, *Wilshire's Magazine*, and it ran in serial form from March 1903 to January 1904; during this time it was published as a book in November 1903, with the title *The people of the abyss*. It was a powerful catalogue of starvation, lack of shelter and a chronic condition of misery. Jack London picked up a then popular theme, the degeneration of urban man:

the London Abyss is a vast shambles. Year by year, and decade after decade, rural England pours in a flood of vigorous strong life, that not only does not renew itself, but perishes by the third generation. Competent authorities aver that the London workman whose parents and grandparents were born in London is so remarkable a specimen that he is rarely found.

(London, 1903; 1978 edn, p. 24)

As a reformist, the author saw the answer in business management:

society must be reorganized and a capable management put at the head. That the present management is incapable, there can be no discussion. It has drained the United Kingdom of its life blood. It has enfeebled the stay-at-home folk till they are unable longer to struggle in the van of the competing nations. It has built up a West End and an East End as large as the Kingdom is large, in which one end is riotous and rotten, the other end sickly and underfed. (London, 1903; 1978 edn, p. 126)

One constant theme in these catalogues of comment and observation was the problem of working-class housing: its physical and sanitary conditions; the intensity with which it was being used (in other words its overcrowding); its wider environment (residential densities); and its rent levels. With regard to public health and sanitation there seemed little more that could be done, though the progress towards the closure and demolition of unfit dwellings was depressingly slow. The target moved, however, from the improvement of the individual house to the enhancement of the wider environment; the argument now was that social betterment might be realized more surely through the benefits of an environment of health obtained through space and sunlight where low-density housing prevailed. In the meantime statistics as to urban congestion and the sheer concentration of numbers of people in London and the larger cities posed the wider dilemma. Amplifying George Haw's influential condemnation of overcrowding, *No room to live* (1985), census figures were particularly revealing (Cherry, 1979). With the official definition of overcrowding fixed at more than two persons per room, the 1901 census revealed that 16 per cent of the population of the Administrative County of London was living in overcrowded conditions. Within the LCC area some metropolitan boroughs recorded much higher figures, headed by Finsbury at 35 per cent, Stepney 33 per cent, Shoreditch 30 per cent and Bethnal Green only marginally under that figure. But there were high proportions elsewhere, typically in the north-east where Gateshead, South Shields, Tynemouth, Newcastle and Sunderland were all above 30 per cent. The larger Scottish cities also recorded notoriously high rates: more than one in five Scottish families were restricted to one room in which to live. However, we should note that by the beginning of the twentieth century the worst of the overcrowding rates seem to have passed: in England and Wales in 1901 there were nearly 600,000 fewer persons than 10 years previously, living in overcrowded conditions.

Census returns also revealed the general levels of urban densities and highlighted particular blackspots. Overall, the Administrative County of London recorded nearly 61 persons to the acre. But within the LCC area many boroughs exceeded overall densities in excess of 100 to the acre; the very highest were Southwark at 182, Shoreditch 180, Finsbury 172, Bethnal Green 171 and Stepney 169. Elsewhere in the country average urban densities were lower: the list was headed by West Ham at 57 persons per acre (on London's edge and sharing its characteristics) and Liverpool at 52 to the acre. But within these averages some highly localized concentrations revealed excessive levels: in the North Everton district of Liverpool for example there were 54,000 people living at a density of 178 to the acre.

The consequences of overcrowding at these levels led to conditions of life which the present day reader can only regard as almost unbearable. The absence of a general system of mortuaries, for example, involved the retention, in the living room of the family, of a corpse until the funeral could take place. Then there was the practice of dwellings being used for various trade practices: rag picking in unventilated rooms and a variety of offensive trades constituted a particularly serious health hazard. As one observer recounted:

> Such trades, such as match box making, requiring the use of paste, especially in warm weather, are especially disgusting. Rabbit pulling is perhaps the most pernicious, as the air is charged with fluff; and when a stray sunbeam shoots athwart the murky room, the atmosphere appears solid enough to be sliced with a bread-knife.   (White, 1886, p. 137)

Inevitably the issues concerned with the late Victorian urban and housing crisis fed a wider debate about social reform and social progress. The American Henry George, economist and social observer, very influential in this country, propagated the view (and it was widely shared by his contemporaries) that the growing cities somehow provided an unnatural condition to man's existence. In his book *Social problems* (1884) we read:

> This life of great cities is not the natural life of man. He must, under such conditions, deteriorate, physically, mentally, morally. Yet the evil does not end here. This is only one side of it. This unnatural life of the great cities means an equally unnatural life in the country. Just as the wen or tumour, drawing the wholesome juices of the body into its poisonous vortex, impoverishes all other parts of the frame, so does the crowding of human beings into great cities impoverish human life in the country.
>
> (George, 1884; 1931 edn, p. 203)

The argument was that a combination of close confinement and the foul air of the big cities was responsible for shortening individual lives and raising up a puny and ill-developed urban race. No wonder there was an increasing interest in fitness: when Captain Webb, for example, first swam the Channel in 1875 his feat was hailed as unparalleled in strength and endurance.

The problem of urban degeneration was a real one, as was discovered by army recruiting stations at the time of the Boer War. Between 1893 and 1902 35 per cent of all men medically examined for enlistment were rejected as medically unfit (Wohl, 1983, pp. 332–3). In 1902 nearly half the volunteers in Manchester were rejected for military service on grounds of physical unfitness. Rates varied from station to station, but figures suggest a high rate of physical deterioration across urban Britain. Hounslow rejected 40 per cent, Liverpool and Newcastle 38 per cent and Belfast 37 per cent. Between 1897 and 1901 Leeds and Sheffield rejected 27 per cent of recruits and accepted another 29 per cent only provisionally. These figures were not much less than had been recorded for urban recruits (but not rural) at the time of the Crimean War. Stunted growth and physical decline fed the spectre of race degeneration. During the Boer War men were enlisted down to a minimum height of 5 ft; in 1845 only one in ten of the men in the army were under 5 ft 6 in. Disturbing evidence was also being recorded by the medical inspection of school children: poor urban environments were clearly producing children of lower height and weight ratios than elsewhere. Agitation led to the setting up of an official government enquiry, the Inter-Departmental Committee on Physical Deterioration, appointed in September 1903.

But the country was one of many contrasts. C.F.G. Masterman's (1909) penetrating observations on the England of his day confirm this and highlight the problems of London on which all reform hinged. England's divergent parts appeared thus:

> There is rural England, still largely unaffected by modern science and invention, except by the loss of population, drained away; the agricultural labourers, the fishermen, and the artisans of the sleeping provincial towns. There is urban England in hastily created industrial centres, vocal with the clanging of furnaces and the noise of the factories; but still a population in manageable aggregation, set in open spaces, never far from green fields under a wide sky. And there is London: a population, a nation in itself; breeding, as it seems, a special race of man; which only is also produced, and that in less intensive cultivation, in the few other larger cities – Glasgow, Manchester, Liverpool – where the conditions of coagulation offer some parallel to this monster clot of humanity.   (Masterman, 1909, p. 99)

Meanwhile social class stratification again pinpointed London as the geographic concentration by virtue of the massing of urban deprivation. Masterman's national analysis was of a

> 'plutocracy' with riches extravagantly accumulated and extravagantly expended; a middle class industrious and a little bewildered; a labouring population industrious, and in times of prosperity contented; below, a life which cries almost unheeded from a condition of perpetual privation.
> (Masterman, 1909, p. 277)

It is at this point that the social, economic, political and environmental questions came together. Housing deprivation, poverty, casual labour, and broadly termed social problems were all part of the same canvas of concern. A cyclical economic depression of the mid-1880s (1884–7) hit occupations in metals, engineering, shipbuilding, chemicals, textiles and printing. The building industry remained slack, there was distress in the clothing industry (exacerbated by an influx of Jews into East London) and depression in agriculture. Some old-established industries in inner London and the older docks exhibited symptoms of structural decline and faced extinction.

Social protest, never far from the surface, erupted in sporadic outbreaks in 1886 and 1887 (Jones, 1971); the newly founded Social Democratic Foundation marked the emergence of a new radicalism.

Other movements at the time attracted their adherents who saw them as correctives to late Victorian urban and industrial life: university settlements, the smallholding movement and the crafts revival. Of these, the Arts and Crafts Movement feeding on the anti-industrialism of Ruskin and Morris, promised a viable alternative to the social and economic conditions of the time. C.R. Ashbee became a leading figure, starting a small craft workshop in East London called the Guild of Handicraft, before moving in 1902 to Chipping Campden (Crawford, 1985).

For contemporary observers the urban crisis focused, however, first on housing, then on poverty. But it reflected wider issues engrained in social structure, class relations and economic power. In a sense not much has changed in the industrial city: the relationship between the spatial organization of urban society, and the social problems of the city remains crucial and is rediscovered in different ways and at different times – today we call it the 'urban question'. At the end of the century there may have been buoyant belief in 'social progress' and perfectibility of man, which sustained the conviction and idealism of many in Europe and on both sides of the Atlantic, but new political realities about equity in human conditions could not long be ignored. Improvements would not just happen, they had to be made to happen.

One question was that of land reform. High land values prevalent in central districts of cities meant that the burden of paying for concentrated urban space fell on the working class – the least likely section of the community to afford it. The Land Nationalization Society was founded and secured an influential following for some years. Henry George in his book *Progress and poverty* (1880) popularized the idea of a tax upon land values as 'the most just and equal of all taxes':

> It falls only upon those who receive from society a peculiar and valuable benefit, and upon them in proportion to the benefit they receive. It is the taking by the community, for the use of the community, of that value which is the creation of the community. It is the application of the common property to common uses.   (George, 1880; 1911 edn, p. 299)

The twentieth century was to hear much of this argument, and the question of land reform as an ideological issue marked the politics of the Liberal Government, 1906–14. The wider issue was the struggle over proposals to use taxation as a new form of intervention against landed property, and town planning was seen as a device to release large blocks of land into the housing market.

But while radicalism was in the air, political initiatives in matters relating to housing and the environment were slow to take place. The Royal Commission on Housing in 1885 adopted a very conservative stance and proposed no new approach, other than to emphasize the importance of efficient administration. As an outcome, existing legislation would be more clearly codified and in London responsibility for the administration of certain acts was to be transferred from the vestries to the Metropolitan

Board. Little was to be done about the rehousing of the central poor. State responsibility for housing was still shirked.

Institutionally the situation was changing, however. The Local Government Act 1888 created a national system of county boroughs, counties and districts, and in London a new approach was signalled when in 1889 the Metropolitan Board of Works was replaced by the London County Council (LCC), and 10 years later 38 vestries and district boards were replaced by 28 new units, given the status of Metropolitan Boroughs. The Board of Works ended its life in disgrace, with charges of corruption pressed against key officials, and a combination of maladministration and ineffective local government elsewhere in London added to the burden of problems experienced by grossly disadvantaged communities. There seemed to be little effective supervision of house drainage by local authorities, and while Inspectors of Nuisances were appointed by vestries and district boards, there were not many of them: in Islington there was one inspector to 56,000 inhabitants, and in Bermondsey one to 86,000. One commentator insisted that:

> The truth must be told . . . vestrymen, voracious, incapable, devoid of public spirit, swarm like locusts on a field of young millet, fatten on the ratepayers, taint the record of public life, check the interests they are elected to protect. Saturated with corruption, and incompetent, the present form of Local Government in London is doomed.   (White, 1886; 1985 edn, p. 151)

Municipal government in London did not in fact stand comparison to any extent with other big provincial cities, particularly Birmingham, Manchester, Liverpool, Glasgow, Leeds and Bradford (Dolman, 1895). For half a century these municipal boroughs had creditable performances to record in respect of improved sanitary conditions, systems of sewerage and removal of domestic refuse, regulations concerning buildings, improvements in water supply, the municipal ownership of water, gas and markets, and the provision of baths, parks, libraries and art galleries. In London the argument was that while medium-sized cities could conduct their affairs in this way, London was too big to follow suit; it was feared that municipalization could not be undertaken by such a large public body and that its managements would be overrun by jobbery and corruption. The fascinating story of the creation of the London County Council as part of the unfolding story of the governance of metropolitan London is well told by Young and Garside (1982).

The first two administrations in the LCC, 1889–92 and 1892–5, formed by alliances of Liberals and early Socialists, under the name of 'Progressives', took immediate advantage of the Housing of the Working Classes Act, 1890, for which they had campaigned. The Act amalgamated earlier legislation, but under Parts I and II rebuilding on cleared sites was made somewhat easier and Part III allowed authorities to undertake further rehousing, where a need was demonstrated, without first clearing the slums. Under the influence of the early Fabians the Progressives adopted a programme of municipalization and on that platform they were returned to power in 1892. A policy of systematic municipal housing was taken up, for the first time in Britain (Beattie, 1980).

A Housing of the Working Classes Branch was set up within the LCC's Architects' Department, and a Works Department formed as an alternative to the use of private contractors. The earliest schemes were blocks of flats built on cleared sites in Limehouse and Poplar, similar in design to previous philanthropic dwellings. But the largest scheme was the Boundary Street Estate in Bethnal Green (1894–1900), comprising 19 blocks of dwellings built under Parts I and II of the 1890 Act. It was as much a social as an architectural experiment, breaking new ground in design and diversity. The Progressives lost office in 1895 but were returned in 1898, whereupon they proceeded to implement Part III of the Act, which crucially permitted the Council to build according to need. The Millbank Estate, Westminster (1897–1902) followed with a simple but confident architecture, probably one of the best of the early inner-city estates.

In conclusion, then, we can see that the 1880s marked a threshold in the development of the housing reform movement: the range of the debate widened, the pace of involvement quickened and a new orthodoxy of reform emerged. The housing problem and its solution in Britain appeared in similar light in both France and Germany (Bullock and Read, 1985); an essentially European debate was conducted in the 10 International Housing Congresses held in the period 1889–1913. Increasingly the housing question was seen not in isolation but as part of the larger problem of urban growth and change. The campaign for sanitary reform had moved into design, environmentalism, land and taxation, and planning.

Environment and design

While the Boundary Street and Millbank Estates were suggesting what advances in architectural treatment might do for the tenement block, and what the committed drive of an elected council might achieve through permissive legislation, a new approach to the solution of working-class housing was being advocated. New forms of low-density housing in locations on the urban periphery now suggested that suburban areas might replace inner-city districts where new development had proved both difficult and expensive. From simple beginnings it would lead to an environmental revolution in the way that the public sector was to engage in its resolution of the housing crisis.

The days of inner-city renewal were clearly numbered. In London the Boundary Street project was the end of an era rather than a beginning. A shift of emphasis was dictated at least on financial grounds, and a switch in policy led to the take-up of suburban sites. In January 1900, just two months before the formal opening of Boundary Street by the Prince of Wales, the purchase of 39 acres of land by the LCC at Tooting in South London for £44,000 had to be contrasted with the £500,000 previously voted for the acquisition of 12 and a quarter acres of central area slum land. Suburbs, cheap land, public transport and initiatives by local councils became the order of the day. As Yelling puts it, clean, efficient municipal estates served by clean, efficient municipal tramways represented a politically useful vision of the future (Yelling, 1986, p. 66).

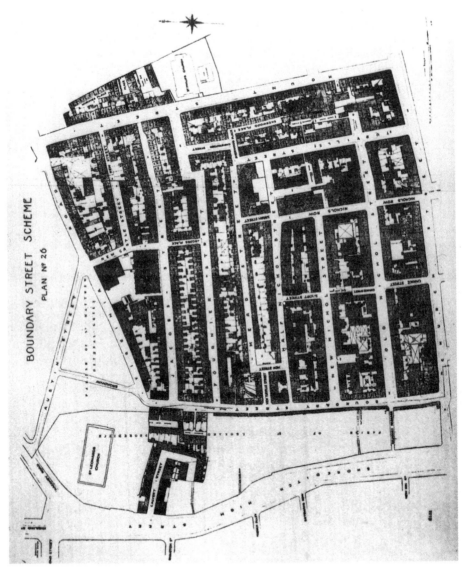

3.1 Boundary Street: the old pattern of development

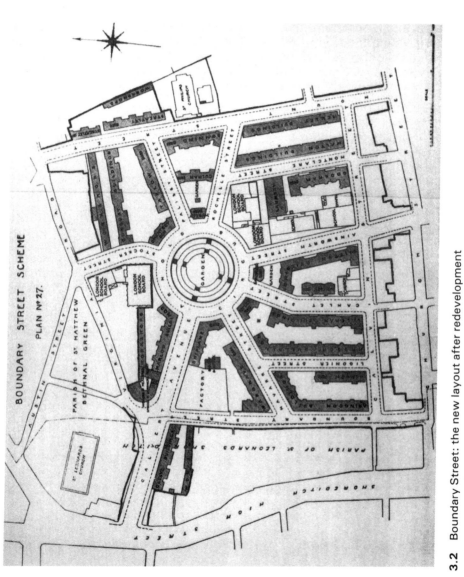

3.2 Boundary Street: the new layout after redevelopment

The message was seen in the provinces too. In Birmingham Councillor John Sutton Nettlefold advocated the opening up of the suburbs as an answer to the problem of working-class housing. In 1901 a new Housing Committee of the City Council was established, forged out of the former Estates and Health Committees. Nettlefold, a ward councillor only since 1898, became chairman; but he had of course the great advantage of family ties with the great ruling families of Birmingham at that time. He stood out against the principle of building local authority houses for the working classes; instead he was to advocate garden suburbs. His Report to the City Council in 1906 makes revealing reading:

> Your Committee are of opinion that a Corporation cannot own too much land provided that it is judiciously purchased. Municipal land could be laid out with open spaces and all other essentials to a healthy, happy community . . . The policy of buying land and encouraging other people to build the houses would enable the Corporation to give a great stimulus to the supply of good, cheap houses on the outskirts of the city, and would thereby benefit a very large number of people. It is now universally recognised to be of the utmost importance to spread the population of our large cities over a greater area than hitherto.   (cited in Cherry, 1982, p. 17)

There were ample forerunners of the low-density estate (Edwards, 1981), but the enterprise of Bedford Park was one which attracted a good deal of attention in the later years of the century. In 1875 a speculative builder, Jonathan Thomas Carr, began building a housing estate adjoining Turnham Green Railway Station in West London; a self-contained middle-class residential area of moderately priced, attractive houses with a basic unity of one architectural style (Queen Anne Revival) was the result (Bolsterli, 1977). By 1880 it had its own church, shops, and tennis courts, and the estate soon gained a reputation for housing artistic, aesthetic and rather bohemian people: a distinctive community in a remarkable suburb.

In generation terms the flight of the middle classes to the suburbs was well under way in the last quarter of the nineteenth century. Masterman noted of the new suburban peoples of London:

> They form a homogenous civilisation – detached, self centred, unosten-tatious – covering the hills along the northern and southern boundaries of the city, and spreading their conquests over the quiet fields beyond . . . It is a life of Security; a life of Sedentary Occupation; a life of Respectability; . . . It finds itself towards evening in its own territory in the miles and miles of little red houses in little silent streets, in number defying imagination. Each boasts its pleasant drawing room, its bow window, its little front garden, its high sounding title – 'Acacia Villa' or 'Camperdown Lodge' – attesting uncon-quered human aspiration.   (Masterman, 1909, pp. 69–70)

It was in this world that new housing opportunities were now sought.

Port Sunlight, founded in 1887, was the creation of a soap magnate, W.H. Lever. A place of wide boulevards, open spaces, gardens and trim lawns it suggested the possibilities of a new environmental setting for industrial housing. Another example followed at Bournville (see p. 11), a green-field site which attracted George and Richard Cadbury when they moved their chocolate and cocoa factory from central Birmingham in 1880. A handful of workmen's houses followed and then from 1895 the Bournville Village Estate proper: tree lined, houses with gardens, low density, picturesque informality. It was a sharp contrast to the regular by-law streets of Selly Oak, the district to the north which it abutted, and also Stirchley and Ten Acres to the east. The housing reformers' ideal of space, open air and sunlight seemed to be met at Bournville, and by the end of the century 300 houses had been built; the Village Trust was created in 1900 by Deed of Foundation (Henslowe, 1984).

But these were just two examples and they were both creations of industrial benefactors. Could the potential be given further expression in different settings? Raymond Unwin proved to be the person as much as anyone to articulate the environmental revolution and to show to both private bodies and public authorities what could be done (Creese, 1966; Day, 1981; Miller, 1981; Jackson, 1985). Unwin was born near Rotherham in 1863 though his boyhood was spent in Oxford, whence, it is said, the quadrangle was to become one of his favourite layouts for cooperative housing. Drawn to the teaching of Ruskin and Morris he espoused socialist thinking, while friendship with Edward Carpenter added to his intellectual liberation. Beginning professional life as an engineering apprentice in Chesterfield, he moved into house design and housing layout with his cousin (by marriage) Barry Parker. Their book, *The art of building a home* (1901) was a clear landmark in the evolution of their approach to environmental design, and Unwin's Fabian pamphlet of 1902, *Cottage plans and commonsense*, showed an intuitive grasp of the importance of the English vernacular tradition in popular housing. Later, Unwin's *Town planning in practice* (1909) became a classic text on the new discipline.

A major opportunity came their way with their commissioned work at New Earswick, a model-village project for Joseph Rowntree on the northern outskirts of York. Unwin prepared the initial plans and he and Parker combined on cottage design. Following Bournville, New Earswick was the second major example of a low-density estate conceived to a picturesque model; begun in 1902 it never achieved the significance of the other, but for its designers it proved an important testing ground.

The Garden City movement soon harnessed Unwin's expertise and the garden suburb offered yet another important challenge and possibility for experiment. A major opportunity was presented with the reservation of a large tract of land for the extension of Hampstead Heath; Mrs (later Dame) Henrietta Barnett (wife of Canon Barnett of Toynbee Hall fame), a persuasive lady of great strength of will, and with social and community ideals close to those of Unwin, chose him to lay out the estate (Green, 1977). Hampstead was the Barnetts' customary retreat from Whitechapel; new development must be quite different from East London. The resultant Hampstead Garden Suburb succeeded in raising the practice of site planning to that of a major art form. Perhaps no other single event conferred upon the new term 'town planning' so much promise: idealism articulated by professional practice. Unwin prepared his first plan in 1905, even though the suburb was not formally founded until 1907, and it quickly took shape in the form of quadrangles, greens and culs-de-sac. The latter was a feature which required special legislation, provided by the Hampstead Garden Suburb Act, 1906. Although by no means an estate for the working classes, it proved to be a very successful adoption of low-density layout norms and standards for suburban development.

A new model had been offered, very different indeed from the conservative, stereotyped layouts of some of the Voluntary Housing societies of the time. A further fillip came with the innovative work of the LCC architects. In addition to the inner-city estates of Boundary Street, Millbank and others, they embarked on a series of cottage estates on suburban land, within the County of London. Available sites were few and it was necessary to obtain new legislation in order to purchase land outside their area. Part of the Housing of the Working Classes Act, 1900 permitted the development of cottage estates under Part III of the 1890 Act at Tooting (Totterdown Fields), near Croydon (Norbury), Tottenham (White Hart Lane) and East Acton (Old Oak), all started before 1914 (and in respect of Tooting, completed before 1914). The later cottage estates developed a free layout style in emulation of Hampstead and elsewhere and some noteworthy developments ensued. One looks with admiration at the small band of public-sector architects, under the leadership of W.E. Riley from 1900 to 1919, who captured a vernacular tradition and applied it to new norms of estate layout in the critical years at the turn of the century.

But the number of people housed by the LCC in its building programmes up to 1914 was small, even insignificant compared with the estimate of one million poor and ill-housed people, as calculated by Charles Booth. Moreover LCC rents were not low: there was no direct subsidization and government approval for financing development was not always easily obtained. The artisan classes may have benefited, but the very poor, displaced by clearance schemes, did not. The 'housing question' remained.

Garden cities

The spatial redistribution of urban population was another element in the search for an answer to the crisis of the late Victorian city. Alfred Marshall (1884), professor of economics at Cambridge, was an advocate of decentralization, arguing that the removal of large numbers of London's population into the country would be economically advantageous. The notion came to fruition in the gospel of an unlikely prophet, Ebenezer Howard (Fishman, 1977). His testament was a book, *Tomorrow: a peaceful path to real reform*, published in 1898, revised and reissued in 1902 as *Garden cities of tomorrow*. His disciples were members of the Garden City Association, founded in 1900. His legacy was not only in England with the building of two garden cities and a lineage which led from satellite towns to new towns, but also a flourishing international movement.

Howard was born in London in 1850, the son of a small shopkeeper. After leaving school he had no settled occupation; at the age of 21 he went to America, but failed in a farming enterprise in Nebraska and became a shorthand writer in Chicago. Returning to England he became an offical parliamentary reporter and to all intents and purposes settled down in this capacity. Moving in reformist circles, he was acquainted with the various urban issues of the day. He was attracted by Edward Bellamy's novel, *Looking backward*, published in Boston in 1888, a vision of that city in the year 2000 as given through the observations of one who falls asleep and awakens more than a century later. The prophecy of a communistic Boston, a Utopia housing a new social order with technological advance emancipating mankind from toil, was part of a common dream extending back over the centuries, but we understand that in this particular case Howard was fired by it.

Howard's singular contribution, influenced by the welter of ideas circulating in later Victorian Britain, was an urban model in the form of an ideal town, built as a satellite. Located at a distance from the parent city, surrounded by an agricultural belt, and developed on land held in common by the community, it was brilliantly conceived. A constellation of such satellites, forming a 'Social City', was in direct answer to many of the problems of the day, both urban and rural. His vision spoke the language of social progress and the perfectibility of man. The Garden city was

> a newer call to build home-towns for slum cities; to plant gardens for crowded courts; to construct beautiful water-ways in flooded valleys; to establish a scientific system of distribution to take the place of a chaos, a just system of land tenure for one representing the selfishness which we hope is passing away; to found pensions with liberty for our aged poor, now imprisoned in work-houses; to banish despair and awaken hope in the breasts of those who have fallen; to silence the harsh voice of anger, and to awaken the soft notes of brotherliness and goodwill; to place in strong hands implements of peace and construction, so that implements of war and destruction may drop uselessly down. Here is a task which may well unite a vast army of workers to utilize that power, the present waste of which is the source of half our poverty, disease and suffering.   (Howard 1902; 1965 edn, p. 150)

Beyond the flowery language typical of his time lay a strategic solution to the problem of the big city. Growth of the parent city should stop, and its surplus population be redirected to planned satellites beyond, the size of which would be limited to 30,000 people. Limitless growth would be replaced by conscious regulation. Small-scale environments, built around wards of 6,000 people each, would overcome the anonymity of the gigantic. Cheap land for housing would mean cheaper dwellings; the poor would have new opportunities for accommodation they could afford. Moreover the land would be in community ownership and profits would be ploughed back to the people who created them; private profit from community development would be a thing of the past.

But it was not only an urban solution; it was a remedy for the ills of the countryside too because it offered new markets for a depressed agriculture. In that, he shared the views of the anarchist Peter Kropotkin, who had urged the more profitable use of rural areas around London. In *Fields, factories and workshops tomorrow* (1899) he bemoaned the poor agriculture in an area north of London:

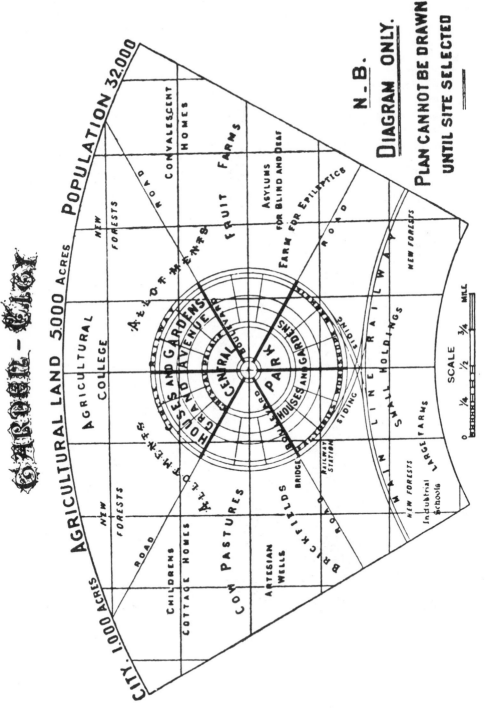

GARDEN - CITY

POPULATION 32.000

AGRICULTURAL LAND 5.000 ACRES

CITY. 1.000 ACRES

N.B.
DIAGRAM ONLY.
PLAN CANNOT BE DRAWN
UNTIL SITE SELECTED

NEW FORESTS

ROAD

CONVALESCENT HOMES

FRUIT FARMS

ASYLUMS
FARM FOR EPILEPTICS

ROAD

AGRICULTURAL COLLEGE

ALLOTMENTS

NEW FORESTS

HOUSES AND GARDENS

GRAND AVENUE

CENTRAL

BOULEVARD

PARK

HOUSES AND GARDENS

SIDING

MAIN LINE RAILWAY

SMALL HOLDINGS

NEW FORESTS

ROAD

CHILDRENS COTTAGE HOMES

COW PASTURES

ALLOTMENTS

ARTESIAN WELLS

BRICKFIELDS

RAILWAY STATION

BRIDGE

ROAD

Industrial LARGE FARMS
Schools

NEW FORESTS

SCALE

0   ¼   ½   ¾   MILE

3.3   Garden City and its agricultural belt

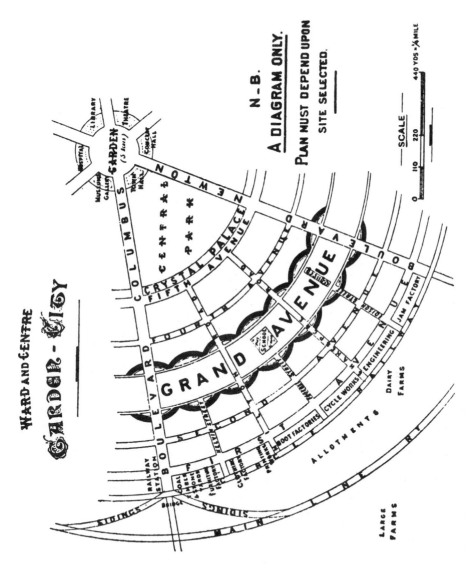

3.4 Garden City: a section

> I could see nothing east or west but meadow land on which they hardly cropped two tons of hay per acre ... And that – within ten miles from Charing Cross, close to a city with 5,000,000 inhabitants, supplied with Flemish and Jersey potatoes, French salads and Canadian apples.
>
> (Kropotkin 1899; 1974 edn, p. 53)

Howard's strategy was a truly metropolitan one, offering a solution to the problems of both town and country as his famous 'three magnets' diagram suggested, though he was much more a socio-economic reformer than a spatial strategist (Beevers, 1988).

> There are in reality not only, as is so constantly assumed, two alternatives – town life and country life – but a third alternative, in which all the advantages of the most energetic and active town life, with all the beauty and delight of the country, may be secured in perfect combination.
>
> (Howard 1902; 1965 edn, pp. 45–6)

This led Howard to assert that . . . 'Town and country *must be married*, and out of this joyous union will spring a new hope, a new life, a new civilization' (Howard 1902; 1965 edn, p. 48).

The book attracted interest, and enthusiasts were recruited as a result of a lecture programme. The Garden City Association (GCA) was founded; the barrister and former Liberal MP Ralph Neville became chairman, with Thomas Adams as secretary. A Pioneer Company was registered and in 1903 a site of nearly 4,000 acres was purchased in Hertfordshire, and the First Garden City of Letchworth was begun. Garden City Associations in other countries were founded and an International Garden City Association (subsequently the International Housing and Town Planning Federation) was formed. It was an astonishingly rapid growth and diffusion.

Howard's gospel was to be powerfully proclaimed by both word and deed. Two men stand out in Britain as advancing his ideas, though neither could be regarded solely as garden city advocates. We look first to Thomas Adams (Simpson, 1985). Born in 1871, the son of a Lowland Scottish dairy farmer, he had writing and political experience before leaving for London in 1900. Appointed to the GCA in April 1901 he had boosted membership to over 2,000 within two years. He organized successful conferences at Bournville (1901) and Port Sunlight (1902), his ability being recognized when he was appointed Secretary Manager of the First Garden City Company in 1903, being given general responsibility for the development of Letchworth. By 1906 he had persuaded eight firms to locate there, while the problem of the provision of workers' homes had been resolved by the sponsorship of a Cheap Cottages Exhibition in 1905, from which the company secured 120 free houses.

Letchworth was not instantly successful in terms of profitability and Adams was relieved of managerial responsibility. But his contribution to new forms of spatial planning had not ended, because between 1906 and 1909, in practice as a land agent and surveyor, he designed a number of garden suburbs. He was in effect the first full-time, town-planning consultant and contributed a strong philosophy to the emergent town-planning movement: low-density forms of layout in sympathy with local topography;

ample gardens, allotments and open space; catering for all social classes; the product of voluntary cooperation between landowners and local authorities; co-partnership housing and self-management by the residents. His seven schemes had mixed success but sufficient experience had been gained to establish confidence in both the philosophy of the new activity and its practice. Two schemes remained on the drawing board: Childwall, east of Liverpool and Newton Moor near Hyde, Cheshire. Only 75 houses were built at Fallings Park, north of Wolverhampton; 50 at Shirehampton, west of Bristol; and 25 at Glyn Cory west of Cardiff. But Alkrington, north of Manchester, and Knebworth near Stevenage achieved modest success. His reputation had been made and in December 1909 he was appointed Town Planning Advisor to the Local Government Board. In 1914 he was the first President of the Town Planning Institute, and although over the next 20 years he made his career first in Canada and then the USA, his formative influences on British land planning and site layout had been firmly established.

Howard's second proponent was Raymond Unwin, whose work in association with Barry Parker at Letchworth was crucial in establishing not only the viability of the garden-city idea but also the new principles of urban design and planning. First Garden City Ltd was formed in September 1903; virtually its first task was the organization of a limited competition for the Master Plan. A number of prominent architects were approached to prepare plans, but in circumstances which appeared to be highly unusual (Miller, 1981) a preliminary plan prepared by Parker and Unwin was accepted early in 1904.

The Plan was carefully related to both topography and landscape. Existing trees and hedgerows were incorporated and the central plateau of the site was marked out for the major axis. A formal geometry was suggested by the major and minor axes but informality was well in evidence too with suggestions for urban quadrangles, village greens and sites for detached houses. An embryo neighbourhood concept appears, with pedestrian walkways. Some of the principles were sacrificed in the haste of early building but design criteria were settled with the uniform use of roughcast brickwork and red-tiled roofs, planting and grass verges to roads. Experiments with cottage groupings and layouts followed, particularly with building by co-partnership tenants, under the chairmanship of Henry Vivian MP. A well-mannered addition to urban Britain ensued, the vernacular tradition nicely balanced by the radicalism of the new drive for population dispersal.

Institutional change

We have already seen that the Hampstead Garden Suburb Act, 1906 conferred powers on the Suburb Trust 'to develop and lay out lands as garden suburbs'. At the same time pressure for national legislation on town planning (a new term seemingly first used about 1906) grew from at least two sources. One was from those local authorities who had already taken an interest in the subject. Councillor Nettlefold of Birmingham was

Chairman of the Town Planning Committee of the Association of Municipal Corporations; a scheme for a draft Bill was prepared in 1907 and a deputation was received by the Prime Minister and the President of the Local Government Board. The other was the National Housing Reform Council which even earlier (November 1906) had sent a sixteen-man delegation led by William Thompson, an alderman of Richmond (Surrey); they advocated a number of reforms including housing and public health, the creation of model suburbs, a simplified procedure for the compulsory purchase of land, a Town and Village Development Commission, the availability of cheaper money and German methods of suburban planning.

A North-country reformer, T.C. Horsfall, had long been an advocate of 'town extension planning' (see his book of 1904) and German experience showed how far Britain lagged behind in proven methods of land regulation. Legislation had given the necessary powers to cities in Prussia and many of the German states after the 1870s. One of the most notable examples of planned city extensions was that carried out by Cologne on land formerly occupied by the city wall and fortifications, which were removed in 1881. Joseph Stübben supervised the planning of Cologne from 1881 to 1898 and was responsible for the city's *Neustadt*. National rivalries were at stake when it was argued that Britain was also falling behind, post-Bismarck, in terms of social and economic legislation. Comparisons with Germany could be sore political points.

In the event a Housing Bill was introduced in 1908, the town-planning sections simply forming a second, short part of a longer piece on housing. Its object was:

> to ensure, by means of schemes which may be prepared either by local authorities or landowners, that in future, land in the vicinity of towns shall be developed in such a way as to secure proper sanitary conditions, amenity and convenience in connection with the laying out of the land itself and of any neighbouring land.

The contrast with nineteenth-century legislation on housing could scarcely be greater. The debate had shifted to land assembly ('the vicinity of towns') and design (issues of layout, amenity and convenience). The local authority role was advanced from oversight of dwelling construction and space standards to guidance as to where dwellings should be built and in what overall manner. Greater clarity of objectives remained to be given but there can be no doubt of the profound change in approach. Municipal power was further extended over private interests, and the battle lines were redrawn for a continued struggle between competing priorities.

A bridgehead of State direction had been formed from which the twentieth century would advance substantially. With hindsight those early years of the 1900s were highly significant: this was the period when disaffection with past approaches to housing reform had given credence to new methods and approaches. It was the period too when the solution to working-class housing appeared not in the centre of cities but on the outskirts; when a free interpretation of environmental quality overtook rigid norms of space standards; when a vernacular tradition in English architecture was reasserted; when the dictates of air, space and sunlight triumphed;

and when spatial strategies of dispersal in the form of satellite Social Cities added such a powerful ideological drive to urban strategy.

But change went hand-in-hand with continuity. The new wine of town planning was contained in the old skins of housing. The Housing, Town Planning, etc. Bill was introduced in 1908. At the end of the parliamentary session it was withdrawn and reintroduced as a 1909 Bill. The town-planning sections merely encouraged local authorities and landowners to adopt future developments through Planning Schemes; the town-planning activity was purely permissive and there were no powers to enable munici-palities to buy land on their urban fringes (contrary to what advocates had urged). This modest legislation attracted opposition by virtue of the exten-sions of bureaucracy implied by the Bill and the problems surrounding claims for compensation. Any landowner could claim compensation for loss of value due to the Scheme; on the other hand a local authority would have power to collect 100 per cent of betterment accruing to a site as a result of a Scheme. In the House of Lords, a 50 per cent betterment levy was agreed. A modest but cumbersome Act was passed.

The legislation needed to be tested in practice. Fortunately there was one city which took up the new powers with some enthusiasm: Birmingham (Cherry, 1974). The first application received by the Local Government Board to prepare a town-planning scheme was from that city in respect of the Parish of Quinton and parts of the Parishes of Harborne, Edgbaston and Northfield – 2,320 acres in extent, located between two already devel-oped areas, to the north at Smethwick and Oldbury and to the south at Selly Oak and Northfield. When submitted, the scheme gave flesh to the provi-sions of the Act in that it provided a framework of development for the area: thus two main roads were indicated as the traffic spines; in land-use terms an overwhelming residential allocation was indicated, with a modicum of open space and parks; and density targets were laid down, with an average 12 to the acre and a maximum of 20 on any one acre.

In a sense, what constituted the new art of town planning was defined in practice. The new activity emerged from no chrysalis of urban theory, rather a womb of local government housing policy, nutured over a long gestation period when the problems of the inadequately housed poor were addressed. Town planning itself remained without definition, but what it actually embraced in practice was listed in the Fourth Schedule to the Act: the raw material of urban development in the form of streets, roads, their construction, stopping up or diversion; buildings and structures; open spaces; the preservation of history and natural beauty; sewerage, drain-age and sewage disposal; lighting; and water supply. These elements could now be consciously controlled by a local authority with the object of creating an environment conducive to good living conditions. The attack on overcrowded, insanitary houses shifted from the old areas themselves to areas of new development on the urban fringe where it was expected that cheaper housing would, over time, syphon off the inadequately housed and ease the problems of the older districts. For a quarter of a century British housing policy was directed essentially to the provision of new dwellings in suburban locations, to new designs, and to historically low densities.

A new era had been entered whereby the issues of housing and land development were fused. The result was the beginning of a conscious exercise in town building, the full implications of which were worked out over succeeding decades. Town planning in a modern sense was born. The origins were clearly rooted in local government practice, fashioned out of concern for health sanitation and housing fitness, but the immediate sparks of originality lay elsewhere in the garden city advocates, the practitioners of garden suburbs, the organizing ability of Thomas Adams and the design genius of Raymond Unwin. Adherents of the new discipline spoke of it with confidence; its claims, after all, rested on common sense. The Secretary of the National Housing and Town Planning Council declared that town planning:

> should come to all clear-headed administrators as an appeal for the substitution of order in place of chaos in town growth. To those members of Municipal Committees who are responsible for the guardianship of the health of the population the appeal should be that of the wisdom of prevention as compared with the wastefulness of cure. The power to plan on right lines in the future, given to them under the Act of 1909, comes indeed as a challenge to their administrative ability.   (Aldridge, 1915, p. 140)

But progress was glacially slow. After 10 years (admittedly interrupted by the Great War) just 172 schemes in England and Wales had been authorized by the Board to be prepared or adopted by local authorities, covering little more than 300,000 acres in all (Cherry, 1974). But in only 13 cases were schemes actually submitted, and of these, five were prepared by Birmingham (and one of those was an amending scheme). The other eight authorities were: Rochdale, Chesterfield and Leeds Corporations; Ruislip–Northwood, North Bromsgrove, Otley and Margam Urban District Councils; and Hunslet Rural District Council. With the exception of Ruislip–Northwood where one major landowner, interested in development, provided the local fillip to Scheme preparation, the outer fringes of London were significantly absent – the very area where perhaps there was greatest need nationally for the Act to be taken up. After falling into the hands of the Municipal Reform Party in 1907 London failed to take any lead in town-planning matters for a generation.

   In Scotland early interest was expressed in Dunfermline, Edinburgh and Dundee, but in the event by the end of the war, not one town-planning scheme in Scotland had been prepared. A large housing scheme for the Admiralty at Rosyth was undertaken under special legislation, the Housing (Rosyth Dockyard) Act, 1915. This development, particularly the way it was carried out, was significant because it implied that new forms of housing layout could quite adequately be provided outside planning legislation; the 1909 Act was not necessary so long as there was an enlightened developer. Another example of this was the development emanating from the Ministry of Munitions during the war, as at Gretna Green (see p. 84).

   With the recording of these initiatives the new activity of town planning was impelled forward, legislation giving justification to changing design practices and strategic concepts. It is a matter of surmise as to what would have happened in later years if changes had been confined to these events. But in fact another major development was to occur: a new profession was founded and over the years it would capture responsibility for the philosophy and practice of the fledgling field. It was to have its own singular contribution to the importance of plan preparation, the way and manner in which plans were prepared, the control of development through local government, and ultimately to the whole process of town building in this country. The professionalization of town planning in Britain imparts a distinct flavour to our story.

By 1913 a group of architects, engineers, surveyors and others, all engaged in the new field of town planning had come together and was holding meetings in London. The first meeting of a Provisional Committee of this body was held in July of that year, and in November a first Council was elected with Thomas Adams, President. The first Council meeting was in December and an Inaugural Dinner was held in January 1914. This was the public launching, but the final membership classes were only adopted in April. The first membership list was dated May and formal recognition of the Town Planning Institute was completed with the signing of the Articles of Association in September 1914 (Cherry, 1974).

The onset of war and the departure of Adams for Canada suggested an inauspicious beginning, but the political balancing act paid off. Without claiming too much for itself in the early days the new body simply brought together the technical professions (architects in the majority, but more than held in check by the combined weight of engineers, surveyors and lawyers), propagandists and public figures as honorary members. Quite quickly the social idealists (the 'planning amateurs') became a distinct minority and the Institute developed as a body for technical people with skills and expertise. The profession inevitably moved to claim unique competence, separate from the other bodies (Hawtree, 1981).

But another contribution came to British town planning which again was to leave an indelible mark. The source was Patrick Geddes and he imbued the new profession and activity with a wider philosophy (Meller, 1980, 1981). Town planning was not to be regarded just as an exercise in building and land assembly; nor was it wedded to one strategic view of dispersed cities (though garden cities met with universal acclaim); neither did it simply embrace new design and layout criteria (though the low-density, cottage-design criterion was a welcome shift of emphasis). His early training as a biologist can be seen in his report on parks, gardens and culture-institutes to the Carnegie Dunfermline Trust (1904), but his wider urban grasp is demonstrated in *Cities in evolution* (1915). Geddes argued that town planning was bound up with changes in society and culture as well as environment. As a sociologist he was not widely understood but he articulated ideas from other contemporaries, particularly the French sociologist Le Play, and succeeded in presenting a kind of integrated philosophy which brought together social evolution, city life, regionalism, culture and town planning. Many of his ideas have lost their force today but in the early years of town planning he was instrumental, both in his concept of Civics and of the Regional Survey, in imparting almost a mystical, unifying force to the professional field. A generalist in a growing world of specialists he was a valuable philosophical spur to the nascent profession.

🖋 An Overview

The years between the mid-1880s and the outbreak of the Great War formed a momentous period. It was one in which the big city became a primary object of concern, from the mid-century onwards popular perceptions growing anti-urban (Lees, 1985). Novelists and men of letters, social theorists and sociologists, historians, clergymen, doctors and sanitary experts, essayists and journalists, municipal administrators, architects and finally planners all played a part in shaping a public consciousness of urban life; they were all instruments of change.

The period experienced the full weight of the late Victorian urban crisis, in which the problem of working-class housing was at the heart. It saw a shift in policy from reconstruction on old sites to new building in the urban periphery. It witnessed the early flowering of new approaches to layout and design, which in the low-density tradition articulated so many of the reformers' ambitions. It was a period marked by economic depression in which the first symptoms of secular decline in the context of international competition were recognized. Consequently, the years demonstrated labour unrest alongside social change (the suffragette movement for example) and disputation (in Ireland). It was a period of international conflict, marked when imperial might was first seriously blunted in South Africa and when European rivalry exploded against Germany. It was a time of technical invention and one, at least, served to introduce a new problem ultimately for those concerned with town design: the motor car. In a remarkably short time the motor vehicle passed from being a rich man's toy to an article of mass production, and traffic circulation in the major cities was a new issue to which the State was inevitably drawn.

In the quarter of a century before 1914 town planning emerged to offer a great deal to the middle and upper classes in Britain, France and Germany, other Western European countries and in the USA. The promise of social peace through a rationalization of the land market attracted a variety of supporters:

> in Germany, an elite of officials and academics; in Britain a dying class of bourgeois social reformers connected with a threatened Liberal Party; in France, a minority of upper-class do-gooders with strong links with the Church and other conservative institutions; and in the United States, urban big business. (Sutcliffe, 1981, p. 208)

In these turbulent years what were the key issues which produced town planning and which ensured that local and central government would become involved with town building? We can identify three: the emergent characteristics of the metropolitan city which seemed to defy the smooth functioning of private markets; developments in housing reform; and trends in the evolution of State apparatus.

By the end of the nineteenth century Berlin and New York had risen from relatively low population levels to join Paris, and notably London, as major world capital cities. The metropolitan city was already identified as a phenomenon of the industrial age (Weber, 1899). Britain's urban characteristics had particular features. London was more than a seat of government, it was an industrial city in its own right, while elsewhere in the country medium-sized industrial cities had their own problems stemming from their manufacturing traditions and mushrooming growth during the century. They were tight knit and high density (though nothing like as congested as Paris, Berlin and New York where apartment living was the norm). They were foci of sustained population growth fuelled by inward migration. Socially they were areas of great extremes, affluence and poverty virtually cheek by jowl as high land values exacerbated the housing problems of the working class.

By the end of the century the reconstruction of cities became a major issue. Innovations neither in building technology nor in street transport seemed likely to suggest any new form of city in the future. Railways were only of limited utility in spreading commuter distances and easing congestion in the centre. Tramway electrification helped marginally but it was the petrol-driven engine harnessed to the motor car which made the breakthrough. Howard's concept of a territorially dispersed city through satellites could not have been more opportune, and remarkably quickly a new urban future was being foreseen, H.G. Wells's *Anticipations* (1902) envisaging a London area extending up to 70 miles from the centre.

The spreading of cities had of course already begun, economic activity taking place increasingly at the periphery of the urban areas, rather than the centre. Market forces, responding both to an accelerating rate of technological change and to a recognition of the inefficiencies of congestion at the centre, now proceeded to deconcentrate the metropolitan city.

It was in this context that measures towards the regulation of the environment, via housing, sanitation and public works, adopted approaches in sympathy with wider market forces of investment. Whether this allows us to say that the emergent town-planning movement, which was broadly to share a decentralist tradition, was (and is) simply an expression of the needs of the capitalist system, or whether the relationship is much more complex than that, is a matter for debate. What we can observe, however, is that town planning proceeded to powerfully reinforce underlying economic trends and societal objectives. The emergent movement seemed to promise socially desirable cities which would also be economically efficient. Moreover, this would be obtained at no great cost to capital or landed property, and this seems to explain the remarkable degree of support to the aims of town planning in the early years of the century from captains of industry as well as social reformers. An ideal future seemed remarkably painless to obtain. There was no need to engage in massive expensive projects either in highway construction or removal of unfit dwellings and subsequent reconstruction on high-cost land. Conscious dispersal, new housing and land planning in the broadest sense seemed to promise all. The State became a willing participant.

The second issue was that of housing. Towards the end of the century new emphases emerged in the housing reform movement. Layout and design was one of them, which in Britain contrasted the drab and utilitarian blocks of model dwellings typical across London from the 1860s with the new enthusiasm for the cottage. The example of the benevolent philanthropists at Port Sunlight, Bournville and Earswick, given greater credence by the garden city protagonists and articulated by Unwin and like-minded architects, served to show that there was another model for working-class housing. Location of course was another emphasis: suburbs at Norbury and Totterdown Fields versus schemes at Millbank and Boundary Street. The debate centred on land costs and the answer was unmistakable.

The question as to who would best supply the new dwellings was another feature. Housing reformers had long taken the view that private enterprise aided by a modest non-profit sector would supply the housing need. But by the end of the century there was an increasing view that government action was more and more necessary if the supply of working-class housing was to be adequate. Government had intervened in public health and in the 1890s legislation significantly extended government powers in the supply of new housing, at least for London.

Ultimately the beneficiary was to be town planning because the debate slipped from the narrow confines of workers' housing to broader issues, first of environmentalism and then social housing and state welfarism. Earlier in the nineteenth century the issue of working-class housing had been a fairly focused one, but by the early twentieth century there was a broad lobby including reformists, house builders, architects and planners. A new consensus on housing matters had emerged from which the integrating movement of town planning would benefit. The housing question was now seen in terms of a quite different urban perspective: city growth, change and the distribution of population. The debate shifted from a concern with individual dwellings, even districts of similar dwellings, to one of cities as a whole where dwellings were simply individual parts.

The third issue was that of the growth of public intervention in areas of environmental management; local authorities were drawn into the regulation of private land within towns. This is not all that easy to explain but it can be argued (Sutcliffe, 1980) that public intervention tended to expand in order to fill the gap between the actual and the desired performance offered by the urban environment. In this way, because of the continued pressure of reformist influences (which assert the importance of the environment for human well-being), government stepped in with actions or investments which the private market or voluntary sectors could not provide. Alternatively, with rather different reasoning some would argue that because of difficulties inherent in capitalism, which results in environmental deterioration, elements in society captured State regulation in order to protect themselves against that deterioration or to impose methods of control over the unruly protests of those who were affected. Both arguments have their merits, but which ever has the greater claim at any one period, the important point is that environmental deterioration in the crisis years at the end of the century was seen as a fundamental problem. New ways in addressing that problem provided the occasion for the rise of town planning.

From many points of view we can say that, with hindsight, all the preconditions for the successful establishment of a town planning tradition were present in this country by the outbreak of the Great War. A favourable set of circumstances provided a springboard for a new coordinated approach to urban problems, which was significantly different from the set of

piecemeal actions characteristic of the nineteenth century. Suburbanization and decentralization were already in evidence. The building boom of
the 1890s coincided significantly with tramway electrification and the
further development of concessionary workers' fares on both tram and
rail. New housing in cottage form was particularly suited to low-density
living, once again encouraging decentralization. Municipal enterprise,
particularly with the creation of the new County Boroughs and the London
County Council was vigorous and respectable, so that an extension of local
authority powers in matters of housing and land was broadly acceptable.
The environmental regulation of the industrial city, shallow rooted for
many years, strengthened and blossomed into a new activity; it became
more scientific and it acquired a social-welfare dimension. The State was
drawn into wider conflicts with private interests and as it adopted measures of regulation over the use of private land within the towns, it became
ensnared and finally took the lead in the town-building process.

4 Between the Wars

In the 20 years between 1919 and 1939 British town planning, while still resting firmly on public-sector housing-led initiatives undertaken before 1914, proceeded both to consolidate its position as a tool of government and to widen its disciplinary and professional scope. The planning of British cities entered a new phase as a consequence. It gained an entrenched footing in local government through the extension of statutory town-planning procedures, which confirmed the bridgehead established before the war; and, largely accidentally rather than by design, the activity of town planning came to involve other forms of public regulation, with the result that its field of concern was enlarged.

Town planning was neither strong nor coherent enough as a discipline and profession for it to stake a claim and take over other intellectual territory; as a movement it was too inwardly diverse to be sufficiently self-willed to embark on aggrandizement in its remit. Rather, town planning became involved in other environmental and social concerns almost by chance, though its claim for a comprehensive, synoptic view of things perhaps made expansionism inevitable. The analogy may be of Britain gaining an Empire by accident, and then losing it; this century, town planning has expanded its subject field, as disciplinary boundaries first collided and then were realigned, at a time when the nature of complex environmental problems was reidentified and expressed again in different terms. A professional cuckoo in the hybrid nest of lawyers, architects, engineers and surveyors was the ultimate beneficiary in a long story of disciplinary realignment. To continue the analogy: the Empire was lost in a pragmatic adjustment to international reality – in the context of late twentieth-century professional demarcations will town planning be the loser in the redefinition of urban problems and preferences for their solution? We shall return to this speculation later (see p. 190).

The inter-war period was one of great change in social and economic affairs. Outwardly Britain may have appeared stable; the class system and its accompanying distribution of wealth remained largely unchallenged. In politics the Conservatives were in power virtually throughout, though not necessarily always directly in office. There were two Labour governments but on each occasion Liberal Party support was necessary to form an administration. The major political event was the split in Ramsay

MacDonald's Cabinet in 1931; the resultant general election returned just 49 Labour MPs to Westminster. Even in 1935, with Labour gaining 154 seats, the party still had fewer than in 1924. On the other hand Labour came to power in London in 1934, re-elected in 1937. Particularly in the 1930s significant shifts in popular attitudes affected political postures, and for a variety of reasons there were calls for increased public sector intervention in a range of national economic and social affairs. Town planning stood to gain accordingly, even if the years between the wars showed no great practical advance in the design, layout and building of towns over what had been achieved before. The period therefore was one of consolidation and cautious experiment, the promise of town planning unrealized in the face of Government apathy.

The town planning infant survived, drip-fed from a number of sources: intellectual, artistic, rational, propagandist, reformist, futurist and legislative. The inter-war years, seemingly uneventful and considered even disappointing for the development of town planning as an activity, did however bring about important changes. Increasingly, the town planning movement came to be dominated by an institutionalized professional ideology. Formerly a disparate collection of enthusiastic amateurs, it became a profession with its own cutting edge. As a body it naturally reflected the dominant interests in society, though it was prone to being strongly buffeted by conflicts of interest in matters of land, property and amenity. Maturity of outlook over the years led it to have a capacity for assuming an independent role, based on its own inherent values. All this is important because it meant that by the end of the 1930s British town planning was in a stronger position than would have been thought likely, to respond to the national emergency of physical destruction, which led to an unprecedented period of planned rebuilding. This is discussed in Chapter 5, but the events of the inter-war years represent an important forerunner, of ultimate significance for the style and nature of plan making in this country.

The context

Enormous changes took place during these years in terms of physical development, which dramatically affected the shape and appearance of cities. National population growth slowed perceptibly, but the major concentrations of population remained, tightly drawn in conurbations as Geddes described them; 'Constellations we cannot call them; conglomerations is, alas! nearer the mark at present, but it may sound unappreciative; what of "Conurbations"?' (Geddes, 1915, p. 34).

In these areas two-fifths of the national population resided in areas which he termed: Lancaston (Manchester, Liverpool and Greater Lancashire), the West Riding, the South Riding (Greater Sheffield), Midlandton (Greater Birmingham), South Waleston, Tyne–Wear–Tees, and Clyde–Forth; in all a 'New Heptarchy' to accompany Greater London. These areas retained the nineteenth-century characteristics which had already focused the reformers' minds: they were tight-knit, high-density, congested, smoky, dirty and they presented a scene of old and obsolete buildings. The challenge of the poverty of environment and of housing conditions remained.

But improvements were to occur, sometimes faster than had been the case before 1914. For example, with regard to overcrowding, 14 per cent of the population of Great Britain lived at more than two persons to a room in 1921; but this proportion had been halved by 1939. The major reason for this was a sustained house-building programme, which contributed nearly 4 million dwellings to the national housing stock between the wars. Of seminal significance, one quarter of these were to provide a new tenure group for British housing: the local authority council house. Of equal significance was the territorial spread of British cities, which massive new house building in a low-density form implied; the decentralizing city was emerging and, with 2 per cent of the entire area of England changing from rural to urban in the 12 years before 1939, a new interest in land use change was shown, not least by the geographer L. Dudley Stamp.

But the dominant urban feature in the inter-war period was the growth and spread of London. The many problems demonstrated by the peripheral development of the metropolis, not to mention the long-standing congestion at its core, and its residual stock of poor dwellings, placed London firmly on the planning agenda. In the nineteenth century it was the squalor and unhealthiness of the northern manufacturing towns, as much as the condition of London's rookeries, that led to measures of sanitary regulation and housing improvement. Between the wars, however, London's problems became national problems: the failure to cope with the onrush of the speculative builder, the frailty of town-planning legislation, the threat of the loss of open countryside, the need for road improvements, and the inadequacy of a multiple number of local authorities without effective coordination. It was to these issues that town planning had to respond.

Another change, which was to have implications for the course of British town planning, lay in the shifts of economic fortune between regions. Britain emerged from war in 1918 both stronger and in a healthier economic state than her European neighbours (Aldcroft, 1986). There had been loss of shipping and sales of overseas assets, but there was no great disruption and dislocation. There was some social and political unrest, it is true, but nothing on the scale seen in Poland, Austria, Germany, Belgium and France. But yet Britain had a poor record of economic achievement in the 1920s, before the world depression marked the years 1929–32.

An economic boom developed in the spring of 1919, but this only lasted a year and when the Bank Rate was hoisted to 7 per cent in April 1920, the short-lived social reform programme was terminated. A sharp downturn in 1920–1 was aggravated and by the middle of 1921 Britain was experiencing one of the worst recessions in its history, with unemployment rising to 2.4 million in May in that year (22 per cent of the insured labour force). Labour unrest followed in the coalfields, in the cotton mills and on the railways. A subsequent economic recovery followed, but unemployment was slow to fall, and 1 million were still out of work in June 1924 (9.2 per cent). In 1926 the recovery was cut short by severe labour troubles, marked by the General Strike and a prolonged stoppage in the coal industry.

The later 1920s reflected a modest boom but the years demonstrated no great grasp of economic analysis (these were pre-Keynesian days), and problems of currency stabilization and national debt management assumed greatest importance. The return to the gold standard, which implied maintaining the £/$ parity, severely limited the range of options for dealing with unemployment because significant monetary expansion would have undermined the balance of payments and would therefore be inconsistent with the fixed parity.

In the event, Britain experienced a fairly modest depression between the years 1929–32, not quite so severe as 1921, but more prolonged. But this period captured the popular imagination because of the very high unemployment figures, the sudden departure from the gold standard in September 1931 and the drama of political events at the time. Weakening British exports, as the incomes of the primary producing countries overseas began to fall, came at a time of a downturn in the US economy which greatly aggravated deflationary tendencies. The US stock-market crash in October 1929 was followed by the international financial crisis in the summer of 1931. Unemployment rose from 1.2 million (9.5 per cent) in the second quarter of 1929 to 3 million (22.7 per cent) in the third quarter of 1932.

When it came to recovery, Britain did rather better than many leading competitors. Between 1932 and the peak of activity in 1937 real income increased by 19 per cent, gross domestic production by 23 per cent, industrial production by nearly 46 per cent and gross fixed investment by 47 per cent. Exports rose too (by 28 per cent) but the recovery was primarily a home market one. But even so unemployment problems remained, with the total out of work numbering 1.4 million (just over 9 per cent) in the third quarter of 1937. The Government stance on monetary and fiscal policy was more relaxed, but the Treasury attitude to public works and reflation by expansionist finance changed only marginally. However, strong natural growth in building and construction trades, and in the consumer industries, provided upward trends in real incomes, home ownership being one of the areas to benefit.

The national situation was overlain by sharp regional differences within the country from the point of view of depression and capacity for recovery. Uneven development marked the geography of inter-war Britain (Ward, 1988). The highest rates of unemployment remained concentrated in areas of heavy industry, including coal mining, mechanical engineering, ship building, textiles, and iron and steel manufacture. The contraction of these high-cost industries proved traumatic. Significantly they were located in areas of nineteeth-century development where the coalfields and tidal estuaries had spawned their great cities. Between the wars, the incidence of regional deprivation heightened the problems of these areas, already afflicted by a backlog of unfit housing, congestion and overcrowding.

Between 1923 and 1939 unemployment rates in these hard-hit industries were high: shipbuilding 36.8 per cent (on average), cotton textiles 20.7 per cent, and coal mining 19.6 per cent. By comparison the figure for vehicle manufacture was 10 per cent. The labour force was being restructured: between 1920 and 1938 the coal industry lost 400,000 of its insured workforce; cotton 230,000; iron and steel 185,000; and shipbuilding 150,000. On the other hand, more than 600,000 were added to the workforces in chemicals, electrical engineering, vehicles, electricity supply, silk and rayon, and hosiery. A distinct shift took place from the staple export industries of the last century to a range of industries more closely linked to domestic markets and reliant on new technologies (Cronin, 1984).

The geography of Britain was changing as population and industry were redistributed. The population of Greater London grew by 2 million between the wars, 1.25 million by inward migration from elsewhere in the country and 0.75 million by natural increase. People followed jobs and moved from the regions of economic decline to the more buoyant areas, typically the outer parts of Greater London and selected centres in the Home Counties. Between 1929 and 1936 unemployment averaged 16.9 per cent across Great Britain, but it ranged from 7.8 per cent in the South-east to 30.1 per cent for Wales, 22.7 per cent for the North-east and just under 22 per cent for Scotland and the North-west.

This novel and distinctive economic backcloth to the inter-war years had a number of important consequences for town planning. Ultimately the regional problem and the changing geography of population and industrial distribution gave the subject field a dramatically widened remit. Another effect was that it engineered a prevailing mood of despair about the quality of urban and industrial life which in turn bred a determination to rebuild and sweep away the past when the time came – which it did, in the 1940s when town planning was able to assume the mantle of the new provider.

Public housing

The war years themselves provided the occasion for a new venture in State intervention in housing: rent control. The Rent and Mortgage Restriction Act, 1915, fixed rents at the levels obtaining in 1914, and although it was introduced as a wartime emergency measure, it became politically impossible to repeal after hostilities ceased. The circumstances of the legislation were that widespread discontent in areas of war industry had resulted from sharply rising rents, and in one locality, Glasgow, a rent strike caused political alarm. Long before 1914 Glasgow had been a pressure point for confrontation between landlord and tenant: collective tenant complaint was commonplace in a situation dominated by communal tenant blocks, administered by tough 'factors' who had extensive powers of eviction and distraint. In 1915 the attempts of landlords to benefit from housing shortages, exacerbated by the cessation of house building and the influx of munitions workers to the Clyde shipbuilding yards and engineering works, led to protest. Melling (1983) has argued that the fight against evictions was not organized by 'Red Clydeside' political activists, but was a spontaneous upsurge by Glasgow housewives: women munitions workers and soldiers' wives and mothers who responded to grievance by witholding rent increases. The dispute threatened to spread to Woolwich, Birmingham, Belfast and other centres of the munitions industry; the legislation of December 1915 was to have a major impact on British housing policy.

An equally long lasting, but more profound government stance came from the perceived need to prepare plans for post-war reconstruction. From Lloyd George's Reconstruction Committee, set up in February 1917, came strong support for a Ministry of Health and an extensive housing programme for the working classes, ideas supported later by Christopher Addison as Minister of Reconstruction. The Report of the Royal Commission on the Housing of the Industrial Population of Scotland (Cmd. 8731, 1917) provided ample justification for a new initiative, in its revelations of the wretched housing conditions inherited from earlier years. Meanwhile successive years of minimal house building had led to a national housing shortage, variously estimated at between 400,000 and 600,000 dwellings. In the period before 1910 about 85,000 new houses had been built each year, but after the introduction of Land Values Duties the building rate fell sharply. The supply problem was further compounded by the fact that during the four years of war only 50,000 dwellings were added to the national stock.

Housing Shortage

Action was called for in matters both of housing quality and quantity, and of distribution according to need. Proposals for qualitative improvement in new dwellings came from a committee set up by the Local Government Board; chaired by Sir John Tudor Walters, an MP and Director of the Hampstead Garden Suburb Trust, it dealt with matters relating to building construction and the provision of dwellings for the working class. The recommendations which flowed from this committee, published in 1919, owed much to one member, Raymond Unwin, and it is from this source that earlier years of experiment in site planning (focusing particularly on density and layout), house design and standards of accommodation finally came to fruition as national policy. For a quarter of a century Britain's housing received a marked Unwin-inspired imprint.

Unwin's early place in British town planning has already been noted (see pp. 63): at New Earswick, Letchworth and Hampstead, where traditions of vernacular architecture, linked to new forms of residential layout dictated by informality, open space and densities lower than had been the norm, provided both a practical base for a newly developing profession and a rallying cry for the future. His pamphlet *Nothing gained by overcrowding*! (1912) may have been based on questionable statistics, but the approach and general philosophy proved increasingly acceptable to informed opinion. Unwin became a national figure of many parts. In 1910 he was one of the prime organizers of the Royal Institute of British Architects' International Town Planning Congress (which attracted an astonishing 1,300 delegates); between 1912 and 1914 he was lecturing at the University of Birmingham; and in 1913 he was playing an active role in establishing a Town Planning Institute. When Thomas Adams left the Local Government Board in 1914, Herbert Samuel, the President, was quick to appoint Unwin as Chief Town Planning Inspector.

The importance of this appointment was quickly recognized. In 1915 he was seconded to the explosives division of the Ministry of Munitions, to lead an ambitious programme of factory and house building. The Office of Works had already commenced construction of the attractive Well Hall Estate, Eltham (the design and layout of which owed much to Unwin's book *Town planning in practice* (1909)), but the building of munitions plants elsewhere in the country was now promoted. The largest was at Gretna on the Solway Firth and it became no less than a State-developed new town, south-west of the existing village. Courtenay Crickmer was the resident architect but Unwin's hand in this early development of a planned settlement with community facilities was well in evidence.

Unwin next joined the Tudor Walters committee of enquiry, providing a major contribution. Miller (1981) acknowledges that the published report (Cmd. 9191, 1918) reflected Unwin's concepts of housing design, garden suburbs, site selection and survey: 'the fragmentary experimentation of Letchworth and Hampstead crystallized into statutory house types and area standards, and a density of twelve houses to the acre, paving the way for an unprecedented municipal intervention into the provision of housing' (Miller, 1981, p. 89). New standards were set for the working-class house in terms of space, WC, bathrooms, sunlight and garden space. The Committee advocated that the density of dwellings in working-class development should not exceed 12 to the acre in urban areas (8 in rural areas). Sites for development should be properly surveyed and selected. In the subsequent layout, road needs and road widths had to be assessed; there should be good access to the rear of houses; the proper orientation of houses should be secured; design elements should incorporate the cul-de-sac, courtyard and green. Generous space standards should attend the dwellings themselves; each house should have its own garden, large living rooms with a sunny aspect, a first floor bath, a WC approached under cover, a larder and a coal store. The Government's own *Housing manual* (1919) adopted these far-reaching recommendations and the pattern for the whole of the inter-war period was set.

Consideration was given to housing need in two Acts in 1919. The Housing and Town Planning Act made it obligatory for local authorities to prepare surveys of their housing needs, to draw up plans to deal with them, and to carry out their schemes. Similar powers in the Housing Act of 1890 had only been permissive and so far only a few councils (notably London) had been active house builders; indeed some, including Birmingham, had regarded the proposition as a matter of last resort.

The Act was passed in July 1919. In retrospect it was courageous legislation but it had curiously little bite. All that the legislation provided for was that any loss incurred by the local authorities, as a result of carrying out the regulations, would fall as a charge upon the Exchequer. Addison was soon persuaded that houses would not be built fast enough without direct subsidy and in December that year a further Housing (Additional Powers) Bill was rushed through all its stages, providing for subsidies (£160 for a four-bedroomed house, £140 for a four-bedroomed house without a parlour, and £130 for a three-bedroomed house) and empowering local authorities to prohibit luxury and non-essential building.

It was Addison, formerly President of the Local Government Board, but with its demise now the first Minister of Health, who introduced the programme which articulated Lloyd George's election promise to the voters of Wolverhampton in November 1918 that returning soldiers should have 'homes fit for heroes'. We might pause at this juncture to ask just why the British Government should assume an obligation to provide decent housing for the working classes, when in other countries rather different policies were pursued; also why Britain embarked, consciously or otherwise, on a massive shift in housing tenure over the next 50 years and more. The factors which lay behind both questions have considerably affected British town planning this century, as the transformation of an old order of private landlords to the new pattern of owner-occupied and council estates has occurred. Daunton asks the searching question: 'did the private market as it existed in the decades before the First World War fall, or was it pushed?' (Daunton, 1987, p. 13). The 'homes for heroes' debate has received full attention (Orbach, 1977; Swenarton, 1981), but the circumstantial canvas of historical explanation extends over some years.

The immediate trigger was that during the last period of the war the Ministry of Reconstruction's Housing Advisory Panel, chaired by Lord Salisbury, was successful in establishing the parameters of post-war policy. The powerful voices of the Fabians, where the Webbs proved insistent campaigners, urged State intervention on a new scale. The Panel argued that private enterprise, which had hitherto provided 95 per cent of working-class housing, could not be relied upon to meet this task after the war. Public utility societies and cooperative schemes, which had previously seemed to offer perfectly viable means of providing housing, were discounted in favour of housing by local authorities. One argument has been that the Government's housing programme was introduced to buy industrial and social peace; it could do this in exchange for really very little, except expense – and when the Treasury found it too costly, the scheme was jettisoned.

But longer-term issues were involved, as reviewed by Daunton (1987). The political explanation runs as follows. For many years before 1914 private house owners had been hit by an increasing share of rate levy, at a time when the costs of urban government were rising; from the 1880s landlords found themselves in an increasingly difficult situation as demand fell and the burden of local taxation mounted. Additionally, private landlords became marginalized politically; industrialists had not extended the housing market and private landlords were drawn largely, though not entirely, from the lower middle class – the very people who found it more and more difficult to establish their position on local councils, bearing in mind, at least, the new element of organized labour via the Trades Councils. The Liberal Party was more interested in shifting the burden of local taxation onto land and tended to regard house property rents as a secondary matter. The Conservatives focused their attention more on the needs of agriculture and the church than urban landlords, but there was a strand in Party thinking which accepted the principle of State aid for housing. All this was before 1914, but the Rent Act, 1915 concentrated the minds wonderfully: State intervention in the provision of working-class housing after the war became much more likely. Interestingly, the Labour Party came to the view that all working-class housing should be supplied through the local authorities. In the final analysis the need for a swift response to an immediate housing shortage after the war pointed almost inevitably to a large-scale local authority housing programme, rather than face a period of delay while housing associations were geared up to the task. It was a crucial decision and town planning in Britain was immeasurably influenced by it.

Lloyd George's Government had embarked on a programme of financing social reform at a time of rapidly rising prices. As economic problems built up in 1920, so the expenses of the housing programme became evident. A shortage of building workers and of building materials compounded escalating costs. In August 1920, the cost of a house which stood at £250 in 1914, had risen to £930 on average. Only 29,000 houses were completed during the year. Addison fell in April 1921, castigated by Lloyd George for waste and lavish public expenditure, and the housing scheme was halted.

Two years later, in 1923, houses were still being completed under the Addison Scheme, under contracts concluded before the cutback. In all, the 1919 legislation was responsible for the completion of nearly 214,000 dwellings, the great majority by local authorities. In 1923 the Conservative Government once again introduced a subsidy scheme, under Neville Chamberlain, and the programme was developed in 1924 by John Wheatley, Minister of Health in the first Labour Government. State-sponsored housing began to reach further down the social scale than previously and house building under subsidy began to increase in the later 1920s. The 1923 Scheme lowered the standards for grant eligibility; the superficial area of houses qualifying for subsidy was also reduced, resulting in smaller houses, let at lower rents. The Housing Act of 1924 restored the local authorities to their former role as house builders, gave higher subsidies and promised a long-term housing programme. The Wheatley Act remained in operation until 1933 (though with a reduced subsidy) and an indelible mark had been made on housing policy. The further reach of State enterprise had been confirmed. Between 1919 and 1934 nearly 2.5 million dwellings were built in England and Wales, 31 per cent by local authorities; and of the rest (largely by private enterprise) a quarter were subsidized.

Visually and socially the local authority houses also had a decisive impact. The council estate became a significant feature in patterns of urban growth. Layouts became standardized and often geometric in design; wide avenues were punctuated (latterly) by roundabouts; and there was an abundance of open space. The larger estates were heavily criticized for absent or late provision of social and community facilities. Becontree in south Essex, as an LCC housing estate then the largest local-authority estate in the world, was a working-class suburb adjoining Ilford, unrelated to industrial development, ill-served by transport and lines of communication, and where schools and shops were late in provision. In Birmingham, Kingstanding, and in Liverpool, Speke, were typical of the one-class, monotone housing estates of the big cities. Rather different was Wythenshawe, south of Manchester on the Tatton Estate, planned as a satellite and enclosed by an agricultural belt, but not distant enough from the parent city to serve that function. Development began in 1928, with Barry Parker as consultant; 10 residential neighbourhoods were laid out with a road layout which followed the American practice of parkways.

Slum clearance

The Housing, Town Planning etc. Act, 1919, (the Addison Act) broke new ground in British housing policy in two related respects: the emphasis on building new dwellings to garden suburb ideals and to a standard hitherto unsurpassed in the public sector; and the neglect of the older slums. For almost half a century the housing question had been dominated by the problems of insanitary, unfit dwellings and the association with over-crowding and ill health. Assumptions and practices changed, with far greater hope now reposing in a massive addition to the housing stock in order to at least begin to tackle the problems of overcrowding and health. Slum dwellers would filter through into better stock, or be rehoused by local authorities in new estates. These rather simple expectations were not fulfilled however: the worst housed were not necessarily relocated and the new estates were associated in due time with their own problems of over-crowding, poverty and undernourishment.

The term 'unhealthy areas' derived from the Housing Act 1875 (the Cross Act) and was retained in common use throughout the inter-war period. An early example of the recognition of the residual problem was afforded by the setting up of the Unhealthy Areas Committee by Addison in 1919. A new Birmingham MP in his first year in the House, Neville Chamberlain, was appointed Chairman (Cherry, 1980). The terms of reference were broadly to consider the principles to be adopted in the clearance of slum areas, but interestingly the Committee's conclusions adopted a city-wide perspective, placing the reconstruction of older areas in the context of territorially diffused urban growth. Chamberlain was broadly sympathetic to the town planning and garden city movements, and his committee included G.L. Pepler, town planner from the Ministry of Health, and Capt. R.L. Reiss, then Chairman of the Garden Cities and Town Planning Association.

Crucially, their *Interim report* submitted in March 1920 noted the inti-mate connection between housing, transport and the ultimate distribution of land uses of all kinds, including residential, commercial and industrial, so that the housing question 'can only be successfully attacked by the simultaneous consideration of all these aspects over a wide area'. Com-pared with nineteenth-century piecemeal projects, such as in Birming-ham's central-area redevelopment, or the Boundary Street scheme in East London, the merits of a twentieth-century comprehensive approach to housing reconstruction and urban redevelopment were advocated. The *Interim report* considered that there were only two alternative methods of relieving the congestion of London: either by vertical expansion in multi-storey buildings, or by removal of part of the population elsewhere, so achieving lower densities and larger open spaces. It favoured the second, advocating the extablishment of garden cities surrounding London: disper-sal and decentralization of both people and employment. A general plan for the reconstruction of London was required. The *Second and final report*, submitted in April 1921, maintained this general line of approach. Specif-ically there was a recognition that delays in slum clearance were inevit-able, and therefore it was still important to achieve improvements of older houses; local authority acquisition was envisaged to achieve this.

Chamberlain's Reports were submitted at a financially unpropitious time, and although the scale of unfit housing was known to be severe, policies for effective remedies were shelved. Garside (1988) has shown how in the period 1919–23 civil servants wrestled with the requirement to indicate action, but without generating demands that could not be satisfied. Government relied on its house-building campaign, postponing action on slum housing, though calling for more information from local authorities to carry out surveys of their areas. In the years of sharp pruning of public-sector expenditure, and at a time when a comprehensive housing programme embracing improvement, clearance, redevelopment and new building lay beyond the grasp of the Ministry of Health, the most that could be hoped for in the 1920s was the amelioration of a small number of the worst houses. In the meantime the relatively favoured escaped to the suburbs, leaving behind the very low paid, especially the casually employed.

It took some years for a lobby to emerge, strong enough to bring pressure to bear on the scandal of the continuing presence of the nineteenth-century slums. E.D. Simon's advocacy was clear (*How to abolish the slums*, 1929): continue to build new houses and relocate the people. As ex-Lord Mayor of Manchester and former chairman of that City Corporation's Housing Committee, his experience led him to demonstrate that:

> the only solution of the slum problem is to go on building new houses, especially what we have called the standard minimum house, gradually transferring the population to these new houses, and at the same time closing down the old houses as they become vacant . . . we ought to aim at building 200,000 new houses each year until we are within sight of a final solution of the problem.   (Simon, 1929, p. 102)

The return of a Labour Government in 1929 provided an opportunity for a different approach. The Housing Act, 1930 (Arthur Greenwood's Act), signalled a move away from State involvement in building additional dwellings, to one of encouraging slum clearance and rebuilding on cleared sites. Local authorities were given extra subsidies related to the numbers of people displaced and the higher price of central area land. Even then, however, there was a preference to use the general subsidies for new suburban houses while ever these remained in force. Slum clearance did not become fully operative until the subsidies were cancelled in 1933.

The major shift in practice came with the Housing Act, 1935. More was clearly needed, for slum clearance since 1930 was regarded as both too limited in scope and too slow in practice to deal with the scale of the housing problem in the big cities. The perceived benefits of large-scale redevelopment were looked at again, costs notwithstanding, bearing in mind compulsory acquisition of housing, industrial and commercial property. There is evidence (Garside, 1988) that ministry officials were influential in their advocacy for a radical, new approach, arguing the merits of large reconstruction schemes such as Kingsway and Aldwych in London and Corporation Street in Birmingham. They had to settle for much less, however, and an understanding was reached with local authorities, in spite of some early reluctance on their part. To meet different points of view and to allay political sensitivities that a radical switch of policy would not imply undue criticism of past failure and neglect, the legislation focused on the establishment and enforcement of an overcrowding standard. In the event, therefore, the Act did not provide for large-scale planning and redevelopment, but stimulated further direction towards slum clearance by extending new forms of subsidy directed to the rehousing of overcrowded families. Local authorities were obliged to carry out overcrowding surveys; to prosecute to enforce the standard; and to define what might be regarded as 'suitable alternative accommodation'. The system depended on local authority action and interpretation.

A compromise situation had been reached. Action was being undertaken, but it was far removed from the radical surgery that seemed to be needed. Official calculations of the number of slum dwellings were continually revised (upwardly) and by 1939 the officially accepted total for England and Wales stood at 472,000. By that date almost half had been demolished or closed. But blackspots remained: one third of the total number of houses in Manchester, for example, were classed as unfit at the outbreak of war.

However, there were some spectacular local developments. The Greenwood Act had provided a special subsidy for flats, and indeed the 1930s produced flat building in British cities in a significant way for the first time. Only in London and Liverpool was there any tradition of flat building that went back to the middle of the nineteenth century. Between the wars, nationally, only about 5 per cent of all subsidized dwellings were in the form of flats; it was 40 per cent in London and 20 per cent in Liverpool. Greenwood's Act finally coerced a number of local authorities into building flats; in the 1920s the majority of English cities had not undertaken high-density redevelopment, confining their use of housing subsidies to suburban estates. London and Liverpool continued to build flats and from 1933 (when the Act became widely operative) many cities built a few hundred flats in large estates: by 1939 Newcastle had built 500, Leeds nearly 1,000, Liverpool over 5,000 and Manchester 9,000 (Ravetz, 1974a).

It was in Leeds that perhaps the most remarkable scheme was undertaken: at Quarry Hill, on 26 acres east of the city centre, from 1934 onwards (Ravetz, 1974b). The site had been in the ownership of the local authority since 1901, but after clearance it was largely empty. A Labour Council was elected in 1933, and under the political influence of a left-wing cleric the city council adopted different policies from the previous Conservative administration. Revd Charles Jenkinson, a Christian Socialist, was appointed to a slum parish in the city in 1927; he was elected to the city council in 1930 and his drive on housing questions made Leeds the leading housing authority in the country.

The Quarry Hill scheme contained 930 flats, progressively occupied from 1938 onwards to a (delayed) completion date of 1941. Designed by the City Architect, R.A.H. Livett who was also Director of Housing, the scheme was linked to a commitment to prefabrication (with implicit promises of speed and economy) and to the architectural ideals of the Modern Movement as represented in the Karl Marx Hof and other Viennese estates. A number of innovations were recorded: the use of lifts (though not the first in

British council flats), the first use of the Garchey refuse disposal system in the country, heights up to 8 storeys, private balconies in the flats and emphasis on community provisions including playgrounds, laundry, gardens, shops and community hall.

Elsewhere slum clearance activity was much more piecemeal and avoided spectacular set pieces. Frequently, the results of clearance activity depended on the strength of key local authority officials and their influence on political decisions. In Liverpool for example the Director of Housing, Lancelot Keay, was a convert from his previous reliance on wholesale decanting of slum dwellers to the suburbs, to a 10-year rebuilding scheme. But in practice it was difficult to acquire sufficiently large sites for the proposed schemes. A number of 5-storey blocks built in brick and concrete were developed, with over 5,500 central-area flats built between 1930 and 1945. Factors such as location, journey to work, allocation and management policies, cost and personal preference meant that different types of households were accommodated in different housing forms; predictably the low-income groups took the poorest quality housing (Pooley and Irish, 1987).

In the meantime, however, while the general lines of policy with regard to public housing switched in favour of slum clearance, significant new evidence from the medical profession served to cast doubt on some long-held assumptions concerning the importance of the environment in matters of health and fitness. Over many years considerable advances had been made in urban environmental quality through better housing, lessening of overcrowding and provision of open space: but national medical standards had not risen accordingly. The claims of the environmentalists had to be looked at again.

Telling evidence came from the Medical Officer of Health for Stockton-on-Tees (G.C.M. M'Gonigle) and his co-author, Kirby (1936). There was no doubting the state of the country's unfitness. In the year beginning November 1917 National Service Medical Boards conducted nearly 2.5 million medical examinations in Great Britain: of every nine men, only three were perfectly fit and healthy, while two were on a definitely 'unfirm plane' of health and strength, three were incapable of undergoing more than a very moderate degree of physical exertion and the remaining one was a chronic invalid. The influenza epidemic of 1918/19 seemed to confirm a national state of unfitness: more than 151,000 deaths were recorded, the highest relative to population for any epidemic since the cholera outbreak of 1849. After the war it was not possible to maintain national service statistics on the earlier scale, but medical records of school children did provide a comparable measure of national health and fitness. During 1933 1.8 million elementary school children underwent 'routine' examinations: 17.3 per cent required immediate medical treatment and a further 14.0 per cent suffering from ailments of a less serious nature, were scheduled 'for observation'. In short, nearly one in three possessed physical defects, a figure which took no account of dental problems or defective vision.

The national picture was augmented by detail from Stockton-on-Tees. In 1927, a district known as the Housewife Lane area was demolished as a slum clearance scheme and its population of 710 (152 families) was moved to the Mount Pleasant Estate, a self-contained municipal housing estate which had been specially built for the purpose. In the next five years (1928–32) the crude death-rate of the transferred population increased from 18.75 to 26.71 per 1,000, and by way of explanation M'Gonigle and Kirby observe: 'It is difficult to come to any other conclusion than that the increased mortality was associated with the dietary deficiences' (M'Gonigle and Kirby, 1936, p. 129).

The argument was advanced that three main factors are responsible for man's health or ill-health: nutrition, infection and external environmental factors. Of these three, bad environment must of course be taken seriously, and it was not suggested that environmental factors did not play an important part in health deterioration, but 'environment is not the only factor so operative and possibly not the most important one' (M'Gonigle and Kirby, 1936, p. 148). The debate progressed to a recognition of the importance of diet deficiency, linked to poverty. Amongst the employed families living on the Mount Pleasant Estate, 51.2 per cent of their total income was claimed by rent and 'other necessary expenditure'; in unemployed families the figure rose to 60.6 per cent. Overall, the amounts which these groups of families were able to spend on food were, in three cases out of four, well below the minimum considered necessary by the British Medical Association Nutrition Committee.

On the face of it, so much for slum clearance and planned redevelopment: community health might even be impaired rather than improved. On the other hand, the issues were now seen broadly in terms of welfare; the physical arrangements of housing and land use had to be part of a wider canvas which tackled poverty and social opportunity. The scene was set for the activity of town planning to move from environmentalism to welfarism.

Land use planning and pressures for development

A major criticism of the town-planning sections of the 1909 Act had been that the provisions were cumbersome and that as a consequence the operation of town planning schemes was slow and protracted. The Housing and Town Planning Act, 1919, simplified the procedures for making schemes. The authority of the Minister of Health (the new Ministry having succeeded the former Local Government Board) was no longer required for the preparation of a scheme; instead, all that was necessary was the resolution of a local council. But otherwise the main principles of planning law, laid down in 1909, were maintained: future development should accord with an approved town planning scheme; compensation to be payable to landowners injuriously affected; and betterment to be payable to a local authority when an increase in land values accrues as a result of planning proposals. Compensation and betterment proved thorny issues and were not totally resolved until 1948, and then only temporarily.

Another criticism was the permissive nature of the 1909 Act, but this was removed in the 1919 legislation. From 1 January 1923 the preparation of schemes was compulsory on all borough and district councils with a population of more than 20,000. The schemes, to be prepared within a period of three years from that date, were still to relate to land in course of development, or earmarked for development. They were little more, therefore, than devices to regulate land development in the suburban areas, to safeguard principal routes of communication and to impart basic characteristics of density, residential character and provision of open space.

Important innovations were introduced by the 1919 Act, which were to have far-reaching implications. First, it enabled Joint Town Planning committees to be established, which assisted in the development of regional planning. Second, it introduced the practice of Interim Development Control by enabling authorities to give consent to development in advance of the preparation of a scheme. In this way development was not delayed and working agreements emerged between developer and local council. This had the effect of statutory town planning taking root in an authority without having to persuade a council as to the merits (and costs) of scheme preparation.

Statutory town planning of a kind therefore got under way after the hiatus of war, with only limited experience to guide it, as summarized by Adshead (1923). Neither was there all that much political interest behind it if the minimal debate during the passage of the Bill through the House was anything to go by (Cherry, 1974). But a new profession was to encourage it; new technical practices such as zoning would foster planning method; and outstandingly George Pepler, now Chief Town Planning Inspector at the Ministry of Health proved a tireless advocate and bridge with local authorites (Cherry, 1981). Wright (1982) confirms his professional enterpreneurship, describing him as 'a John the Baptist. He made converts, and prepared the way for the real planning that began with the bombs of 1940–41' (Wright, 1982, p. 9). Meanwhile, overtones of a moral crusade were maintained by the garden city movement, both at home and overseas in the form of the International Garden Cities and Town Planning Association.

In spite of the hopes of the new legislation, progress in scheme preparation, the show piece of statutory town planning, was still slow. By 1928 there were still 98 out of 262 urban authorities of 20,000 population size in England and Wales which had not submitted any proposals, in the form of either resolutions, preliminary statements or schemes. The date for the submission of obligatory schemes had already been extended and the Local Government Act, 1929 extended it again to 1 January 1934, with power for the Minister to further extend it, but not beyond 31 December 1938. In Scotland progress measured by submission of schemes was even slower, with only two small schemes in Edinburgh submitted by 1929.

The basis for statutory town planning was changed in the Town and Country Planning Act, 1932. The origins of this legislation were particularly protracted, and concerned the question of rural amenities; 'town and country' now became the customary title for Planning Acts. The 1932 Act repealed and consolidated almost all general and local enactments relating to planning. It materially extended the powers of local authorities by authorizing the making of schemes for any land, whether urban or rural, though requiring ministerial approval. But the Act broke with the 1919 precedent by reverting to making scheme preparation voluntary rather than obligatory. This move was bitterly attacked by the planning profession, though in the event the process of scheme preparation quickened during the later 1930s; by the end of the decade London and most of the large towns were wholly or almost wholly under planning control. Even in Scotland there was developing interest, particularly in Glasgow with four major schemes in the 1930s.

A rudimentary system of land-use control had been partially developed by the outbreak of war. In March 1938 in England and Wales, 24 million acres were under planning control, but only 236,000 acres of this total applied to approved schemes actually operative (92 in number). The rest of the land was covered by local authority resolutions and draft schemes not yet submitted.

Much has been made of the importance of the 1919 and 1932 Acts in establishing a nationwide system of supervision over building development, based on local authority scheme preparation and the twin sanctions of by-law and planning control. Together with the hold over council housing, it could be said that there was a measure of guidance and control over suburban building, its location, layout and design, as never before. True, but in some cases that did not amount to all that much, and while inter-war legislation obviously provided the experience for the post-war Planning Acts which followed, the development of statutory land-use control took place at a time when particular environmental changes seemed to be little affected by formal planning powers. There are three aspects which deserve attention: the enormous surge of private house building between the wars; the concern over scenic protection; and the search for wider regional, strategic models for planning.

Private housing.   There were a number of preconditions for the advent of mass owner occupation, which first characterized the inter-war years (Ball, 1983). A gradual growth in owner occupation was already in evidence before 1914, but a spectacular rise was assisted from a number of different directions. First, during the 1920s it became easier to transfer freehold land, as long-standing solicitor resistance to changes in property law broke down; a series of Property Acts from 1910 to 1925 facilitated the free and rapid transfer of small plots and single dwellings. Second, there was an acute housing shortage, for virtually all classes of society, hence speculative house builders were in a unique position to take advantage of this and other conditions. (For example, the late 1920s and early 1930s were years when building construction was cheap, with a fall in commodity prices.) Third, the position of landed property was precarious, which depressed land prices, kept farm rents low, and encouraged the selling of land for residential purposes. Whole farms and landed estates at the edge of urban areas came on to the market; suburban land prices therefore were very low.

There were other factors too to explain the veritable explosion of building for owner occupation. There was for example the capacity of an expanding middle class to afford their own homes. The salaried groups were expanding as employment grew in professional and administrative services; for every two civil servants in 1929 there were three in 1938. Furthermore, income tax was relatively low; it did not rise above 4s 6d to 5s in the pound during much of this time, and middle-class incomes of £250 p.a. to £1,000 p.a. enjoyed the lowest percentage burden of both direct and indirect taxation combined.

Perhaps more importantly there was the sustained expansion of the building societies, a factor which permitted house purchase at attractive terms. The 1930s particularly was an era of cheap money. While the scope for profitable investment in manufacturing industry was limited, the owner-occupied housing market seemed ideal for loan capital. There was no competition either from demands for overseas investment, and a large-scale property market did not exist. As a consequence direct mortgage lending to owner occupiers increased sharply. Ninety-five per cent mortgages were permissible and interest rates were low, falling to 3.25 per cent in 1934. A new house, costing let us say £480 (higher than the national average cost of houses being built in 1937, then £427), could therefore be purchased for a deposit of £24, with repayments of 13s 6d per week over 20 years.

Some speculative builders boomed in these conditions, few having been active prior to the 1920s, though their characteristics suggest some link or other with housebuilding:

> The largest of the 1930s house builders, New Ideal Homesteads, was set up by an ex-local authority surveyor in the late 1920s. Laing and Costain had been medium and small building firms respectively in the north of England before both moved south to London and prospered . . . Taylor Woodrow was set up after the unintended sale of two houses by a 16-year old greengrocer's son and his solicitor uncle. Wates was a small family concern, two members of which owned a furniture shop in south London. Wimpey was a small stone masons and road building firm until acquired in 1919 by an ex-army major with the support of his quarrying merchant father.   (Ball, 1983, p. 34)

The building industry at this time created a distinct suburban environment, with the prevalence of the three-bedroomed, semi-detached house. As Oliver, Davis and Bentley (1981) remind us: 'The "suburban semi" is a cliché which summons up a mental picture of rows of red-roofed, rough-cast pairs of houses, each with its bay windows, its porched entrance, its "third bedroom" above', (Oliver, Davis and Bentley, 1981, p. 11), recalling images of small front gardens and bigger rear ones, side garages and garden gates.

A boom period of speculative house building peaked between 1928 and 1936 when construction of 118,000 dwellings annually increased to 293,000. Market saturation caused a subsequent downturn as working-class wage levels proved too low to enable the market to be extended further. But this was not before State subsidies, both direct and indirect, had first fuelled and then maintained a remarkable period of private development. State grants to builders initially induced the builders to build; thereafter local authority provision of basic services was readily forthcoming; and in London at least, the Transport Executive spread its underground (and overground) railway lines north in advance of development.

A sociological revolution was also taking place as the social status of owner occupation proved increasingly compelling. Linked to the new fashions of semi-detached houses with private gardens, and perhaps a drive and garage for a car, in a setting of more abundant open space, in an environment of modernity where new schools were particularly welcome by a child-rearing local population, and in a social milieu of middle-class respectability, the private building boom created ever-expanding suburban estates.

The territorial expansion of the big cities, and the further metropolitanization of London itself during this period, represents a fascinating period of land-use change and urban transformation. London was the prime example (Jackson, 1973). Middlesex bore the brunt of the tide of development where the flat claylands in the centre and west lay open, with accessibility already afforded by railways constructed earlier; its pasture was no longer needed and neither were the market garden plains of the south. The population of the county increased by 1.64 million between 1921 and 1931, five times the increase for England and Wales, and the highest recorded for any county. The district of Harrow received the largest influx of any local authority in Greater London between 1921 and 1938 (134,480 persons), though as a percentage increase that for Wembley was greater than for Harrow. Hayes and Harlington, Ruislip–Northwood and a host of other districts leapt in population size. By 1939 all but the northern and north-western parts of the county had been built over. North-west Surrey expanded with equal vigour, particularly around Merton and Morden, which had the benefit of an underground railway service to complement the frequent electric train service elsewhere. In Essex, development was concentrated in Becontree and around Dagenham, Hornchurch, Romford and Ilford. Expansion in Kent was slower to materialize but, when it did, Bexley was the main growth point. On the edge of London, Hertfordshire and Buckinghamshire showed significant growth around Barnet, and particularly Slough, respectively.

Scenic preservation. Inter-war Britain was notable for a generation which sought to emphasize the principles and practicalities of the protection of natural beauty. It made its mark on an emergent philosophy of town and country planning (Sheail, 1981). The desire to return to past simplicities was marked, given the successive disappointments after the war, with slumps and uncertainty. The appeal of natural beauty may have been strong precisely because it was free of argument and doctrine; it became a common denominator in the drive for moral and spiritual recovery. So it was that the scenic heritage of coast and countryside took on a special significance. There was also an urgency to protect and preserve while it was still possible to do so: the countryside was in change and this seemed to invigorate the various lobbies which fought for their special interest: flora, fauna, landscape, outdoor recreation and protection from development.

One of the features of change was the emergence of a unique landscape along the coast, on the riverside and in the countryside: 'a makeshift world of shacks and shanties, scattered unevenly in plots of varying size and shape, with unmade roads and little in the way of services' (Hardy and Ward, 1984, p. vii). These were the 'plotlands' of Jaywick Sands, Canvey Island and Peacehaven, which became bywords for the desecration of the countryside.

The pace of land use change over many areas was certainly striking, and town planning, because of the statutory system which emphasized land use control, was drawn into an imprecise area of wider policy and prescription. By 1939 one third of all the houses in England and Wales had been built since 1918; and extensive urban land absorption was in evidence particularly in the 1930s. The geographer L. Dudley Stamp fashioned his land use survey in this context to capture for the first time since the Domesday Book an impression of how the land of Britain was used (or misused). The town planner with no prior guidelines from the history of his own practice, readily subscribed to the intellectual fashion of preservation. Certainly there was widespread dismay at the destruction of the country-side. This was well captured by George Orwell who, in *Coming up for air* (1939), describes the return of George Bowling, after 18 unimaginative years in insurance and marriage to the joyless Hilda, and now shaken by the fear of a future war, returns to the village of his childhood: Lower Binfield. Disillusionment was complete: 'But where was Lower Binfield? Where was the town I used to know? It might have been anywhere. All I knew was that it was buried somewhere in the middle of that sea of bricks' (Orwell, 1939; 1962 edn, p. 117).

One of the most important new groups to emerge during this period was the Council for the Preservation of Rural England (CPRE), formed in 1926 as an initiative   in part, of the President of the Town Planning Institute, Patrick Abercrombie. The Council was merely an umbrella organization for a large and expanding number of countryside and amenity organiza-tions, but it became an invaluable integrator, particularly on the issue of National Parks when it set up its own Standing Committee.

Meanwhile more flamboyant voices were raised. The architect Clough Williams-Ellis of Port Meirion fame published his influential *England and the octopus* in 1928 – 'an angry book, written by an angry young man' as the author confessed in a Preface added to a 1975 edition. The octopus was urbanization and Williams-Ellis conjured up the vision of the tentacles of urban growth with their strong hold over the countryside. His target was 'the spate of mean building all over the country that is shrivelling up the Old England – mean and perky little houses that surely none but mean and perky little souls should inhabit with satisfaction' (p. 15). A book in similar vein was his edited volume *Britain and the beast* (1938) in which his assem-bled contributors reviled the symptoms of Britain in the modern age and offered a nostalgia for the past. The town planner Thomas Sharp made an eloquent plea in *Town and countryside* (1932) for the clear separation of urban and rural. The geographer Vaughan Cornish tried to establish a scientific basis for the study of scenic heritage. For the popular reader the British countryside held appeal: the new magazine *The Countryman* was founded in 1927 and from the Batsford press came a stream of illustrated regional books on the British landscape.

On the face of it, the statutory town-planning system of plan preparation and development control could meet the requirements of this new challenge. But urban sprawl and rural decay and disfigurement was often taking place in areas where local authorities were weak and where traditions of council control over development had not yet been established. Possible claims for compensation could not be faced by most councils, and in any case, there still had to be worked out a coherent land use strategy for the development of the urban fringe. The confusion over the Restriction of Ribbon Development Act 1935 did not help: there were uncertainties between the Ministries of Transport and Health, delay over necessary action and ineffectiveness once it had been taken.

One focus within the countryside lobby was the agitation for a green belt around London. Local authorities began to acquire properties as a response to the inadequacies of the 1932 Act and even before the LCC announced its green belt scheme in January 1935 some authorities, notably Middlesex and Surrey had commenced acquisition on a large scale (Thomas, 1970). All authorities had some sort of proposal on paper by that year, derived in part from the regional advisory reports of earlier years. But authorities had differing aims for the green belt. Middlesex sought to prevent urban development, with the secondary purpose of preserving amenity and providing recreational facilities. On the other hand the aim of the LCC was to secure a reserve supply of recreational land within easy access of the urbanized area of London.

The LCC grant aid scheme offered £2 million to local authorities to buy up land for green belt purposes, and a vigorous period of purchase ensued between 1935 and 1939. The Green Belt (London and Home Counties) Act, 1938, was necessary to legitimate the LCC grant being made available to authorities outside its jurisdiction. The fact was that the London green belt estates represented probably the largest single initiative by local authorities in the face of the inadequacies of planning legislation prior to 1947. Local authorities around London simply took matters into their own hands, either by using other legislation such as the Open Space Act, 1906, or by introducing local powers (Sharp, 1986).

Regional planning. After the First World War the term 'regional planning' was used extensively, the new practice representing a significant extension to planning practice. The term 'regionalism' was itself in vogue in a number of related disciplines, particularly geography and sociology. In a short period of rapid theoretical development the emergent core of regional planning principles and practices strengthened considerably.

Ebenezer Howard's concept of the social city was of course essentially regional in territorial scope, and with the founding of Welwyn Garden City in 1920, the advocates of planned satellites had a second success to record (Purdom, 1925; Macfadyen, 1933). The Garden City implied the primacy of the central city over a surrounding hinterland, but the subsequent contribution of Patrick Geddes was more explicit, advocating civic and regional surveys to demonstrate the interlinkages between a town and its region.

The linkages were already in evidence from one point of view: road traffic. As early as 1913 a conference was held of all local authorities in Greater London to plan comprehensively for arterial roads. Another practical application soon followed, in the field of public administration. Within geography, where a vigorous regionalist theme was in evidence, the work of C.B. Fawcett was influential in relating town planning to local government hierarchies (*Provinces of England*, 1919); significantly C.B. Purdom's book *The building of satellite towns* (1925) was subtitled 'a contribution to the study of town development and regional planning'. Purdom, the Financial Director of Welwyn Garden City Ltd, recognizing that satellite towns were part of the process towards city decentralization, postulated the idea of new regional and provincial authorities in order to assist in the more effective development of such settlements.

In this context town planning was a beneficiary of a number of important developments, which gave to the evolving discipline and profession a distinctive recurrent theme, that of a regional perspective. For central government the region became a convenient administrative unit. During the First World War a number of Ministries set up regional offices and the newly created Ministry of Health set up nine regions – an experiment to be rudely terminated in 1921 as an economy measure. As early as 1920 the Ministry set up a committee to study the regional problems of South Wales: the first example in Britain of *ad hoc* regional planning.

In the event, however, regional-planning practice developed under the aegis of Joint Town Planning Committees (JTPCs). Under the 1919 Act local authorities were permitted to establish such bodies, and they could be either advisory or executive as the constituent authorities wished. The setting up of these committees (largely advisory) proved to be a popular and widespread development, though only two in the 1920s were sufficiently large to be considered 'regional': the Midlands and the Manchester JTPCs. But they gave opportunities for the advancement of town planning, facilitating consultancy work and (so ably fostered by Pepler) encouraging individual local authorities to take the first steps in scheme preparation in their own areas. The JTPCs became instrumental in preparing the ground for district councils to engage fully in the statutory proceses. By 1931 (after 21 years of town-planning legislation) 104 JTCPs had been established and there were very few urban areas not covered at least partially by them (Cherry, 1974).

The notion of regional planning received a great fillip from Unwin's proposals for London prepared between 1929 and 1933. Unwin's work has to be placed in context not only nationally, but internationally. Other big cities in the world were the subject of plans, often decentralist in nature, of which Thomas Adams's *Regional plan of New York* was a celebrated example, issued in two volumes (1929 and 1931) and backed by eight subject reports. London had been given no such attention, but The London Society since 1912 had been undertaking work which was brought together in essays edited by Sir Aston Webb (1921). In one of them Unwin suggested the setting up of an authority to prepare a broad plan; a mile-wide green belt with garden cities beyond would be an essential feature of the strategy.

In November 1927 the Greater London Regional Planning Committee was constituted by the then Minister of Health, Neville Chamberlain. An advisory body, it had 45 members representing the LCC, the City of London, six county councils, the Standing Joint Committee of Metropolitan Boroughs and 129 local authorities ranging from county boroughs to rural districts. The area covered the London and Home Counties Trafffic Area, more than 1,800 square miles in extent, within 25 miles of Charing Cross. Unwin was appointed Technical Advisor to the Committee (chaired by Sir Bannister Fletcher, President of the RIBA and representative of the City of London) in January 1929 for two years.

We should note the miniscule operation: Unwin had assigned to the project the part-time services of G. Montagu-Harris (a past president of the TPI), an assistant and three draughtsmen. But Unwin and his son Edward tackled the challenge with vigour and imagination (Miller, 1981). By the end of 1929 the First report was published: slim and hastily written it yet established a frame of reference for the London region. Philosophically and technically town planning demonstrated in Britain, as elsewhere, an operational capacity to conceive and prepare a metropolitan plan, robust enough to stand the test of time. Unwin's analysis depended on four rings for the Greater London region: belts of population of decreasing density from core to periphery, separated by belts of open space for recreation purposes. These were expressed in schematic diagrams showing the relationship between building development and open land. One showed a background of potential building land with reservations of open space upon it; the other reversed the image by suggesting a green setting within which building areas would be reserved in a pattern of satellites. Of enduring significance was the concept of a green girdle around the perimeter. Within the total spatial concept, proposals were made for the decentralization of industry and the eradication of ribbon development on main roads.

Two Interim reports were published in January 1931 which further developed the principles, but economic retrenchment cut back the work. Many local authorities withdrew or reduced their contributions and for a while Unwin financed the continuation of the Committee's work himself to publish a Second and final report in March 1933, which made a more detailed proposal for a narrow green girdle around London. The Greater London Regional Planning Committee was reconstituted in 1932, and survived as an umbilical cord to commission Abercrombie's work on Greater London 12 years later (see Chapter 5).

Unwin's work mirrored the firmly held decentralist view in town-planning circles (Warren and Davidge, 1930). Although Welwyn Garden City was only the second (and last) of its kind, in 1920, Howard's propaganda remained persuasive. Chamberlain's Unhealthy Areas Committee had accepted the principle and Unwin's Greater London Plan offered a spatial model for its attainment. Meanwhile with the sprawl of burgeoning London, and the perceived frailty of statutory town planning procedures to contain it, pressure for more determined action mounted. One illustration of this was the organization called the Hundred New Towns Association, formed by the architect A. Trystan Edwards in 1934, which advocated, as the term suggests, 100 new towns to relieve pressure on the metropolis; the migration of 5 million people was proposed to 100 new settlements: 40 south of a line from the Wash to the Severn, a further 36 to the rest of England, 15 to Scotland and 9 to Wales.

There was a response from Government. The Interim report of the departmental committee on regional development (Cmd. 3915, 1931) chaired by Lord Chelmsford, had looked at the Reports of the Regional Planning Committees. Where the Reports had dealt with satellite towns, the Committee was 'attracted by the possibilites of future usefulness in these forms of development'. Rather more forthright was the Report of the Departmental Committee on Garden Cities and Satellite Towns, chaired by Lord Marley. Reporting in 1935 it advocated the fullest adoption of the planned distribution of industry and population based on garden city development.

So far, developments in the field of regional planning related to two matters: the application of statutory procedures on a territorial scale larger than a single local authority, and the pursuance of dispersal and decentralization to form the basis of a spatial model for big city growth. Little had been said about the other regional aspect represented by unemployment and economic decline in the Special Areas. The Special Areas (Development and Improvement) Act, 1934, provided for measures of assistance to facilitate the economic development and social improvement of areas affected by industrial depression; it also provided for the appointment of two Commissioners (one for England and Wales, and one for Scotland) to prosecute that assistance. The Commissioners' annual reports make fascinating reading. The particularly incisive Third report of the commissioner for the special areas (England and Wales) (Cmd. 5503, 1936) was instrumental in relating the question of the economic and social problems of the Special Areas to the wider issue of planning for the accommodation of growth elsewhere. The key lay in the uncontrolled growth of London. The Report of P.M. Stewart, the Commissioner, exposed the problem starkly:

> The majority of those who have studied the problem of the location of industry may reasonably be assumed to agree that the colossal post-war growth of Greater London is the aspect of the problem which occasions most concern, and can be rightly regarded as calling for control in the national interest. (para.20)
>
> The macrocosm of London grows with a rapidity which is beginning to cause alarm. Its sheer magnitude and density of population are such that, in the event of a hostile attack, it is doubtful if it could be assured of adequate protection or food supplies. (para.21)
>
> Is it in the national interest that this phenomenal growth should be allowed to proceed unchecked? Much of the growth of Greater London is not based on strictly economic factors; psychology plays an important part in the matter. There is a considerable portion of industrial production not dependent on considerations which are absolutely essential to its location in London. It is this part of the industrial flow which might reasonably be directed elsewhere. Industrialists should be required to state their reasons for seeking to

establish themselves in Greater London; if these reasons are not found to be valid, then they should be restrained from so doing, but, left free to make their choice elsewhere. (para.21)

By the late 1930s, therefore, the scene was set for town planning to incorporate a wider frame of reference. Forty years earlier the promise of town planning was that it could address the urban housing problems of the day, but the principles of environmental regulations were now seen to relate to a quite different set of questions: the problems of regional economic development. The *Third report* introduced a beguiling relationship: on the one hand, the need to establish new and to expand old industries in the Special Areas, and on the other, the need to control the post-1918 growth of Greater London. At one and the same time advocacy for dispersal from big cities was related to proposals for planned development in the depressed regions. Another role for town planning beckoned; it took some years for regional economic planning practice to take coherent shape, but the gauntlet of the conceptual challenge had been thrown down. In the future, town planning was not just about scheme preparation for coordinated development, or the rational control of land use, or even spatial strategies for cities; it was now to be involved in regional economic affairs, though just how had yet to be demonstrated.

Transport

The question of road traffic was another area which brought town planning a wider frame of reference, by virtue of the profession's overall concern for cities in their totality, and its claim for a comprehensive approach to all major development. The Arterial Roads Conference for Greater London in 1913 was in fact a regional plan, but the link between transport, city planning and civic design remained imperfect both in principle and practice. The formation of the Ministry of Transport in 1919 separated the function of traffic and planning in different ministries for half a century.

At the beginning of the First World War there were nearly 140,000 motor cars on British roads. By March 1918 this figure had dwindled to 78,000, but within two years the number had more than doubled. In addition there were nearly as many buses and goods vehicles and an even larger number of motor cycles. The problem was obvious: how to control the fast moving vehicle, to limit the damage it caused both to person and amenity, and to provide new or widened roads in areas of congestion. The layout of roads was a technical matter for surveyors and engineers, though new highways had town-planning significance. But for various reasons a specifically town-planning view of the roads question was slow to develop; emphasis seemed to lie elsewhere.

One factor was that although the motor car made up only one third of all motor vehicles, it was yet seen as the crux of the motor problem (Plowden, 1971). The 'politics' of the motor car throughout the inter-war years depended to a large extent on the vigorous leadership given by the private motorists' main organization, the Automobile Association. With a membership of 100,000 in 1914 its numbers had doubled by 1924 and again by 1931; it waged vigorous self-interested campaigns on such matters as the petrol tax, the Road Fund, speed limits and compulsory insurance.

Another factor was that the inter-war governments were anxious to cut down expenditure on roads. It was not until the Trunk Roads Act, 1936 that anything like a national roads strategy was suggested, with a rational division of roads into four: Trunk, Class I, Class II and unclassified – and even then Britain declined to embark on motorway building, in sharp contrast to Germany's *autobahns* and Italy's *autostrada*. Highway expenditure was firmly linked to local government spending. The most that was achieved was in a few examples of new highway construction (in London the long-standing schemes of the Great West Road and the North Circular came to fruition); and in the bigger cities, there were road-widening schemes, some stretches of dual carriageway and the occasional new project (such as the Headrow in Leeds linked to redevelopment) and some spectacular new projects (such as the new suspension bridge over the Tyne at Newcastle and the Mersey Tunnel at Liverpool/Birkenhead). Perhaps there was a wider Government view: limiting expenditure on the roads enabled the railways to survive the pressure of growing competition from road transport.

A further aspect is that with public attention focused firmly on the statistics of road accidents, many traffic issues became matters for the Police. Fatal accidents involving motor vehicles rose from 373 in 1909 to 1,154 in 1913 and to 2,010 in 1920; in 1926 road deaths rose to 4,886 and to 7,300 in 1934 – a figure that would not be reached again until the early 1960s. For many, the roads debate therefore rested on measures of speed restriction and road safety, but with 2 million motor cars on British roads in 1939, and urban congestion a growing problem, this was scarcely a satisfactory situation. We remember the 1930s for a set of very general measures, rather than for any inter-professional work on traffic and roads as part of a comprehensive view of urban development and planning. Instead, more typical of the time was the innovation of painting white lines along the centre of roads, the more extensive installation of traffic lights, the coming into force of the 30 m.p.h. speed limit, the inauguration of driving tests and the innovation of pedestrian crossings marked by the Belisha beacon, named after the Home Secretary of the day, Sir Leslie Hore-Belisha.

But a wider view was emerging, albeit gradually. In 1934 the Minister of Transport, then Hore-Belisha, inaugurated a comprehensive survey of highway developments required in the London traffic area for the next 30 years, and an Origin and Destination census was conducted in June 1936 at London Docks (note the then fixation in London road-traffic circles of facilitating good road communications to the Docks). A Highway Development Survey was prepared in 1937 by consultants Sir Charles Bressey (a former Chief Engineer at the Ministry of Transport) and Sir Edwin Lutyens (a leading architect of his day).

A specifically town planning approach to road transport matters was still awaited though there were indications of changing attitudes, particularly in other parts of the world, providing examples for emulation in this country. For example, the principles of segregating pedestrians from motor traffic were illustrated by S. Stein and H. Wright in their design for a new city, Radburn, 16 miles from New York. Proposed for 25,000 people, the building of the city was stopped because of the economic crisis after two 'superblock' units had been constructed, but sufficient was shown that a quite different form of residential layout was possible from that dependent on the provision of estate roads and traditional house frontage. Later the master plan proposed for London in 1939 by a Committee of the Modern Architectural Research Group (MARS), chaired by Arthur Korn showed traffic considerations as an integral part of the conceptual design. However, it is fair to conclude that town planning practice had not yet made any significant contribution in Britain to dealing with traffic question; this remained for the future.

A concluding view

Developments in planning history have a frame of reference which is social, political and institutional, rather than technical and professional. Earlier chapters have demonstrated this assessment, and the inter-war period confirms it. The town planning movement emerged out of a consideration of housing, health and social betterment; new forms of housing layout and design and planning of the wider environment were the new solutions. Town planning legislation ushered in a rudimentary form of statutory planning based on local authority scheme preparation and control over building development. That was the situation at the end of the First World War. Twenty years later that same movement, and the legislation which anchored it to statutory process, had secured a firmer foothold and had begun to flirt uncertainly with wider issues.

In 1939 British town planning was poised to expand its traditional remit. But this was as a result of no great advance in the technical skills available to the discipline, nor of any weight accorded to the profession in recognition of its claims, although the garden city lobby nationally and internationally was vociferous enough and attracted figures of influence. Rather, British town planning, both as a movement and as a profession, found that it had a relevance to wider questions to which it could respond. It had begun to claim a concern for cities as a whole: how they looked, how they functioned and how people lived in them. However, cities were not all equal; some were in decline economically, others were booming, and town planning was drawn into a view of regional and national spatial distributions of population and industry. The inter-war period, then, released a set of environmental issues different from the past; the new questions were economic, technological and political. The discipline and profession of town planning became a beneficiary of this wider frame of social concern. The perception of urban problems changed; in due time the nature of planning response changed with it, and it is in this context that explanations may be sought as to how and why the tempo and style of the public regulation of the urban environment changed so markedly at this time.

The backcloth to the period is dominated by the restructuring of the labour force during these years, and the geographic redistribution of the population. It has been summarized as follows:

> It thus mattered a great deal where one lived and to what sort of job one became initially attached. For those in growing industries and areas, regular work and wages combined with falling prices and shorter hours to produce a style of life involving considerable scope for leisure and consumption. For the many who were tied by reasons of training, sentiment or simple inertia to declining industries stagnant areas, the period between the wars was marked by bitterness and fear, hunger, ill health and desperation.
>
> (Cronin, 1984 p. 54)

In the nineteenth century the range of urban problems had been perceived as essentially local and place-specific; health, sanitation, housing fitness and environmental squalor related to often quite narrowly defined areas. They were problems which demanded technical solutions, locally applied. This is not to deny of course that there were some who saw housing inequalities and poverty unescapably linked to underlying economic and class structures, but essentially nineteenth-century public regulation of the environment was a matter for the local amelioration of a particular problem. In the twentieth century, and particularly after 1918, spatial inequalities nationally and regionally attracted more attention, and in tackling problems of town growth and redevelopment, a much wider frame of reference became obvious. Town planning was not just place-specific; it was inescapably linked with questions of distribution and equity.

The nature of the urban crisis, to which town planning was addressed, also changed in that housing solutions increasingly had to be prepared in recognition of public opinion. The issue now was seen not just in terms of provision of new housing or the simple eradication of the slums as a technical exercise; housing likes and dislikes had now to inform town planning of preferences in provision. Recognition of this new client awareness came fairly late and it served to liven the 'flats versus houses' debate at the end of the 1930s and into the 1940s. Mass-Observation's inquiry which resulted in the report *People's homes* (1941) revealed contrasting views from 12 working-class communities. Five were older working-class neighbourhoods in Birmingham, Fulham, Ilford, Portsmouth and Worcester; three were LCC estates at Becontree, Roehampton and Watling; two were blocks of flats in Fulham and Kentish Town; and Bournville and Letchworth completed the list. People living in new housing, whether estates, flats or garden cities, were more satisfied with their houses and neighbourhoods than were those living in the older areas, although there was more than a hint at the loss of street-corner sociability. The powerful drive for new homes and the rejection of the old was confirmed in Bournville Village Trust's own survey *When we build again* (1941).

This sense of the need to depart from the past was reinforced by a prevailing sense of gloom in certain intellectual quarters about the city; over time this informed the professions of architecture and town planning in particular. Lewis Mumford's *The culture of cities* (1938) confirmed a pessimistic scenario with a concept of the rise or fall of cities in six stages. The rise of the village community was a phase termed 'Eopolis', followed by

'Polis', and association of villages. 'Metropolis' was where a city merged within its region and 'Megalopolis' marked the onset of decline through the consequences of size. 'Tyrranopolis' was the period of moral decadence and a failure of governments, terminating in 'Nekropolis' where war, famine and disease racked the city. In the politically charged and uncertain years of the late thirties this imagery was very powerful.

This cultural context which affected attitudes towards the city and how it might be planned was built up from a number of sources and expressed in the literature of the day (Timms and Kelley, 1985). T.S. Eliot's *Waste land* (1922) offered a vision of urban dereliction and corruption. James Joyce's *Dubliners* (1914) portrayed another sordid city and *Ulysses* (1922) put stress on the futility and anarchy of modern city life. How different it all was from the romanticism of the Georgian poets; Rupert Brooke, W.H. Davies, Walter de la Mare, John Masefield and others made their escape to the romanticism of the English countryside. The predominant mood of rural England was replaced by the sharper view of vagrant cosmopolitans like Eliot and Ezra Pound, and of course the European expressionists who came face to face with social realism.

This quite different context allowed some observers of the city to communicate a view about the squalor of the Victorian legacy. George Orwell in *The road to Wigan pier* (1937):

> As you walk through the industrial towns you lose yourself in labyrinths of little brick houses blackened by smoke, festering in planless chaos round miry alleys and little cindered yards where there are stinking dustbins and lines of grimy washing and half ruinous w.cs. The interiors of these houses are always very much the same, though the number of rooms varies between two or five . . . At the back there is the yard, or part of a yard shared by a number of houses, just big enough for the dustbin and the w.c.
>
> (Orwell, 1937; 1962 edn. p. 45)

Another influential observer was J.B. Priestley; his *English journey* (1934), 'being a rambling but truthful account of what one man saw and heard and felt and thought during a journey through England during the Autumn of the year 1933', evoked another angry response to his urban world. In the Midlands he took a tram in Birmingham:

> There is something depressing about the way in which a tram lumbers and groans and grinds along, like a sick elephant. Undoubtedly the tram helped. But it was Birmingham itself that did most of the mischief. In two minutes, its civic dignity, its metropolitan airs, had vanished; and all it offered me, mile after mile, was a parade of mean dinginess. I do not say that this was a worse tram-ride than one would have had in Manchester, Liverpool, Glasgow, any of our larger cities, or smaller ones either for that matter; I am not making comparisons between cities now. I only know that during the half-hour or so I sat staring through the top windows of that tram, I saw nothing, not one single tiny thing, that could possibly raise a man's spirits. Possibly what I was seeing was not Birmingham but our urban and industrial civilisation. The fact remains that it was beastly. It was so many miles of ugliness, squalor, and the wrong kind of vulgarity, the decayed anaemic kind.
>
> (Priestley, 1934; 1968 edn. pp. 85–6)

These were years then of a heightened dissatisfaction with our towns and cities, and every-day lives and attitudes of the British people; the social history of the 1930s is one of bitter years (Branson and Heinemann, 1971). The poverty, unremitting daily grind of hardship, poor food, pawnbroking, unemployment and hopelessness, had all been chronicled before in the London of Henry Mayhew and Charles Booth. The squalor was still there, but with East London there were now the old industrial towns of the North. A committee chaired by the Archbishop of York studied the effects of long-term unemployment in six towns: Deptford, Leicester, Rhondda, Crook, Liverpool and Blackburn. Their report *Men without work* (1938) gave new insights into poverty, household budgets, working-class life-styles, health and a range of psychological problems. Even a popular novel of that decade had a title *Love on the dole* (Walter Greenwood, 1933). It did not take much to reason that international capitalism had failed and that a new order must replace it. Jarrow, became 'the town that was murdered' (Wilkinson, 1939); its industrial history, the recent closure of Palmer's shipyard and the march of 1936 evoked this bitter conclusion from its MP:

> This island is too small, its economic life too precariously balanced, its geo-graphical situation too vulnerable, for its fate to be left to the casual workings of chance, or the unsatiable unheeding drive of the profit-markers. Jarrow is an object lesson of what happens then . . . It is time now that the workers took control of this country of ours. It is time that they planned it, organized it, and developed it so that they all might enjoy the wealth which we can produce. In the interest of this land we love that is the next job which must be done.   (Wilkinson, 1939, p. 284)

This sense of failure was accompanied even in the prosperous areas by a disenchantment with what 20 years of new building had achieved. Betjeman captured the concern in 1938 in his poem *Slough*:

> Come friendly bombs and fall on Slough,
> It isn't fit for humans now.
> There isn't grass to graze a cow.
> Swarm over, Death.

What had appealed so much to a previous generation was no longer a cause for pride. Observers ridiculed the semi-detached house and the suburban environment with its social sterility.

Uncertainty and unfocused disillusionment can be read into the social restlessness of the later 1930s. Other countries seemed to be doing so much better. America had its New Deal, and fascist and communist dictatorships were not slow to publicize their public works–led recovery. Britain by comparison still relied on the democratic traditions of local government, as fictionally portrayed in Winifred Holtby's *South Riding* (1936). Some looked for new political initiatives, particularly from the left: a survey of the 'condition of Britain' led Cole and Cole (1937) to advocate a Popular Front, with a programme embracing both an international policy of democratic defence and economic collaboration.

For professionals the Modern Movement offered new opportunities. In the nineteenth century architects had largely been concerned with special buildings produced for civic, commercial, ecclesiastical and landowner clients. In the twentieth century the field of concern for architecture broadened to the everyday living environment; housing for example was no longer a question of designing a single house, or even a group, but a whole estate or neighbourhood. Between the wars the idea of modern architecture was a heroic adventure which could actually improve man's condition. A powerful imagery of both the physical form of the future city and the shape of the society likely to live there was built up particularly by European architects. Science and technology would be harnessed and a political dimension was introduced with the belief that the full potential of the new architecture could only be realized if established traditions were overthrown. The future city was seen as massive, comprehensively and rationally planned, using new materials (steel and concrete), new technology and new forms of energy, particularly electricity.

The accompanying revolutionary fervour for a general reconstruction of society scarcely extended to Britain, and the Modern Movement was strangely muted in this country, where the *beaux-arts* tradition remained strong. Plans for British cities were hardly affected by the radical experiments and literature of some other countries. Britain remained wedded to its Unwin-esque traditions in housing design and layout and to the statutory town planning which we have described. But in Europe particularly, town planning and architecture were in relative turmoil, invigorated with new concepts (Ostrowski, 1970). In the Soviet Union the early post-revolutionary years saw a flowering of creativity; Le Corbusier had novel ideas on the construction of cities and from 1922 onwards in presentations, conferences and publications he attracted a world-wide following; and in Germany the social housing programme of the Weimar Bauhaus, directed by Gropius, was architecturally distinctive, and in Frankfurt on Main the housing estates of Ernst May attracted great interest. In America Clarence Perry was working on the design principles of a 'neighbourhood unit', and Frank Lloyd Wright advocated the ultimate in decentralized living in 'Broadacre City'.

Town-planning ideas were in ferment from another direction too. The Congrès Internationaux d'Architecture Moderne (CIAM) had been set up in 1928. A set of principles of 'functional' town planning was established, enshrined in a document drawn up at the fourth congress held aboard a liner cruising between Marseilles and Athens: hence the Athens Charter, 1933. It formulated a programme for the rational layout of towns, preceded by analytic study. The Charter had a negligible effect on Britain: it was only published in Greek and French, with Warsaw being the first city for which a plan applying the Charter's principles was drawn up.

By comparison, the British tradition had already been established and was not yet to be moved. But intellectually, on this and a number of different fronts, town planning was on the frontiers of change. The circumstances under which the actual change was to take place were cataclysmic, and it is to these that we must now turn.

5 Britain at War: Plans for Reconstruction

We have seen that during a period of twenty years between the wars, town planning in Britain consolidated its position in local authority practice, consultant advocacy and professional solidarity, though little was achieved by way of addition to intellectual content or method. By comparison, the 1940s proved to be a remarkable decade of innovation and advance. Town planning came into its own through a set of totally new factors, when a remarkable social and political consensus flowered briefly to provide authority and legitimation. A new planning system was worked out and new research methods forged. The State took a very considerable leap forward in establishing the rudiments of central planning in land use management, resource allocation and the distribution of population and industry. In the new activity of urban reconstruction, plans were prepared to sweep away the inadequacies of the past and heal the scars of war damage.

Superficially the story might appear a simple one of challenge and response: aerial bombardment and the need to redevelop provided a situation in which Government at a time of emergency understandably took the initiative. But it was not as straightforward as that, and we need to unravel the various strands of influence and persuasion. The chapter unfolds as follows. First we consider the demands for renewal and redevelopment, as expressed at the very beginnnig of the war years. Second we turn to the war itself: the shock of destruction, the determination to rebuild and the emergence of consensus over central direction. Third: the years of plan making for British cities. Fourth: new found techniques of operation.

The call for action

Let us recap: intellectually and in terms of technical content town planning had not advanced all that much since the remarkable flowering of the early years of the century. The underlying approach was still remarkably uncritical and very much a matter of assertion and appeal to reason, the message couched in fairly bland terms and over-reliant on a concept of progress from a philistine past. Patrick Abercrombie's gentle overview, *Town and country planning*, published in 1933 (significantly, in view of the new interest taken in planning in the wartime years, with a second edition in 1943 and three further reprints by 1945), declared that:

> Town and Country planning seeks to proffer a guiding hand to the trend of natural evolution, as a result of careful study of the place itself and its external relationships. The result is to be more than a piece of skilful engineering, or satisfactory hygiene or successful economics: it should be a social organism and a work of art.   (Abercrombie, 1933, p. 27)

Historic examples showed what had been achieved in the past, but Abercrombie stressed the degradation of industrialization which the country had experienced in the nineteenth century. Enlightenment now revealed what could and should be done, planned town life offering 'Beauty, Health and Convenience' (p. 104). This was to be achieved through a theory of civic planning which controlled and guided directions of external growth. The method relied heavily on prior survey, which was supposed to reveal the directions which the plan should take, the plan being essentially of allocating land (zoning), establishing patterns of communication, ensuring open space provision and giving coherence to community grouping. It was all a matter of common sense: planning (which was the only possible way forward) or *laissez-faire* (which had failed).

All this was little more than the Ministry of Health could offer in 1935 as advice for scheme preparation, in guidance which remained in force for the remainder of the decade. Local authorities should begin with a general review of the area concerned before work on the scheme proceeded, when the essential elements would be established: use zoning, roads, reservations and preservation of trees and protection of woodlands. Significantly (in comparison with the advice for wartime Britain, and the new planning problem that was then urgently confronted) suggestions for the planning of developed areas were cautious in the extreme and hedged about by restrictions due to liability to compensation. For the 'planning of developed areas' (redevelopment) for example, we read:

> A new necessary rearrangement of buildings may involve expenditure – not necessarily either immediate or unprofitable – but in many developed areas the advantages of planning control can be secured without substantial initial expenditure or immediate interference with their existing state. It may be sufficient to ensure that on redevelopment general characteristics shall be maintained and that any necessary changes shall be carried out in an orderly and balanced manner.   (Ministry of Health, 1935, p. 20)

This was hardly encouraging to any local authority, nor suggestive of a planning system which could deliver much. Town planning, it seemed to say, was an eminently sensible activity, governed by technical considerations, but its achievements would be limited. In truth, for the most part, town planning at the outbreak of the Second World War had become little more than a token regulatory hand, useful in developing areas, but of little consequence in the existing areas. Much still rested on the provisions of local Acts for improvement schemes.

The Barlow Report of 1940 (Cmd. 6153) brought the arguments for a more positive planning approach to a new head. The *Third report of the commissioner for special areas (England and Wales)* had provided the opportunity; Barlow now took it. The Royal Commission on the Distribution of the Industrial Population was set up in 1937; the terms of reference were:

> to enquire into the causes which have influenced the present geographical distribution of the industrial population of Great Britain and the probable direction of any change in that distribution in the future; to consider what social, economic or strategical disadvantages arise from the concentration of industries or of the industrial population in large towns or in particular areas of the country; and to report what remedial measures if any should be taken in the national interest.

The long years of economic depression and high unemployment rates, the sharp divide between favoured and unfavoured regions, and the drift of population from 'north' to 'south' combined to supply the political pressure for enquiry.

The industrialist Sir Montague Barlow was appointed Chairman of the Commission, whose members included Professor Abercrombie, then the most influential academic planner in the country. The evidence taken by the Commission sustained a generally decentralist line for the further development of big cities, powerful advocacy coming from Frank Pick of the London Passenger Transport Board and Frederic Osborn of the Garden Cities and Town Planning Association. The need for planned dispersal, the reduction of overcrowding and congestion, and by implication the redevelopment of the central parts of cities was strongly expressed. The contrast between these recommendations and the then enfeebled state of planning practice was striking.

The consequences of unrestricted outward growth of cities were stark to the observers of the late 1930s. Barlow summarized:

> The larger the town grows, the greater – in the absence of special provison – becomes the traffic converging upon the central areas, and the higher the land values in the central area tend to become. Traffic congestion grows more acute, and the remedying of defects – such as inadequate roads and lack of open spaces – arising from the unplanned character of the centre becomes increasingly difficult by reason of the rising land values. At the same time the countryside recedes further and further from the inhabitants of the centre, and access to it which is most desirable – indeed some would say indispensable – in the interests of health and general well-being becomes more and more difficult.   (Royal Commission 1940, para. 139)

This general statement of disadvantage was reinforced by more specific observations on both social and economic disadvantage. For example, Barlow observed that the inhabitants of large towns and areas of industrial concentration

> suffer certain disadvantages due to bad housing, lack of space for recreation, difficulties of transport, congestion, smoke and noise. These disadvantages, which are often accentuated in the case of large towns by unsatisfactory economic conditions, are the result of the haphazard manner in which urban development has proceeded in the past, and which has been marked by:

(a) densely built inner areas of badly constructed and unplanned housing;

(b) an increasing density of industrial and commercial development and consequential transfer of land from housing to industry and commerce in the cores of the towns.

The disadvantage of concentration could be remedied or greatly reduced by good planning.   (para. 172)

Furthermore, there were significant economic disadvantages:

(a) heavy charges on account mainly of high site values, (b) loss of time through street traffic congestion in the very large towns, which can hardly fail to offset to some extent the advantage of lower transport costs, (c) the risk of adverse effects on efficiency and output on account of the fatigue incurred by work-people through having to make long daily journeys between home and workplace, often under conditions of considerable discomfort

(para. 202)

In addition, there was the new problem of danger from air attack, and on strategic grounds there was good reason to advocate policies of decentralization and dispersal.

Barlow succeeded in establishing the case for radical, remedial measures to deal with the problems of London and the big cities. The standard of health in the large towns still lagged behind the country as a whole, in spite of substantial improvements from the last quarter of the nineteenth century onwards; but this disadvantage need not be, Barlow argued, given good planning. Likewise it was possible to overcome the adverse features of slums and overcrowding, lack of open space, and the smoke, dirt, fog and noise of big cities. Transport congestion and long journeys to work could also be overcome. It was all possible (and the problems of the regions could be addressed too) with spatial planning, summed up in two principal objectives: continued and further redevelopment of congested urban areas, where necessary; and decentralization or dispersal, both of industries and industrial population, from such areas.

The package, submitted in 1939, but published in 1940, was well argued, coherent and compelling. The argument for the adoption of national spatial policies was persuasive, the latest of a long line of advocacy for a programme of urban rebuilding which would consciously reconstruct older areas to different patterns. The importance of Barlow was that the attitudinal preconditions for urban renewal were established as never before; a tide of opinion had been caught. The report demonstrated that Britain's cities could and should be improved from the point of view of economic, social and environmental conditions.

Supportive evidence had been plentiful and even now fresh arguments were forthcoming. One source was a body working at the time of the publication of Barlow, in association with the National Council of Social Science: the Hygiene Committee of the Women's Group on Public Welfare which met between 1939 and 1942. Margaret Bondfield, a future Minister of Education, expressed the hope in a preface that its Report, *Our towns: a close-up* (1943), would be 'the last of its kind'. It represented an attempt of a small group of working professional women to make a nationwide survey of the conditions of town life in England which might be held responsible for particular characteristics of wartime evacuees. It highlighted all the issues of the unhealthiness of industrial towns, of poverty, bad housing and squalid environments. Its conclusions repeated a long-standing cry:

> There is need for a far more equal distribution of the amenities – all town children need public parks and gardens, not only for play, but to ensure for the human spirit its right to feed upon the beauty of the trees and grass, flowers, water, clouds and the miracle of the changing year. There should be beauty in the design of even the humble dwellings and measures to ensure that their seemliness is respected.
>
> (Hygiene Committee of the Women's Group on Public Welfare, 1943, p. 110)

Social vision and a collective determination was added to the rational argument of Barlow. In the context of war the fusion was to be explosive. A past system had failed; a new approach must succeed. The failings of the international economic order, the power of the private sector and the strength of individual interests had prevailed too long; corporate interests represented by government and the community sector would replace them.

The vision and the hope of new ways of doing things were there, but they were grounded in little reality as to actual implementation. The fact was that the activity of town planning had little specific to say about urban reconstruction. Certainly there were the broad guidelines of dispersal and decentralization. But on what principles was the redevelopment of the old, the obsolete and the outworn to proceed? What kind of central cities were envisaged?

There were merely glimpses here and there. The Swiss-born architect Charles Edouard Jeanneret, the adopted Frenchman Le Corbusier, proclaimed his new architectural style of tall buildings, but it did not readily strike an echo in Britain. The Modern Architectural Research Group (MARS) of London architects put forward a scheme in 1938 for the total renewal of London on radical lines, but it was a futurist fantasy. Occasionally British cities hinted at new urban forms: in Leeds, the Headrow was a new traffic artery in the central city, and in Birmingham a combination of inner city slum clearance and a long-proposed inner ring road promised much change, while in Coventry a young city architect, Gibson, saw the possibilities of a new central area. But no coherent approach to the design of the new cities had yet been worked out, even if the problem of compensation, which made the task of land assembly by any local authority almost impossible, could be overcome.

In short, therefore, by 1939 pressure had built up for certain strategic solutions to the problems of London and the big cities. These solutions implied considerable redevelopment in the central, older parts, but it remained unclear as to just what form of renewal was to be adopted either in land use or visual terms. Town planning as an art form may have taken considerable strides in suburban or garden city situations, but there had been no practical progression to the redevelopment of commercial areas; there was only a handful of local authorities which seemed capable of making design and environmental advances in planning practice. There was an enormous gap between the possibilities of radical architecture and the strategic thinking of a few academic planners on the one hand, and the practical capabilities of planning staffs at local government level, on the other. But the situation was soon to change.

The war

The onset of hostilities, in particular the incidence of aerial attack on British cities, changed matters very considerably. The aerial 'Battle of Britain' having been won by RAF Fighter Command in August–September 1940, the German *Luftwaffe* switched its attention to the bombing of London and industrial towns. Between September 1940 and May 1941, 141 major air raids were made on 21 cities. Night attacks continued in 1942 and day attacks started in 1943. Altogether there were 85 major raids on London, and eight each on Liverpool/Birkenhead, Birmingham, and Plymouth/Devonport. The scale of physical destruction was such that of 98,000 dwellings administered by the London County Council in 1939, just 9,250 escaped unscathed. The vast majority of course needed only minor repair, but 25,113 were seriously damaged or rendered uninhabitable and 2,487 were totally destroyed (Bullock, 1987, p. 73). In England and Wales the number of dwellings destroyed or made permanently uninhabitable totalled 475,00.

The bombing was concentrated both in terms of space and time; a small number of East End London boroughs bore the brunt of the damage, typically Stepney and Bermondsey, during the first few weeks of the Blitz in late 1940. From June 1944 the flying bomb attacks were less concentrated spatially, but even more destructive. Commercial and manufacturing premises were also widely damaged, and swathes of war-damaged land were for years eloquent testimony to both the urgency of the problem, and of course the potential scope for imaginative solutions. Moreover, the problem was not confined to one city (London), it was an issue for the whole country: Belfast, Clydeside, Merseyside and a range of industrial and port areas, and city centres as at Sheffield, Coventry, Plymouth, Hull, Bristol and certain cathedral cities.

War damage gave the opportunity to rebuild, and a new social psychology in wartime Britain provided the determination. There was an overwhelming drive to win the war: Britain was not the aggressor and the country could think of itself once more as a nation with a mission. Britain stood for political ideals that must prevail if western civilization were not to break down; Britain could carry the torch of freedom, truth, toleration and peace. The enemy stood for different things and must be defeated.

But if Britain spoke with a moral voice, it had to put its own house in order. Moral and spiritual renewal went hand in hand with economic and social renewal, and past practices and systems, with which the traumas and the injustices of the inter-war years had been associated, had to be overturned. It was increasingly argued that the international capitalist order had had its day and that post-war recovery would be achieved rather differently, through much greater State involvement. Planning was winning the war, it would win the peace. Moreover, greater centralization in national affairs and a greater exercise of State powers would not be accompanied by any loss of democratic freedoms. Remarkbly, in a short time, war-torn Britain had compulsory direction of labour, it re-established its crippled industries, depressed agriculture was revived, population was relocated (1 million schoolchildren were evacuated) and industry steered. It was all possible, though it took a war to make it so.

The literature of the time provides ample evidence of a dramatic shift in public attitudes. The popular press, even a special issue of *Picture Post* ('A plan for Britain', 4 January, 1941), the activity of pressure groups and the findings of special conferences: all echoed a determination to rebuild, reconstruct and renew. One of the popular books at the very outbreak of war captured the mood, *Mrs Miniver* (1939); an American best seller and subsequently a most successful film, it is said that it hastened America's entry into the war. In a romantic, rather cloying story of an English family, the authoress Jan Struther (Joyce Anstruther) showed how things had changed:

> I can think of a hundred ways already in which the war has 'brought us to our senses'. But it oughtn't to *need* a war to make a nation paint its kerbstones white, carry rear-lamps on its bicycles, and give all its children a holiday in the country. And it oughtn't to need a war to make us talk to each other on buses, and invent our own amusements in the evenings, and live simply, and eat sparingly, and recover the use of our legs, and get up early enough to see the sun rise. However, it *has* needed one : which is about the severest criti-cism our civilisation could have.   (Struther, 1939, 1980 edn, p. 286)

A new community feeling was being expressed and those keen to work for the development of State initiatives were quick to feed on it (Marwick, 1968). For example, demands for a national enquiry into schemes of social insurance and allied services led to the appointment of an inter-departmental committee of civil servants under William Beveridge; their subsequent report in December 1942 had a major impact; 'freedom from want' finally seemed to be a real possibility.

Political change helped to articulate the drive for reform. Intellectual fascination with communism had been a feature of the 1930s (naturally enough given the gloom and despair of that period) and Communist Party membership surged during the war in response to admiration for the Russian military effort. But in Britain Marxism still had no more than minimal adherence and we must look rather to the re-emergence of the Labour Party from a decade in the shadows, when it was riven by international faction and uncertainty over international pacifism and rearmament. Conservatism went into relative eclipse, while Labour under Clement Attlee was able to wield influence in the coalition government.

After 1942 programmes for economic and social reform after the war began to take shape; they had popular appeal and Labour was identified with them rather more than the Conservatives, whose ministers sometimes appeared reluctant converts. Between 1943 and 1945 four Conservatives loyal to the Government were defeated at by-elections by Commonwealth or Independent Socialist candidates, and there was a general tendency for the Conservative share of the vote to fall (Addison, 1977). A major leftward swing in British politics was taking place. The coalition government broke up and in May 1945 Churchill resigned as leader, to be reappointed as head of a 'caretaker' government of Conservatives, National Liberals and non-party functionaries. Parliament was dissolved in June and polling took place in July. Labour won a massive victory being returned with 393 seats to the Conservatives' 213 and the Liberals' 12. Attlee's party had markedly broadened its class appeal and won handsomely in 'white collar' constituencies in the London suburbs, also in the West Midlands and East Anglia. Trades Union leaders and the Labour Party successfully projected an image of moderate, social patriots, committed to reform on a broad front. A new political consensus had emerged, with the promise of a social revolution.

Political change nationally was to make certain things possible, and town planning found itself elevated to a new position of responsiblilty with regard to city reconstruction. But much had to be done before any real progress could be made, and essentially this lay in the problem of land acquisition and assembly. The fact was that the central parts of cities had confused land-use patterns and other features which rendered necessary some new, speedy coordinating hand to control the renewal process. The problem pointed to local government as the most likely actor.

The City Engineer of Birmingham, H.J. Manzoni, speaking at the 1941 Conference of the Town and Country Planning Association (under its new name, the 'Garden City' appellation having been discarded) described the problems of large-scale redevelopment under existing legislation. In an area of 300 acres he catalogued:

> Nearly 11 miles of existing streets, mostly narrow and badly planned. 6,800 individual dwellings, the density varying locally up to 80 to the acre. 5,400 of these dwellings classified as slums to be condemned. 15 major industrial premises or factories, several of them comparatively recent in date. 105 minor factories, storage buildings, workshops, industrial yards, laundries, etc. 778 shops, many of them hucksters' premises. 7 schools. 18 churches and chapels. 51 licensed premises. Many miles of public service mains, water, gas, and electricity including over a mile of 42-inch trunk water main, nearly all laid under carriageways and consequently in the wrong place for good planning. Add to these a railway viaduct, a canal, a railway goods yard and a gas works, and you have a beautiful problem in redevelopment.
>
> (Manzoni, 1941, p. 98)

This was a sober assessment, and resolution of the 'beautiful' problem was far from easy. It was of course a political problem because it concerned property, land and land values; its resolution was equally a political matter and has proved on more than one occasion to be a fundamental point of divide between Conservative and Labour attitudes. Inexorably the State was involved in this aspect of environmental planning.

As early as February 1941 the Minister of Works and Buildings (Lord Reith) was being advised that post-war reconstruction would proceed on the basis of some central planning authority (Cullingworth, 1975). An Expert Committee on Compensation and Betterment had been set up in January under the chairmanship of Mr Justice Uthwatt with terms of reference 'to make an objective analysis of the subject of the payment of compensation and recovery of betterment in respect of public control of the use of land'. In April of the same year it was clear from the interim report of the committee that recommendations would be proposed whereby building development would be controlled throughout the country and that compensation for the public acquisition of land would be set at the standard of 31 March 1939. It was already being alleged that speculation in bombed cities was going on. Events moved quickly, though as Cullingworth's history reveals, not without great uncertainty and confusion in Whitehall. The final report was published in September 1942 (Cmd. 6386).

Meanwhile, in February 1942 town planning powers (except in Scotland) were transferred to the Ministry of Works and Buildings, whose title was changed to the Ministry of Works and Planning. In January 1943 the Ministry of Town and Country Planning Bill was introduced, providing for the appointment of a Minister whose 'sole ministerial responsibility is in connection with town and country planning'; the Bill was passed in February and W.S. Morrison was appointed first Minister. But any notion of a central planning authority, with if not exactly omnipotent powers over other government departments, soon foundered.

In July 1943 the Town and Country Planning (Interim Development) Bill received the Royal Assent, legislation which effectively extended planning control to the whole of the country not so far covered by a planning scheme, nor by a Resolution to prepare one. It was now possible to take immediate enforcement action against development prejudicial to a longer-term future; uncontrolled rebuilding would have been very unsatisfactory. Almost at a stroke Government had moved town planning into a higher gear, with a national system of development control, ubiquitous in operation.

During 1943 and 1944 Government wrestled with the recommendations of the Uthwatt Report; a Town and Country Planning Bill would centre on the level of compensation to be paid for land and property acquired by local authorities, and the procedures to be followed. The political battle lines were drawn (Cherry, 1982). In November 1944 the Town and Country Planning Bill passed through all its stages, but the political objections to the compensation provisions caused great difficulty to the end. Local authorities were now permitted to buy land, simply and expeditiously for certain planning purposes, notably in areas of extensive war damage, and areas of bad layout and obsolete development. Quickly dubbed the 'blitz and blight Act', it was the resolution to Manzoni's 'beautiful problem'. These new sweeping powers opened the door to planned redevelopment on an extensive scale, an important forerunner to the Town and Country Planning Act, 1947, which effectively set up the post-war statutory planning system.

During the war when so much was happening in terms of national legislation, the extension of planning powers and the marked widening of Government involvement in affairs of land and development, there was a growing acknowledgement in professional and related circles as to the new place of town planning in national affairs and its potential for post-war recovery. An influential research study from the Bournville Village

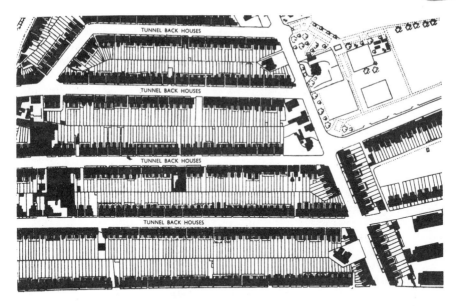

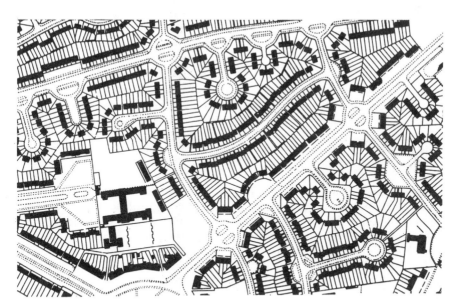

5.1 Birmingham: Middle Ring and Municipal Estate

Trust in Birmingham, *When we build again* (1941), proclaimed the message that it was vital to ensure that the redevelopment of cities should not perpetuate the faults of the old cities. Town planning was more than ever seen as a standard bearer for recovery, and the determination to rebuild pervaded the planning literature of the day. For the lay reader, Geoffrey

Boumphrey's *Town and country tomorrow* (1940) had three sections: 'Things as they are', 'Things as they could be' and 'Things as they should be', and the contrasts were made to speak for themselves. It was argued that Britain stood at a historic point; a new urban future was at hand. The confidence was breathtaking:

> In the frank use of new materials, new processes, and new methods of planning there was the near possibility of greater improvement in living conditions for all classes than have been brought by the last two thousand years. We can only realise these by setting to work with the boldness and single-minded purpose of the old master-builders.   (Boumphrey, 1940, p. 72)

Beauty, convenience and comfort lay in the promise of new ways of doing things in rationally planned large towns, where the public would now be protected 'from the results of selfish or short-sighted exploitation' (Boumphrey, 1940, p. 152).

Another commentary on the future, published in the same year came from a professional, Thomas Sharp (1940). His highly successful *Town planning* which in the Pelican Books series cost 6d. and sold a quarter of a million copies, was a technician's plea for the quality of urban townscape as a worthy setting for community. The subtlety of his disagreement with the garden city lobby may have been lost on many, but the message in his final chapter was clear and unequivocal: 'Plan we must'.

> It is no overstatement to say that the simple choice between planning and non-planning, between order and disorder, is a test-choice for English democracy. In the long run even the worst democratic muddle is preferable to a dictator's dream bought at the price of liberty and decency. But the English muddle is nevertheless a matter for shame. We shall never get rid of its shamefulness unless we plan our activities. And plan we must – not for the sake of our physical environment only, but to save and fulfil democracy itself.   (Sharp, 1940, p. 143)

The language belonged to a forthright, dogmatic man, but it captured the spirit of the time: confidence, determination, a radical zeal for rebuilding.

Another view of the need to rebuild British cities came from an old school: the garden city movement. The onset of war and the urban destruction that followed breathed new spirit into a flagging crusade. Suddenly the urgency of new building was on the national agenda and the question was double-edged: what sort of dwellings, and where would they be built? The satellite solution in the hands of the British garden city tradition had the answer to both. It was significant then that F.J. Osborn's *New towns after the war*, first published in 1918, was revised and reissued in 1942 with little amendment. Again, change was in the air; the chance had to be seized; it was now or never.

> We are not any of us so satisfied with our old cities that we want to rebuild them just as they were. Loosen out congestion, to substitute gracious and healthy surroundings for dark, drab, and debasing streets, tenements and

slums, to give better working conditions for industry and greater security for agriculture, to think of the requirements of our people as individuals, as families, as workers, as citizens, and to shape our cities and protect our countryside in the best interests of all.   (Osborn, 1918; 1942 edn, p. 13)

The challenge to sweep away the old was unmistakable.

These three publications, and their extracts, have been chosen deliberately to give a flavour of the planning viewpoint of the time, from very different perspectives. As a conscious exercise in boosting public morale at a difficult time there was a real danger of over-indulgence in wishful thinking; it would be a cruel delusion to anticipate too many rabbits out of

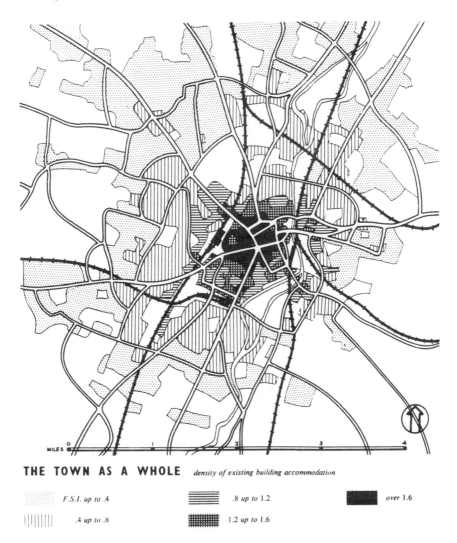

THE TOWN AS A WHOLE   *density of existing building accommodation*

F.S.I. up to .4   .8 up to 1.2   over 1.6

.4 up to .8   1.2 up to 1.6

5.2(a)   Town centre building accommodation – existing

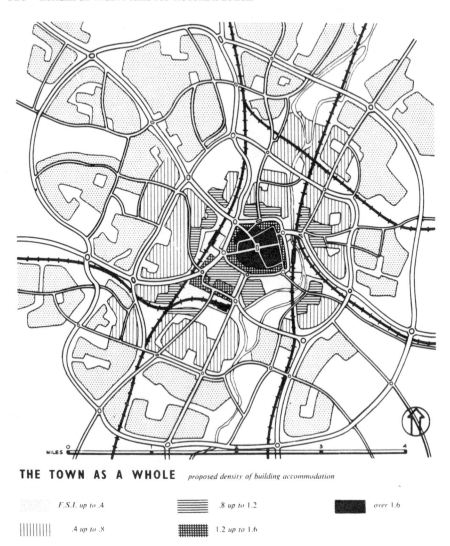

THE TOWN AS A WHOLE   *proposed density of building accommodation*

F.S.I. up to .4		.8 up to 1.2	over 1.6
.4 up to .8		1.2 up to 1.6	

5.2(b)   Town centre building accommodation – proposed

the hat, only to be fobbed off by the patter of the conjurer. But even the most hardened, seasoned observers, aligned with no particular planning faction and having seen it all before as civil servants, could demonstrate sober conviction as to the power, promise and reasonableness of planning as a State activity. Sir Gwilym Gibbon (1942), a former Permanent Secretary, in *Reconstruction and town and country planning* had no doubts as to the efficacy of good planning and the need to follow important principles in the redevelopment that was to come.

By the end of the war the British public seemed ready to accept the

notion of planning as a State activity, and warmed to the particular promise of town planning, with its profession harnessed to the requirements of
government. It recognized the need to rebuild the nation's cities and to
sweep away the old, guided by principles of economic, social and spiritual
renewal, though there was no commitment yet to any one particular model
of urban design and it was ignorant, so far, as to just how it would all be
done and with what consequences. But in any event the hand of the State in
the exercise of rebuilding had become uncontestable. Towards the end of
the war the expectations of reform reached new peaks; the increasing
prospect of peace focused the mind.

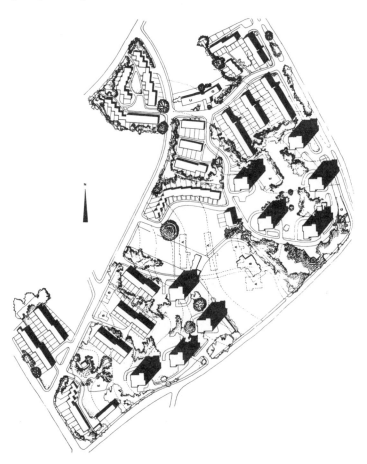

5.3 Layout plan, Alton, London

The most strident voice was that of the decentrists in the garden city/
new town tradition. One has only to read the correspondence of F.J.
Osborn with Lewis Mumford over these years (Hughes, 1971) to appreciate
the single-minded zeal that could be generated for the attainment of the

new Jerusalem. One example of this was a remarkable collection of essays, compiled by Elizabeth and Gilbert Glenn McAlister (1945). 'Positive planning' would open up a dream future:

> We shall be able to open up London, Manchester, Liverpool, Newcastle, Sheffield, Glasgow and the other great cities so as to permit rehousing of reasonable densities. We shall be able to provide houses with gardens for at least 80 per cent of the population and enough flats to satisfy the demand for flats. We shall be able to provide open space for the inhabitants so that all citizens will be within reasonable distance of parks, playing fields, tennis courts and the other amenities necessary for healthy, open-air recreation. We shall be able to give dignified settings to the more important public buildings, while the everyday streets of houses and shops will have a beauty hitherto reserved for the luxury developments characteristic of less democratic periods.   (McAllister, 1945, p. xxvii)

The nation was to be planned, as the McAllisters' distinguished contributions proceeded to demonstrate: towns, agriculture, land use, industry, transport, fuel, homes, the arts and planners themselves. As the Archbishop of York observed: 'they have shown that it [planning] should embrace the whole country, and that without it we cannot make the best use of the limited space in our small island' (p. 160).

An old campaigner maintained his position too. E.D. Simon, Chairman of Manchester Housing Committee (1919–23) and Parliamentary Secretary of the Ministry of Health (1931) was confident of being able to rebuild Britain within 20 years: 'If we can tackle the problems of peace with anything like the same sense of purpose, the same devotion, and the same efficiency as we have shown during the war, the Rebuilding of Britain will be child's play' (Simon, 1945, p. 228).

It seemed self-evident that in the welter of these breathtaking claims, the case for planning no longer needed to be argued. Nobody had criticized the Government for 'planning' the Normandy invasions, as Simon tersely argued, so it was perfectly reasonable for the Government to continue to plan after the war. Furthermore, the political economists had a relatively easy time pointing to the failings of the economic system of earlier years in terms of disorganization and inefficiency and the imperfections of the free market (Cole, 1945).

The contrary arguments were there, and indeed cogently argued, but were almost silenced by the clamour for State socialism. Friedrich Hayek, an Austrian economist living in England, issued a seminal warning: full employment, social security and freedom from want could not be had unless they came as by-products of a system that released the free energies of individuals; furthermore planning created not certainty, but uncertainty. *The Road to serfdom* (1944) carried a standard that was unfurled again a generation later. In the meantime the anti-planners were relatively few, though titles like *Ordeal by planning* (Jewkes, 1948), a furious onslaught on the experiences of the recent past, fuelled the deep-seated convictions of the political Right.

Plan making

We must now turn to see how these ideas were translated into practice via
the great wartime plans. Some of these proved to be classics in their own
right and became accepted as models for others to follow. Two names stood
out : Patrick Abercrombie and William Holford, and their work in respect
of London deserves close examination.

A plan for London was long overdue. Throughout the inter-war period
there had been no effective plan, merely Unwin's work and sporadic activity in the preparation of statutory planning schemes by the London boroughs. In 1941 Lord Reith, as Minister of Works and Buildings, asked the
LCC for a reconstruction plan for the County of London; this was undertaken by the LCC architect, J.H. Forshaw, in conjunction with Patrick
Abercrombie, then professor of Town Planning at University College,
London. Their *County of London Plan* was published in 1943. The authors
identified three options before them: first, 'planning', starting again with
no preconditions; second, total dispersal; and third, 'conditioned yet comprehensive planning' – retaining the old structure and making it work
under modern conditions. Forshaw and Abercrombie opted for the third.
The garden city lobby alleged that the vested interests of London had
worked against a decentralist approach, for which it had been striving for
many years, and F.J. Osborn acknowledged in correspondence with Lewis
Mumford that the Plan was a bitter disappointment to him and the Town
and Country Planning Association (TCPA):

> the work was done, not in Abercrombie's private office, but in the LCC office,
> with the maximum daily influence of the old point of view and at very close
> quarters with the housing and planning schemes already on the table and in
> the files in 1939. Though I was, having expected one of the great historic
> documents of planning, bitterly disappointed with the Plan when I first stud-
> ied it, I now think that in the circumstances Abercrombie did as well as any
> man, of the type who can survive in planning practice, could have done. But it
> was quite impossible for the TCPA or me to bless the Plan unreservedly. We
> applauded its general boldness and frame-work, and in very plain terms
> objected to its housing standards and to its 'back pedalling' on industrial and
> business decentralisation.   (Hughes, 1971, p. 45)

The *County of London Plan* was not radical but it was honest, pragmatic
and logical enough. Its major weakness was not of its own making; rather it
lay in the narrow geographical confines to which it was addressed: the
Administrative County of London, whereas territorially what was in fact
London spread far wider than that. Forshaw and Abercrombie focused on
four major problems: traffic congestion, poor housing, inadequacy and
maldistribution of open spaces, and land use intermixture – what they
termed 'indeterminate zoning'. Almost as a throw-away they added a fifth,
the outward sprawl characteristic of outer London. For solutions they
thought that London could be considered from three points of view: as a
community – where people live, work and play; as a metropolis – the seat
of Government and a great cultural and commercial centre; and as a
machine – of locomotion.

A number of detailed policies were proposed. With regard to reconstruction and decentralization of congested areas, the Plan contemplated the conservation or creation of communities which would be divided into smaller neighbourhoods of between 6,000 and 10,000 persons, related to the elementary school and the area it served. In this way the social and functional structure for London became a constellation of residential areas in map form appearing as eggs in a basket, against a backcloth of open space.

For the centre of the metropolis the aim was to define the function of the various component parts and, while making them more efficient and dignified, to free them from damaging intrusion. The answer lay in a 'fast motor ring road', to which the principal radial roads of London would connect; within the ring, 'tunnel-cross-roads' would be essential. It was acknowledged that within the heart of London there were areas which required remodelling and these would offer opportunities 'for a fine architectural treatment'. One of these was Piccadilly Circus, the authors observing that: 'here the architectural setting becomes a major consideration, although this must not preclude a satisfactory traffic solution' (para. 32) – an almost prophetic comment, bearing in mind the events relating to Piccadilly in the 1960s (see p. 168). Two areas in particular required renewal, it was thought, namely the West End and the south bank of the river.

The concept of London and the machine revolved round two problems: journeying to work and the obsession with the notion of through traffic from West London via the centre to the docks. The plan therefore built on the proposals put forward in 1937 by Sir Charles Bressey and Sir Edwin Lutyens for London's traffic, and proposed to add to the two already partly-built outer ring roads (the North and South Orbital and the North and South Circular) with two corresponding inner rings – 'the fast traffic ring-road and (innermost of all) the sub-arterial station ring'.

So much for the County of London. A plan for Greater London was also commissioned, this time carried out by a small team led by Abercrombie. The territorial spread and regional significance, up to 30 miles or so beyond the LCC boundary, now provided the occasion for a planning study of seminal importance, updating that by Unwin of ten years past. Beyond the compact unity of the City of London and the LCC (and its constituent metropolitan boroughs) there lay a multiplicity of administrative units, extending over almost 2,600 square miles divided amongst no less than 143 local authorities, nearly every one of which had a planning scheme prepared or in course of preparation, independently of its neighbours. Additionally there was a vast number of statutory authorities ranging from the Port of London Authority to the Thames Conservancy, Drainage and Hospital Boards, Gas, Electric Supply, Railway and Canal Companies. The challenge for coordinated planning could not have been greater.

The Greater London Regional Planning Committee, set up in 1927, and which Raymond Unwin had served, came to an end in 1931; it was replaced in 1937 by a Standing Conference on London Regional Planning. In 1942 Lord Reith asked the Standing Conference if they would agree to his appointing an expert to prepare an Outline Plan and Report for Greater

London. Abercrombie was appointed to work in collaboration with the Technical Committee. So while the *County of London Plan* was still in preparation, Abercrombie was at work on his wider remit. The *Greater London Plan 1944* was actually published in 1945. It was a very different report indeed.

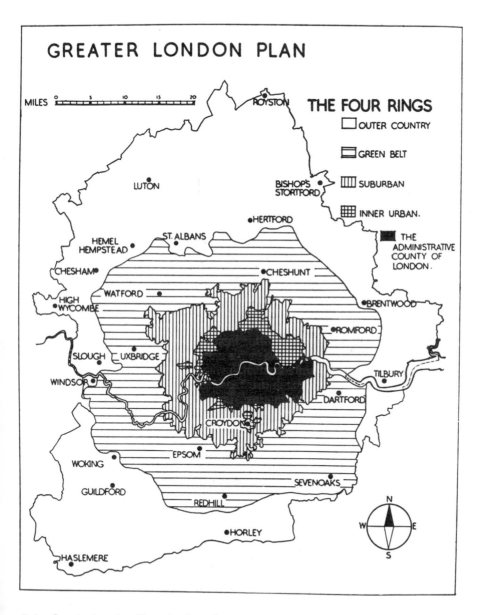

5.4 Greater London Plan: the four rings

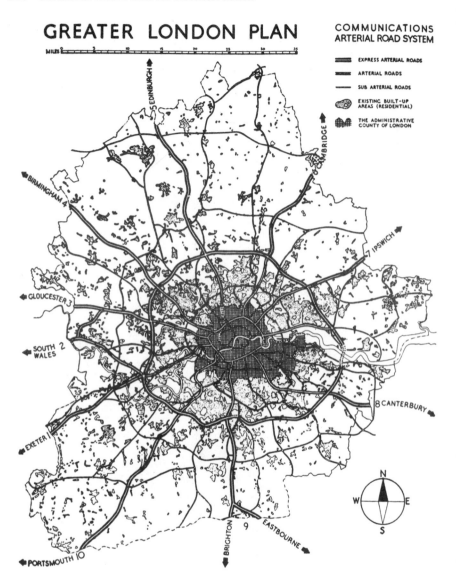

5.5 Greater London Plan: road proposals

All plans are based on assumptions and Abercrombie disarmingly revealed five. The first followed the Barlow Report in assuming that 'no new industry shall be admitted to London and the Home Counties except in special cases'. The second concerned the scale of decentralization of people and industry from a congested centre. A recommended density of 136 persons per acre (up to 200 in parts) would involve the decentralization of 618,000 people, to which would be added a further 415,000 people for decanting from overcrowded places outside the LCC, giving a total of 1,033,000 in all. This figure would increase to 1,232,750 should a density of 100 persons per acre be adopted for the central area. Either way, it was a figure of about 1.25 million that was implied, for a further 214,000 was added in order to allow for a measure of free choice. The third assumption was that the population of the whole area would not increase, but would be somewhat reduced. Fourth, the Port of London would continue to be one of the world's great ports. Lastly, it was assumed that new powers for planning would become available, including powers for the control of land values.

The plan fell into place. Functionally it was an interlocking web of economic and social purpose of great imagination: a masterly bringing together of a number of town planning themes. The overall design for Greater London took shape in the form of concentric rings according to population numbers and density, industrial location and use of open land for agriculture and recreation. The inner ring comprised the older areas built up to around the turn of the century, which because of their high density and lack of open space required 'decentralizing', involving 415,000 persons. The second ring was in effect suburban London, representing the ribboning, scatter and sporadic development of the inter-war years. By no means an exact circle, it had an approximate radius of 12 miles from Charing Cross, though with a few wedges penetrating into inner London, most notably at Totteridge and Mill Hill. Aiming at densities of 50 persons per acre, the area would receive no additional population.

The third ring included most of the land already acquired for green belt purposes under the 1938 Act, but it would also include other open land, not necessarily in public ownership but permanently safeguarded against building. Within this green zone, which included old towns like Watford and Reigate and new communities such as Hornchurch and Upminster in the east and Banstead and Orpington in the south, there would be no further urban expansion except for very special cases.

The outer country ring would be the chief reception area for overcrowded London. A more generous expansion of exisiting centres would be permitted and the zone would provide the sites for eight new satellites (ten sites being suggested), while the general character of a prevailing agricultural use would be secured. Overall, the figures of population movement are summarized as in Table 5.1

Ten years earlier Unwin had faced the alternative to London's outward spread: either a continuous zone of free entry at varying degrees of density, its continuity broken by areas of public open space; or a continuous green background as the setting for occasional development. Abercrombie followed Unwin in advocating the second alternative for the two outer rings, and in fact his plan put great store on both the scenic aspect of regional open space and the detailed design which would knit the whole together into a continuous system by footpaths, riverside walks and bridleways. Overall it offered a strategic solution to many of London's problems – though, as it was realized later, only if the world would stand

Table 5.1

(a) *Decentralization In and Near the Region*		
	Persons	Persons
(i) Addition to existing towns largely in the outer county ring	261,000	
(ii) New sites (eight new satellites)	383,250	
(iii) Quasi-satellites (immediate post-war housing programmes of LCC and Croydon)	125,000	
		769,250
(b) *Dispersal Outside the Region*		
	Persons	Persons
(iv) Additions to towns mostly between 40 and 50 miles from the centre of London	163,750	
(v) Beyond the metropolitan influence	100,000	
		263,750
Total number of regrouped population		
		1,033,000

still long enough for desirable change to be effected without being over-taken by other events. Schematically the concentric form for Greater London was compelling: clear, easy to understand, and appealing in its simplicity. This time Osborn was much more generous in his comments to Mumford: 'a far better statement of the problem than the LCC Plan . . . It is so great an advance on any other big regional plan that one must be enthusiastic about its general pattern' (Hughes, 1971, pp. 71–2).

With regard now to transport, Abercrombie built on the work contained in the *County of London Plan*. He took the ten radials, previously selected, and projected a system of 'express arterial roads', including a new outer ring (the D ring), placed on the inner edge of the green belt. In other words a dart board, or spider's web design was superimposed on his concentric rings: ten radials and two rings, the inner (B ring) within the LCC boundary, the outer (D ring) just outside the built-up area. There were of course three other rings: the North and South Orbital (E), the North and South Circular (C) and the A ring, which connected the terminal railway stations. Thirty years later London's traffic planners were to be haunted by the ghosts of these proposals.

Just as in the *County of London Plan*, the *Greater London Plan (GLP)* included some detailed design examples of redeveloped areas and new communities. Essentially, however, both plans were land use and trans-port strategies, the *GLP* particularly magisterial in its approach. It seemed to represent the last word as a model for other cities to follow. For Glas-gow, for example, the parallels were obvious. Abercrombie and Matthew's *Clyde Valley Regional Plan 1946* followed the principle of decentralization from redevelopment areas, thus meeting the long-standing problem of overcrowding, congestion and unfitness of dwellings (Wannop, 1986). The Clyde Valley Regional Planning Committee had been constituted in 1943, and Abercrombie was appointed Principal Consultant; Robert Matthew was his deputy. Population dispersal followed the Greater London model: town expansion and the building of three new towns (East Kilbride, Cumbernauld and Bishopton), and the possibility of a fourth at Houston, and a green belt covering the agricultural land in the middle and lower Clyde basins.

Later, for the West Midlands, two plans also followed the decentralist model, though this time without any requirement for new towns: *Conurbation* (1948), produced by the West Midlands Group on Post-war Reconstruction, and the *West Midlands Plan* (1948), prepared for the Minister of Town and Country Planning by Abercrombie and local consultant Herbert Jackson. The authors of *Conurbation* were particularly interesting in their treatment of the urban fringe. In the 1930s the beginnings of a green belt for Birmingham were contained on land to the south of the city, provided by the Bournville Village Trust. A rather different strategic view from London now emerged:

> The redevelopment pattern which the Group has in mind is of an *archipelago* of urban settlements, with each settlement isolated from its neighbours and set in green, open land, from which all development other than for agriculture or amenity is rigidly excluded. Seen from another aspect, the redevelopment pattern is a system of green strips running uninterruptedly through the Conurbation, with existing towns and townships shaped into tidy units, each surrounded by its green border.   (West Midlands Group, 1948, p. 200).

But regional strategies were one thing, detailed design for redevelopment was another. A number of commissioned reports provided opportunities for consultants to bring together the disciplines of planning, architecture, and road engineering to suggest new forms of urban layout. New life was breathed into the practice of civic design: Abercrombie's plans for Plymouth, Hull and Edinburgh, and Sharp's plans for Oxford and Exeter were notable products of the genre. But even where local issues were paramount, Abercrombie, for one, could not resist the wider regional view. At Plymouth, for example, where in 1941 he was invited to prepare a redevelopment plan for the city, in cooperation with the City Engineer, H. Paton Watson, his starting point was that he should not be constrained by local authority boundaries: in his view Plymouth extended six miles and more beyond the city centre and should be planned on that basis. What followed was a proposed 40 per cent increase in shopping provision with a new central area layout replacing the haphazard medieval street pattern (though elsewhere in the city, in the Barbican area, the old intimacy was retained).

It was the plan for the City of London (1947), presented to the Court of Common Council by consultants Charles Holden and William Holford, Professor of Town Planning at Liverpool University, which took the furthest strides in design proposals. Though only 677 acres in extent, the area was one of great complexity, and heavy war damage meant that about one third of the pre-war commercial and industrial floor space was

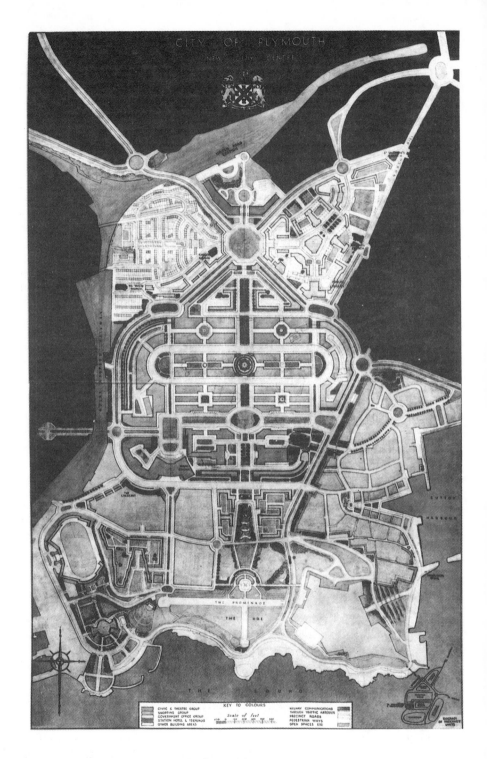

5.6 Plymouth: Abercrombie's Central Area

destroyed. Significantly their Plan, in the form of a final report (1947), was published in a book *The City of London* (1951), which was subtitled 'a record of destruction and survival'.

Against a long-term plan of redevelopment (perhaps 30 years, and therefore with inherent flexibility) Holden and Holford sketched a 10-year programme for definite action. For rebuilding, it was recommended that existing clauses governing the height and site coverage of buildings should be reviewed; a revised table of heights and angles of set-back was put forward and a new code of daylighting adopted. Streets, from sub-arterial to local should be classified according to function. New thoroughfares were proposed, together with a variety of measures for street widening, parking and design of intersections. Functionally the whole city was proposed as a 'one-use zone' for offices and business premises, but secondary uses such as shops, public buildings, light industry and warehouses could be admitted according to detailed location and access. There was an emphasis on precinct development, notably around St Paul's Cathedral, and the city churches. A Declaratory Order covering 270 acres was proposed with a view to designating extensively war-damaged land, subject to compulsory purchase; this was required for essential improvements to be carried out over the next 15 years. The Minister subsequently approved the Order for all but 40 of the acres applied for.

It is impossible to do full justice to the elegance and sensitivity of this volume which contained the final report. It had a depth and penetration which separated it from most other consultants' reports of the time. Moreover it is important to appreciate the breakthrough in planning methodology which Holden and Holford effected. The key was the institution of a density control based on a normal limit of floor space five times as great as the plot on which building was to take place. This was the 'standard plot ratio'. Before the war there had been 85 million square feet of floor space; in 1947 it was 59 million. Much would depend on the way in which floor-space control would operate, and the relaxations from the standard ratio. In the event the plot ratio proved to be one of the major devices whereby the city was prevented from turning into a minature New York (Cherry and Penny, 1986).

Techniques and methods

Notwithstanding the success of the new generation of plans, much remained to be done in fashioning the methodological tools which the planners needed to engage seriously in the job of urban reconstruction. Here we have to turn to developments in design practice, road layout and housing.

One of the key people to chart the course of reconstruction and development practice was William Holford (Cherry and Penny, 1986). After early work on the design and building of hostels for the Ministry of Supply, Holford was recruited to the Reconstruction Group to serve Lord Reith at the Ministry of Works; his job, together with that of a team assembled under him and a career civil servant, H.L.G. Vincent, was no less than to secure an immediate strengthening of the planning system and the encouragement of planning work in local authorities. In fact it took some time to make effective progress, in part because of institutional changes; Lord Portal replaced Lord Reith, and in 1943 a separate Ministry of Town and Country Planning was set up. Another problem was the uncertainty surrounding city-centre planning, when it was apparent that there was little likelihood of an early resolution of the financial, administrative and political issues involved. But local authorities were anxious to make a start on tackling their blitzed areas, though central area redevelopment was a matter where they were almost entirely without expertise. There was merely conventional wisdom about such questions as principles of road design, use zoning, building heights and controls over the external appearance of buidlings. The Ministry's technical guidance was urgently required. While road layout and zoning problems may have sufficed as techniques for suburban planning, centre reconstruction (three dimensional as opposed to two) required something more.

Holford supervised a small team in the Ministry of Town and Country Planning which prepared the advisory handbook on *The redevelopment of central areas* (1947). The key instrument of control became the Floor Space Index (FSI), a disarmingly simple measure which expressed the relationship between the curtilage of a site and the floor area of the buidlings erected on it. The derivation was made by calculating the usable floor area of the individual building and dividing the sum by the total area of the site, including (where appropriate) half the width of the adjoining streets.

The full power of the FSI was seen in the practice of development control. An index value could be fixed by a local authority for a particular planning area; in other words no development within an area zoned for office use should exceed a certain value as measured by the index. When a development proposal was submitted, the maximum permissible floor space was calculated by multiplying the area of the site by the FSI applicable, and consent given on condition that the area of floor space should not be exceeded. In other words, it became possible for the intensity of development to be determined in advance by a local authority. The index was also a flexible tool, allowing certain freedom to both architect and developer: for example for a ground area of 10,000 sq. ft and an FSI at 2, either the site could be covered at two storeys to yield the permitted 20,000 sq. ft, or the same floor space could be obtained on a smaller part of the site by building higher, and so releasing land for car parking and other uses. With tall buildings a daylighting indicator was a further safeguard against very high structures.

The handbook, available to local authorities in advance of publication, was well received. It represented something new, sophisticated yet practical: guidance of great utility by the Ministry on how to handle problems of redevelopment, which gave a common, technical template to urban centres with similar problems. A framework of procedures was suggested, beginning with surveys, both local and regional. The next stage was a matter of taking 'the main decisions', particularly in respect of land-use zones, the amount and distribution of accommodation and the main street layout; a hierarchical road system and tightly drawn ring roads were made a feature in the generalized depiction of city-centre plan (actually it was the reverse image of the town centre of Leicester). Then followed guidance on layout and development: streets, car parks, street blocks, the control of the external appearance of buildings, and open spaces and street planting. Finally there was guidance on a phased programme of realization: first and later stages of redevelopment. Throughout, the ideal of comprehensive planning was thoroughly endorsed, although there was little acknowledgement of the economic issues for the redevelopment process. The handbook must be seen as a major step forward in British planning method, and although the results were slow to be realized, one city at least, Coventry, perhaps shows in plan form what the authors might have envisaged.

The second guidance was in respect of roads, and much needed to be done in this regard. The highway development survey commissioned for Greater London in 1936, and carried out by Sir Charles Bressey and Sir Edward Lutyens, addressed the problem of the flow of commercial traffic in London, but said nothing about the reduction of central area congestion nor about the relation between traffic circulation, land use or environmental design. The breakthrough came from an unlikely source: an Assistant Commissioner of Police at Scotland Yard, Alker Tripp.

Road traffic had long been a matter for the police because of the very great concern over road accidents. Perhaps it was appropriate, therefore, for a police administrator with considerable experience of controlling traffic movement in a big city to provide a new perspective: that of bringing road planning and town planning together. His book *Town planning and road traffic* (Tripp, 1942) proved of seminal importance. Tripp's starting point may have been road accidents, but his overall grasp of the problem took him into wider fields. More than 68,000 persons were killed and more than 2 million injured on British roads in the 10 years prior to the outbreak of war, but Tripp was able to advocate not just improvements to major roads as one way of reducing the number of fatalities and accidents, but complete road systems. 'The whole trouble originates in unsuitable layout; the problem is fundamentally one of design and planning' (Tripp, 1942, p. 16): this was his starting point. The principles fell into place:

> It is wrong to have the local groups of population clustering about conduits that carry high-speed traffic; it is equally wrong to lead the heavy traffic-flows through places where shopping crowds congregate; and these things must not be allowed to go on happening just because they have happened for years and years past. Replanning is the only cure. (Tripp, 1942, p. 17)

There were two major features to Tripp's proposals: the acknowledgement of a hierarchy of roads and the creation of precincts in urban layouts. He saw three classes of road: arterial, sub-arterial and local. The arterial road was to be reserved for heavy traffic between towns; restricted points of access to twin carriageways would permit no building frontages, no standing vehicles and no pedestrians. The local road, including country lanes and town roads, was to be reserved only for traffic which had business in the locality; it should be designed to discourage through traffic. The sub-arterial road was to be an intermediate class of road designed to link up the main arterials to the local roads.

Such a hierarchy confirmed that the ideal town plan was a gigantic cart wheel with several rims, a loose arrangement of radials and circular ring roads: a feature which Abercrombie stressed for London. For smaller cities tight inner ring roads were advocated, Tripp suggesting that in a city of 100,000 population the radius of the inner ring road would probably be a quarter to half a mile, while in a ctiy of a million, the radius would be a mile or more.

Tripp's ideas for reformed urban layouts focused on 'pockets' or 'pre-cincts' of local roads from which through traffic would be deflected. Within towns they would be little systems of shopping, business, industrial and residential streets. He took his example from the Inns of Court, London, an enclave where general traffic had been excluded.

From Tripp and the applied work of Abercrombie it was a logical step to an official stance of the Ministry of War Transport. A Departmental Com-mittee, having been appointed in 1943, published its report in 1946: *Design and layout of roads in built-up areas*. It was not so much a guidance note as a review; the Committee's terms of reference had been to consider the design and layout most appropriate to various types of roads in built-up areas, with due regard to safety, the free flow of road traffic, economy and the requirements of town planning, and to make recommendations. The broad lines of advice had in fact already been established: the deflection of arterial traffic from built-up areas as far as practicable; failing this, traf-fic should be either elevated or sunken when passing through urban areas; vehicles, cyclists and pedestrians should be segregated on important traf-fic routes; frontage access should be restricted; fly-over crossings should be provided. Importantly, however, the report gave weighty endorsement to the principle of inner, intermediate, and outer ring roads. Such advice was fully taken in the preparation of the first generation of development plans in the late 1940s and early 1950s.

The techniques of urban renewal remained to be filled in with regard to housing design and layout. The Tudor Walters Report (1918) had shaped the form of housing after World War I; it was the Dudley Report (1944) which performed the same function after World War II. Early in 1942 two committees were set up by the Central Housing Advisory Committee to report to the Minister of Health (the minister responsible for housing) on the question of post-war housing rebuilding. One (the Burt Committee) looked at the solution of prefabrication and other forms of non-traditional construction. The other (a Committee under the chairmanship of Lord Dudley) laid down the forms and the space and equipment standards for post-war housing, and in conjunction with a team from the Ministry of Town and Country Planning, examined matters such as housing layout and densities. This was published as *The design of dwellings* (1944).

The report was by no means as radical as that of Tudor Walters a quarter of a century earlier; rather it confirmed the pre-war ideal, emphasizing the virtues of family life and the design of houses most likely to foster those virtues (Bullock, 1987). However, the Committee did emphasize the need for a much wider range of accommodation than had been provided before the war, and so they were drawn into the sharp debate about densities and preferences as between flats and houses – and this is where the link with the Ministry of Town and Country Planning proved so important. To accommodate the different types of housing required, the Committee recommended a range of densities: from 30 persons per acre for suburban development to 100 persons per acre for town centres, rising to a maximum of 120 for the largest cities. Building flats seemed inevitable if these higher densities were to be achieved. At densities of 120 persons per acre it was estimated that between 25 per cent and 30 per cent of the population would have to be flat dwellers.

These were statistical norms, but what would the post-war housing layouts actually look like? Concepts of neighbourhood planning prevailed. Mixed layouts of flats and houses were advocated for an area of different types of household with a range of facilities for local use, including schools, shops, open space and a community centre. Abercrombie and Forshaw had already applied this model in the *County of London Plan*, and before the war the idea had been fed from at least two sources: from the continent there were the large building blocks of Vienna and elsewhere with their community facilities, and from America there was the wider practice of according suburban districts a measure of identification as neighbourhoods of 5,000 to 10,000 people. Before the war Young's study of life at Becontree (1934) and Durant's study of the LCC's Watling Estate (1939) had both been critical of the lack of social and community facilities. During the war the National Council of Social Service (NCSS) strongly recommended neighbourhood planning and the Dudley Committee suitably responded.

Finally, the architecture of mixed development was put forward officially in the *Housing manual 1944*. Prepared jointly by the Ministry of Health and Ministry of Works, with advice from the Ministry of Town and Country Planning on matters of site planning and layout, it was intended for the guidance of local authorities – who, it was presumed would be undertaking most of the post-war redevelopment. It was unexceptional, and largely reproduced ideas already incorporated in the Dudley Report and the *County of London Plan*. In practice, for inner London at least, a trend was set for forms of mixed residential development in which blocks of flats were conspicuous: Churchill Gardens Estate, Pimlico, designed by Powell and Moya, contained 2,000 dwellings which combined eight-storey blocks of flats and maisonettes and three-storey terraces of housing and flats at an overall density of 200 persons per acre; and the Somerford Grove Estate in Hackney, another layout of flats and houses, designed by Gibberd at a density 104 persons per acre. While the flats versus houses issue remained hotly disputed, London at least demonstrated in schemes shortly after the end of the war that the flat combined with mixed development would be an essential ingredient of post-war central cities.

And so the components of post-war redevelopment fell into place: central area design to a comprehensive plan; ring roads and a functional road layout; new standardized housing forms; the neighbourhood unit; overall the dispersed, decentralized city. New powers for speedy land assembly, for plan making and the control of development were given to local authorities, consumated subsequently in the Town and Country Planning Act, 1947. The planner was elevated to the role of a coordinating 'technician-craftsman'; the practice of civic design as perceived by Holford would 'elevate the plan from technical, functional competence to the level at which it might cater for the cultural, emotional and aesthetic needs of a civilised society' (Cherry and Penny, 1986, p. 158). The next 40 years were to show how far this ideal would be achieved.

6 The Post-War Legacy

The period since 1945, a stretch of rather more than 40 years, may be considered as a whole, though in fact during that time the unfolding story of the public regulation of the urban environment has been far from one of even continuity. Its unifying feature has been the consistency of the form of statutory town planning derived from the Town and Country Planning Act 1947 and its successors, primarily the Acts of 1968 and 1971. This legislation ensured that the whole of Britain has been subject to compulsory land planning based on the application of two simple practices: the preparation (including revision and updating) of plans for the future allocation of land uses, and the control of development to accord with the provisions of those plans. The system has been flexible and robust enough to respond to changing conditions and circumstances, and there has been sufficient political and institutional stability with regard to attitudes towards, and assumptions about, planning during much of the period to give some measure of consistency to public policies and programmes.

The period began with town planning elevated in the public mind by virtue of the favourable reception accorded to the various plans for city reconstruction drawn up during the war years and immediately afterwards. Both the proposals and the practice met the spirit of the age: new cities planned to be environmentally attractive, socially acceptable and economically viable gained support from both public opinion and commercial interests. The period continued in the 1950s with the operation of the planning system proving capable of responding to a range of local situations, before, in the 1960s, it had to cope with the pressures of a housing boom, commercial redevelopment, a feared city thrombosis through increase in traffic circulation, and renewed problems from regional disparities. In the 1970s differences *within* cities became more pronounced than those *between* regions and the focus shifted to dissatisfaction with forms of public provision, particularly housing, and to concern over inner city decline. In the 1980s a change in political attitudes affected a long-standing commitment to public-sector plan making, and different policy initiatives have sought to reduce local authority provision of housing and play down other forms of local planning.

This is not an easy period to encapsulate in a short chapter, and in any case there is abundant literature, none more comprehensive than

Cullingworth (1988). However, to maintain the balance and the style of the account of earlier periods, we can adopt a similar approach. The principles and practice of plan making, and the various ways in which government, both local and central, has intervened in environmental affairs, have always been dependent on the context of the time: political, institutional, social, economic and technological. We begin therefore with an outline of the political background and an indication of the nature of urban and regional change during the period. We then consider the objectives and operation of the post-war planning system. The various aspects of planned development then unfold: housing, new towns and expanded towns, aesthetics of control, transportation, regional strategies and inner-city planning. We conclude with an overview.

Political background

Clement Attlee became Prime Minister in July 1945. His administrations (1945–50; 1950–1) completed and consolidated the work of the coalition government in establishing a managed economy and expanding the welfare state. The notion of town planning and its profession of technically qualified practitioners inevitably stood to be beneficiaries in this context. Attlee's Labour Party had broken out of the ghetto of solidly working-class support, its 1945 victory being based on the electoral sympathy of a broad section of the middle class. In the general election Labour won 79 seats for the first time; it carried 10 out of 13 seats in Birmingham, 9 out of 10 in Manchester and 48 out of 62 in London. With enormous gains in the white-collar suburbs, Labour became the party of bureaucrats, administrators and a progessive intelligentsia, all predisposed to seeing a greater share of public control over an increasing range of national affairs.

The National Insurance Act, 1946, implemented the Beveridge plan, though with some modification. The nationalization programme quickly accounted for the Bank of England (May 1946), coal (January 1947), electricity (April 1948), gas and railways (both May 1948). A National Health Service was introduced in July 1948. Steel nationalization followed in February 1951. In the middle of all this, the New Towns Act, 1946, and the Town and Country Planning Act, 1947, took their logical place.

But the physical direction of the economy through manpower planning did not last all that long, and after 1947 the financial budget was restored as the principal means of economic guidance. However, the Conservative Party in opposition made it clear that they too would maintain a strong central guidance over the economy, when returned to power. The two main political parties had converged and when the Conservatives won the general election of October 1951, the main lines of economic policy were maintained. The continuity was impressive, brought about by a reformed style of capitalism on the one hand and a moderate Labour Party and a cautious trades union movement on the other.

Political sentiment was captured and articulated by a band of upper-middle-class reformers of the kind earlier represented by Beveridge and Keynes. Socially concerned professional people came into their own: these

were the days of professional experts; architects and planners were typical of the humane technocrats who had won the war and had a vision of the
skills to win the peace. Politically the Conservatives integrated many of
Labour's demands into their own pragmatic philosophy. But these
demands had first found expression in a world of thought provided by
non-socialist intelligentsia, first in the 1930s and increasingly during the
war. These were the conditions of a new consensus; far-reaching proposals for redistribution and public control over private interests, which could
have been dangerously aligned to one political party, became shared by
both main parties.

In these circumstances it might have been expected that town planning
would be guaranteed a fair wind for many years while the consensus
survived. In a sense this was so, but on the other hand the activity of town
planning soon got bogged down in a technical bureaucracy, losing the dash
and verve which sustained it during the 1940s. Plans for the better distribution of population and employment were still needed, but one academic
observer reported in 1957:

> there is now not much enthusiasm. Town planning questions are no longer in
> the public eye. They seldom figure in party manifestos or wireless debates,
> and they arouse hardly any political controversy – more as a result of
> indifference than agreement. Planning controls are coming to be viewed as
> necessary evils, rather than as instruments for forging lasting benefits. A
> dead hand grips the spirit of planning, and issues which once engaged lively
> public interest are left to the anonymous decisions of officials whose consci-
> entiousness is only matched by their caution.   (Self, 1957, p. 166)

After 13 years the Conservatives lost office; in the general election of
October 1964 Harold Wilson won power with a slender majority of four
over the other parties. In March 1966 Labour was returned with a massively increased majority: 100 over the Conservatives, 97 overall. In June
1970 Labour surprisingly lost and an eventful six years of Wilson administrations came to an end. During this time many aspects of town planning
received a considerable boost, particularly in local authority house
building, the development of regional strategies, new policies for the
disadvantaged regions, transportation and a new attempt to control the
land market. More money was available for State development projects
and an emphasis was given to science-led growth.

The 1970s are more difficult to categorize from the point of view of
planning and national politics. After the administration of Edward Heath
(1970–4), Labour replaced the Conservatives again, winning two elections
in 1974, and Wilson returned to power for two years until he was succeeded on his retirement by James Callaghan. The Labour government fell
in May 1979, thrown off course by labour and economic problems, and
Margaret Thatcher and the New Right gained office, to be re-confirmed in
power in 1983 and 1987. The most significant development in this period
was the profound shift in attitudes towards the State: against the exercise
of public control and more sympathetic towards the operation of the free
market. It was increasingly argued that unnecessary State control of personal and community affairs was wrong in principle, serving merely to

weaken the capacity of the individual to enhance life chances; arguments not heard for perhaps half a century were rehearsed.

Environmentally it was reasoned that the consequences of State control have often been unpalatable: where were the beautiful cities that had been promised? Planning, after all, did not always solve problems; it could also create them. Moreover the massiveness of the planning machine, and the insensitivities of the bureaucrats who operated it, were surely counter-productive. The inefficiency of State power in regulating development and in providing guidance for the future was compared unfavourably with more adaptive private market intelligence. The free market had virtues too long eclipsed by slavish conformity to collective ideals that no longer seemed relevant. Pressure for 'retreat from government' gathered pace across the western world: opposition to rates and taxes, resentment of the over-abundance of officials, attacks on State waste and inefficiency. In these circumstances the conditions for unquestioned support for the statu-tory town planning system, which had lasted for over 30 years, were now considered debatable. It was no longer obvious that public-sector envi-ronmental planning of the old style need be maintained. The town planning ship ran into choppy waters and it remains in uncertain seas.

The other political factor against which town planning has to be seen in context in the post-war period relates to the local government and the institutional setting it has provided. The twentieth century had already seen the steadily increasing scope of local government. The dual nature of British governance (local and central), in spite of the inbuilt tensions, had proved durable and effective. The system of counties and districts, and county boroughs, established before the end of the nineteenth century, had provided an acceptable setting for the exercise of local powers by local authorities over the control and regulation of the environment. Dur-ing the 1930s there was a general belief in a vigorous system of local self-government and the maintenance of free democratic institutions (Young, 1985). A book published in 1935, *A century of muncipal progress* (edited by Laski, Jennings and Robson) as the title implies, had a tone which was optimistic and self-confident – in sharp contrast to the many threats to world peace at that time, indicative of a breakdown of effective law and order elsewhere: the Japanese invasion of Manchuria, the rise of Hitler, the failure of the Disarmament Conference, the progressive decline of the League of Nations, the assault on Abyssinia and the Spanish Civil War. In Britain local government could bask in a sound record of development of urban public services. The arguments for the increasing assumption of public responsibility for matters hitherto considered more appropriate to the private domain were largely won, it being held that private enter-prise and voluntary organizations were either inadequate or inefficient in supplying local services.

All this stood town planning well, as we have seen in Chapter 4, when the early forms of the statutory planning system were established. The wealth and power of the Victorian cities and the civic pride expressed in their impressive town halls, first enabled them to pioneer public services; later it permitted them to build up teams of technical staff and take on a range of tasks of increasing complexity and sensitivity. In the 1930s, for example, planning had become involved in the problems of servicing development and mediating between conflicting interests as to how land should be used: an important operational advance from the earlier bridgehead of scheme preparation and interim development control. After 1945, and with the Town and Country Planning Act, 1947, local authorities were the natural agency for the discharge of town planning powers. It could have been different (as it was with New Towns) but it was not: town planning was massively buttressed throughout the post-war period by becoming an integral part of local government.

While local councils were popular, all was well, even though town planning was often seen as yet another irksome irritant in the exercise of personal choice. But within a few years of the end of the war, responsibility for trunk roads, gas, electricity, national assistance and hospital services had been transferred from local to central government control. In 1974 further functions were taken away: 10 regional water authorities became responsible for water supply and sewerage. So we had a paradox: local government was losing functions, yet the continued exercise of monopoly power by local authorities attracted increasing opposition. Special interest groups, particularly in regard to roads, housing and the protection of amenities clashed with established practices of local government, and planning policies were less and less understood. When it came to slum clearance, opposition came not from slum landlords but from the residents themselves. Finally, as local authorities needed more and more Exchequer money to deal with urban problems of environmental decline and a welter of economic and social problems, new tensions in central–local relations unfolded in the 1980s. Local government ceased to be regarded as an indispensable deliverer of services; it had become part of the intractable problem of the late twentieth-century urban crisis. The promise of town planning itself was tarnished in this context.

Another development, within local authorities, served to weaken the traditional view of town planning as a place-orientated, coordinating activity for corporate affairs at the local scale. In the late 1960s and early 1970s there were significant shifts in British local government towards public policy making, during which time the role of the statutory Development Plan was weakening. The emphasis now was on lessons learned from American experience with PPBS (planning–programming–budgeting-systems.) Local authorities took to the fashion of developing management and political processes, and institutional structures, which would make them more able to plan, control and review their activities, commensurate with their resources. Policy planning was rethought, and local land-use planning had a rather different context (Hambleton, 1986).

Tinkering with local government boundaries did not seem to help either, although it was clearly necessary from time to time to take steps to match the changing facts of social geography to local authority boundaries and status. The Attlee government baulked at local government reform by boundary revision, the Local Government Boundary Commission which it had set up, proving to be of short-lived duration. Between 1949 and 1953 Ealing, Ilford and Luton failed in their bids to achieve county borough status, but in 1957 a Royal Commission on local government in London was appointed and, by the Local Government Act, 1958, a series of commissions was set up to consider the problems of particular localities, particularly those of the major English conurbations. The major recommendation of the former came to fruition: the establishment of an enlarged Greater London Council to replace the old London County Council.

New enlarged county boroughs for Luton, Solihull, Teesside and Torbay were established, together with a rationalization of boundaries in the West Midlands conurbation. Much more was to follow: a Royal Commission chaired by Sir John Maud (later Lord Redcliffe Maud) recommended the creation of a small number of two-tier authorities for the metropolitan areas of England (plus Hampshire) with the remainder of the country divided into 52 single-tier, unitary authorities. An influential minority report by Derek Senior advocated a map involving solely two-tier regional authorities, 35 in number. In the event, although the Labour government opted for the two-tier metropolitan counties (without Hampshire), the returning Conservatives (in 1970) went further, establishing a two-tier county-district relationship elsewhere in place of the unitary authorities. The operative date was April 1974. In Scotland the pattern followed was for Regional Councils and constituent Districts. Nonetheless there were certain similarities: Glasgow was a District in the massive Strathclyde Region; Birmingham a dominant District in the West Midlands County.

A new pattern of inter-authority rivalry ensued and in the upheaval town planning was a loser. A new fractiousness between authorities, together with an indication of a sharp increase in the politicization of local government, diminished the standing of British local government, and many of its services suffered. In many cases the professional certainties of a former generation of town planners were overridden by strident political voices and the activity fell increasingly into some disrepute. Finally, in April 1986 the Greater London Council and the metropolitan county councils in England were abolished: the last formal vestiges of strategic planning over the old conurbation areas were removed.

Changes in urban geography

Abercrombie and fellow practitioners who prepared plans for the reconstruction of British cities after the war, and planning officers up and down the country who drew up the first batch of development plans after 1948, worked to a common assumption: once the new urban land use pattern had been established, city form and structure would settle down into a steady state. Their plans were strategic in the sense that an idealized future (say 20 years hence) was projected which would accommodate all assumptions as to likely change: there would be no great population growth (why should there be? – the 1930s had been a decade of population stagnation, if not decline); inter-war regional drift would be halted; the housing shortage would be made good; the necessary population redistributions would be implemented, so reducing densities to an acceptable level in the inner districts; areas for suburban expansion would be identified and selected against a background of open space and protected countryside; lines for improved road communication would be safeguarded and the commercial areas, particulary town centres, would be better defined and made architectural show-pieces. Above all, urban Britain would be 'contained' (Hall et al., 1973) and its internal structure managed over time to a determined land use pattern.

How different it was all to be, and the marvel of it is that the plans prepared in the period after 1945 proved as robust as they did for so long. The fact is that urban Britain faced not a period of standstill but of dramatic growth and reordering. The context for the drawing up of plans and the management of on-going change proved quite different. Since the war urban Britain has experienced a rate of change unparalleled since the early days of the Industrial Revolution. A radically new urban experience was presented: whereas in the nineteenth century the major urban change was in the formation of tight-knit, high-density conurbations, and between the wars it was in the first flowering of low-density peripheral suburbanization, the second half of the twentieth century has seen metropolitanization as the essential phenomenon. Plan making in Britain and other schemes for the public regulation of the urban environment have responded successively to these three phases of urban change.

Statistical analysis by Hall et al. (1973) on the 1951, 1961 and 1966 Censuses revealed the early post-war experience, based on an examination of population change in new geographical units ('building blocks'): these were the Standard Metropolitan Labour Area (SMLA) and the Metropolitan Economic Labour Area (MELA). Hall et al. identified that in the period 1951–66 two different spatial tendencies were operating in England. One was regional: the metropolitan dynamism of the South-east and the Midlands compared with the sluggish tendencies of Lancashire and Yorkshire. The other, particularly striking in the South-east was a local decentralization effect, with very rapid growth on the outer periphery of London. There was a clear tendency for population to decentralize from the core of the metropolitan areas to the ring; in 1931 71 per cent of the total metropolitan population of England and Wales was found in metropolitan cores, whereas in 1966 the proportion was 60 per cent. So far, employment had shown less tendency to migrate from the central cities, but this process was soon to quicken.

By the middle 1960s the new urban map of Britain was being consolidated. Metropolitan clusters were clearly in evidence with their own internal dynamics of change dominated by a trend to loosen and shed population from the core to the periphery. The primary concentration consisted of London and the 25 contiguous SMLAs, in a dispersed area extending up to 60 miles from the centre, containing nearly 37 per cent of the population of England and Wales on less than 10 per cent of the land area. A second concentration was represented by the 40 SMLAs occupying the East and West Midlands, Lancashire and the West Riding of Yorkshire: another 33 per cent of the population of the country on 14 per cent of the land area. With the break between the two concentrations, soon to be filled in by Milton Keynes and Northampton's expansion, a virtually unbroken stretch of metropolitan areas promised to stretch from Sussex to North Lancashire.

Elsewhere metropolitan Britain existed in isolated outliers: including the Hampshire coast, parts of East Anglia, Bristol/Bath, North-east England, South Wales and the South Devon coast. In Scotland the central valley was filling in with massive expansions particularly around Glasgow, while growth around Edinburgh, Dundee and Aberdeen maintained a long-standing pattern. Metropolitan Britain had arrived.

It was already clear that Britain's early post-war experience bore similarity to that of the United States, and it was not too long before it was evident that Britain's experience was part of a wider set of tendencies to be seen not only in Europe but also in other world urban systems. Hall and Hay (1980) identify 539 separate metropolitan areas in the 15 countries of western and central Europe. Their study shows that between 1950 and 1975 an already urban continent underwent further urbanization, with metropolitan areas gaining over 39 million people. During this period the pattern and timing of change was striking. In the 1950s European population was still concentrating into metropolitan cores (perhaps in part as a process of adjustment to rebuilt cities), but by the 1960s a reversal had taken place, with people decentralizing from cores to rings, a process which accelerated in the 1970s. Britain was the fastest to decentralize, suggesting perhaps that it is in an advanced stage of industrial-urban evolution compared with much of Europe, though behind the trends observed for the United States.

In the process we have observed, two new urban phenomena have come to the fore: the outer city and the inner city, both urban environments with distinct challenges for planned regulation. Herington (1984) has drawn attention to the quite different urban form now represented by the dynamic periphery of the dispersed city, with its suburban nodes, its declining reliance on the central city, its dependence on private transport and its monotone socio-economic composition. Hall (1981) has described the deprivation and disadvantage now characterizing the inner city, confirmed by a series of reports commissioned by the Economic and Social Research Council (Cherry, 1987).

The facts of economic change have helped to produce a new urban crisis situation. After a boom period in the 1950s and 1960s, when real wages grew by more than a quarter between 1950 and 1965, and when earnings rose by more than 40 per cent, the later 1960s ushered in years of intermittent depression. London has seen the disappearance of more than three quarters of a million manufacturing jobs in 20 years: an aggregate figure masking stagnation and decline in an inner south-east zone, and growth in the west, in part related to Heathrow Airport, as a 'high-tech' crescent (Hall et al., 1987). During the same period Glasgow and its conurbation have gone from being an industrial city with 60 per cent of its labour in manufacturing to a service centre with 60 per cent of its labour in service occupations. The West Midlands has seen a remarkable economic collapse: Birmingham and Coventry were second and third only to London in the growth of new jobs between 1951 and 1961, but between 1970 and 1983 relative earnings in the West Midlands fell from being the highest to being the lowest of any region.

With economic change has come the emergence of both areas and social groups of disadvantage, which have attracted the attention of analysts and observers with an intensity accorded to the social and environmental problems of deprived London a century ago. In London an area forming an arc east of Charing Cross, from Lambeth through Docklands to Islington now represents a major concentration of deprivation, the dominant characteristics being high rates of unemployment (racially concentrated), high population density, a poverty of housing stock and a disadvantaged environment for a population with its distinctive sub-class of welfare dependents. In the West Midlands, Birmingham's area of deprivation extends in a boomerang-shaped district around the city from the north west in Handsworth to the east in Small Heath and to the south in Sparkbrook.

Overall, then, we can say that profound changes have occurred in the form, shape and structure of British cities since the war. We are now confronted with the phenomenon of the post-industrial city, with a quite different set of problems for public regulation (Young and Mills, 1983). Meanwhile the process of 'de-industrialization', typified by the shift of employment from manufacturing to service industries and the related growth of female participation in the labour force, and of white-collar as opposed to manual occupations, has been accompanied by fundamental changes in the location of economic activity, both locally and regionally. Significant trends are now working their way through the specific conditions prevailing in different cities and regions in Britain (Goddard and Champion, 1983). Slow, though sustained, improvements in economic performance and rates of unemployment from late 1986 onwards will not reverse the urban changes which have taken place.

Latest census figures (1981) confirm the pattern established over the last 20 years. In the decade 1971–81 the population flight from the cities continued. A preference for country living is clear, and in some remoter rural districts there was even a significant growth in population. The absolute loss of population from the cores of Greater London, Greater Manchester and Merseyside was less than in the previous decade, but population growth is now firmly identified with smaller towns and accessible settlements in the countryside. Data assembled by Chisholm (1983) for local authorities in England and Wales for the last inter-censal decade illustrates this point conclusively (see Table 6.1).

The relative population positions of Inner and Outer London in the 20-year period 1961–81 has been compared by Morrison (1982). Inner London lost 1 million inhabitants and Outer London 30,000 in a global decline for Greater London of more than 1.25 million. In every one of the 13 Inner London Boroughs the population decrease exceeded 10 per cent between 1971 and 1981; in Kensington and Chelsea the actual decrease was almost 29 per cent. On the other hand, while all the 19 Outer London Boroughs also lost population in only two cases (Brent and Richmond) did the decreases exceed 10 per cent (10.2 per cent and 10.4 per cent respectively).

The pattern of population redistribution around the country's metropolitan regions is best seen as an evolving one (Champion, 1983), though the broad picture is one of absolute loss of population from the older urban cores in favour of the newer suburbs and (increasingly) the surrounding towns. The inter-censal decade 1961–71 saw some very heavy losses

Table 6.1 Population Change for Different Categories of District 1971–81

Category of district	1981 No. of districts	pop. present on census night (000s)	1971–81 pop. change 000s	%	1961–71 pop. change %
England and Wales	403	49011	262	0.5	5.7
Gtr. London Boroughs	33	6696	−756	−10.1	−6.8
1. Inner London	14	2497	−535	−17.7	−13.2
2. Outer London	19	4199	−221	−5.0	−1.8
Met. Districts	36	11235	−546	−4.6	0.5
3. The principal cities*	6	3486	−386	−10.0	−8.4
4. Others	30	7749	−160	−2.0	5.5
Non-met Districts	334	31086	1564	5.3	11.8
5. Large cities**	11	2763	−149	−5.1	−1.4
6. Smaller cities	16	1687	−55	−3.2	2.2
7. Industrial districts					
a) Wales and the 3 northern regions	39	3348	42	1.3	3.7
b) Rest of England	34	3320	158	5.0	12.1
8. Districts with New Towns	21	2165	283	15.1	21.8
9. Resort and seaside retirement districts	36	3335	156	4.9	12.2
10. Other urban, mixed urban rural and more accessible districts					
a) outside the South-East	42	3793	307	8.8	21.9
b) in the South-East	57	5656	354	6.7	22.1
11. Remoter, largely rural, districts	78	5013	468	10.3	9.7

* – Birmingham, Leeds, Liverpool, Manchester, Newcastle upon Tyne, Sheffield

** – over 175,000 pop. in 1971.

Source: Michael Chisholm, (1983) p. 40.

Liverpool recorded a population loss of 18.2 per cent of its population in the 1960s, Manchester 17.9 per cent, Newcastle upon Tyne 17.6 per cent and Birmingham 8.6 per cent – much higher than the losses of the 1950s. Population redistribution trends in the 1970s were affected by both changing demographic and economic factors: Scotland and the Northern Region improved on their earlier poor out-migration losses, while in-migration surged in the less urbanized regions of southern Britain, such as East Anglia and the South-west. The cores of the metropolitan regions continued to lose population, though the gains registered by the surrounding counties were rather more subdued. Overall, in the 1970s the main areas of rapid population growth tended to lie just beyond the traditional suburban counties: in southern England as a broad arc to the north of the Home Counties from Norfolk to Northamptonshire and Buckinghamshire.

The planning machine

In Chapter 5 we saw that two people were pre-eminent in influencing the ways in which planning after the war would be determined. One was Abercrombie, who left an enduring stamp on broad strategy, as reflected in his regional plans for Greater London, Clydeside and the West Midlands, and his city plans for Plymouth, Hull and Edinburgh. The other was Holford, who, as head of a technical department within the Ministry of Town and Country Planning, fundamentally altered the technical basis of planning, and later as an academic consultant prepared plans with a distinctive contribution to civic design. Meanwhile, in his final years before retirement, Pepler contributed to procedures, bringing his experience to bear for over a quarter of a century on government departments and officials in them, and between local and central government.

Together with advice and guidance on housing, neighbourhood development and the layout of roads, this amounted to a total visualization of urban form at a regional scale. Abercrombie's broad-brush strategy was now filled in with the complementary prescriptions for design at the local scale, both central areas and residential districts. It is difficult to over-estimate what a transformation in the scope and purpose of physical planning this represented, far surpassing anything that had been achieved before. The garden city ideal as expressed at Letchworth and Welwyn, the garden suburb at Hampstead, Bournville and Wythenshaw, the planned estate either suburban or redeveloped, or the MARS group's proposals for London just before the war were no more than partial concepts by comparison. A total comprehensive view was now available complete with a repertoire of techniques for implementation. Moreover there was an established wisdom about it all.

However, it demanded an administrative and political will, and the cultivation of inter-departmental and inter-disciplinary cooperation, for the integrated development strategy to succeed. Experience was quickly to show that these conditions were not forthcoming; neither have they been realized throughout the post-war period. Whitehall officials have often found the concept of regional planning complex and imprecise, discovering that the necessary coordination between departments could not be relied upon. Moreover, the lack of precision and the subtlety of the overall vision of the city development strategy, as Holford outlined, was not all that easy to articulate either, or to communicate to others with conviction (Cherry and Penny, 1986). The Holford concept was not an Abercrombie-like statement; it was sensitive to local conditions and circumstances, it relied on process rather than programme, it was pragmatic, and it was a social art, informed by knowledge, technique and values. Holford's planners had to have a broad cultural background and were to be 'enablers', building up from research and synthesis to a design end-product.

This was too vague and imprecise. Most local authority staff found it difficult to interpret, seeking more specific guidance. The Holfordian approach to civic design withered on the vine and the operation of planning for the most part relapsed into a much more mundane, bureaucratic system based on plan making and development control, guided by adherence to normative values and adherence to scientific criteria – ironically of the kind that Holford's team in the ministry had drawn up.

The nub of the technical job to be done was the control of land use. This had already been established in the White Paper, *The control of land use,* (Cmd. 6537) in 1944, with the unequivocal statement:

> Provision for the right use of land ... is an essential requirement of the Government's programme of post war reconstruction. New houses ...; the new layout of areas devastated by enemy action or blighted by reason of age or bad living conditions; the new schools which will be required ...; the balanced distribution of industry ...; the requirements of sound nutrition and of a healthy and well-balanced agriculture; the preservation of land for national parks and forests ...; a new and safer highway system ...; the proper provision of airfields – all these related parts of a single reconstruction programme involve the use of land, and it is essential that their various claims on land should be harmonised so as to ensure, for the people of this country, the greatest possible measure of individual well being and national prosperity.   (para 1)

But this matter was part of a wider exercise. For many years both during and after the war the government wrestled with the principles of post-war reconstruction, and it was not until 1947 that the mammoth Town and Country Bill passed into law. It began as a Bill primarily to deal with the recommendations of the Uthwatt Report (1942) and the question of compensation and betterment was the cause of most of the indecision and uncertainty. The resultant financial provisions of the 1947 Act need not detain us too much, save to summarize the radically different position plan making experienced compared with the earlier situation. Whereas the problem of payment of compensation by local authorities to a developer refused planning consent had always proved a great obstacle to effective control, the new situation was that where land was developed, the increase in its value resulting from the grant of planning permission was secured for the community by the imposition of a development charge (equivalent to 100 per cent of the increase in value), to be assessed and collected by a Central Land Board. Landowners refused permission to develop land were not entitled to compensation, because the development value of the land had been invested in the State. (To be more explicit: landowners were to be compensated for lost development value as it existed in 1948, out of a fund for £300 million reserved for this purpose.)

The actual stages whereby the financial provisions of the 1947 Act were decided were extremely tortuous (Cullingworth, 1975) and the interplay of forces within the Government, between ministers and between officials had their effect too on the much more straightforward development plan provisions. One interesting aspect was that during the war the lines of debate were largely settled by civil servants; the effective opposition was not a political party, but the Treasury and other departments who saw themselves threatened by a new, upstart Ministry of Town and Country Planning. The detail of planning legislation by and large fell to a number of able officials who had a remarkably free hand. A major problem was what to include in the Bill and what to leave out. After the 1944 Act, issues including both the *Control of land use* White Paper and the restriction of ribbon development had to be taken into account.

The Act introduced a new development plan system as successor to that based on planning schemes: obligatory but more flexible, the plan was intended to outline a basic framework of future land use against which development proposals might be considered. All development was brought under control; with certain exceptions, it was made subject to the permission of the local planning authority. Only the larger authorities – counties and county boroughs – were entrusted with planning powers, with the consequence that 1,441 planning authorities were reduced to 145.

The Act required these authorities to submit their plans to the Minister by July 1951. Only 22 managed to meet this date, but by 1955 a good submission record meant that about half the country's plans had been approved, and the bulk by the end of the decade.

Land-allocation maps were the main feature of plan preparation, no longer simply for land in course of development but for the whole of a local authority area. But the system was bifurcated, because side by side with the making of development plans went the granting (or refusal, or granting with conditions) of planning permission for development. The system is a remarkable one and says much for our political culture: land ownershp of itself conferred no right to develop; development could only take place if a developer had obtained planning consent, and if permission was refused there was no payment of compensation.

It was through the control of land use that post-war cities would be given their orderly structure; major activity zones, such as residential, commercial, industrial and open space, would be sharply separated from each other. Furthermore, the careful delineation of neighbourhoods, typically of 10,000 population size with their standard provision of schools, open space and shops, and with roads deflecting through traffic to the edge of the residential area, also served to impart a new spatial order to the urban environment. But by the early 1960s planners were being charged with an over-obsession with neatly packaged land parcels, and this came to a head with Jane Jacobs (1961), an American journalist married to an architect, living in New York. Her thesis was that cultural and physical diversity was important in the life of a city, and she charged planners with pursuing policies which had the effect of eradicating it. The argument held that in the past, cities had been regarded as disorganized complexities, and that the objective of planning was to impose rational patterns of simplicity; Jacobs saw cities as organized complexities, and hoped to keep them lively, diverse and intense. Her model was Greenwich Village, New York, not readily transferable to British urban experiences, but her book *Death and life in great American cities* struck a chord in British planning. Jacob's strictures served as a reminder that neat and tidy land use arrangements may have been over-emphasized. Great diversity was important; a city after all was more than a set of carefully structured spatial patterns, it was a social system where environmental disorder might have a place in reflecting cultural diversity. The pendulum of opinions swung back, if only a little.

These various basic principles which underpinned the planning machine have survived throughout the post-war period. The resolution of the problem of compensation and betterment, which has changed on a number of occasions according to political philosophy, has not affected the system of plan and control. However, in the 1960s there was a major revision of the provisions for plan making in order to meet alleged deficiencies of the 1947 system which had emerged: slowness, alienation of the public, a focus on land use detail rather than broad strategy, and an increasing difficulty in using two-dimensional land use maps to represent three-dimensional, multi-use development proposals. The Minister of Housing and Local Government (as his Planning Ministry had been called since 1951), Richard Crossman, set up a Planning Advisory Group in 1964, chaired by a civil servant, I.V. Pugh, with members drawn from local government. Its Report *The future of development plans*, published in 1965, recommended changes, basically that a number of different types of plans should replace the development plan and the comprehensive development area plans. The need for flexibility in plan making was stressed; something more than land use maps were required and they had to be more responsive to the rapid changes then being experienced in the 1960s in terms of economic and social trends, population forecasts and traffic growth. The recommendations were largely followed in the Town and Country Planning Act, 1968, which established a two-tier system of plan making: structure plans as statements of intent and broad policy relating to spatial development, and major objectives in housing, employment and traffic; and a variety of local plans to show detailed proposals in respect of small areas.

There was another feature of the legislation, in that it provided for new ways of involving the public in plan preparation. With the old development plans, an appeals system entailed a confrontation between an appellant and the local authority over a disputed proposal, before an inspector appointed by the minister. With the new structure plan/local plan system, the preparation of planning proposals was done in two stages: draft and final, with exposure to public consultation. A further refinement is that the Secretary of State (through a panel of inspectors) conducts an examination in public into the proposals, rather than adjudicates on objections in an appeal system. The late 1960s threw up extensive demands for public bodies to be more open and responsive to community groups and sectional interests; the demand was for plan making to be a negotiable activity between interested parties, rather than a matter of technical decisions handed down from a monopoly elite in government. The Report of a government-appointed committee, chaired by Arthur Skeffington MP, *People and planning* (1969) was sympathetic to these demands and advocated new ways in which community involvement in planning might be conducted.

Some of the early structure plans were extraordinarily ambitious in their scope: land use plans promised just for a little while to become all-embracing social, economic and 'physical' documents, with a further clear relationship to transportation matters. But comprehensive data collection ran ahead of a capacity for meaningful analysis, and prescriptive content was disappointing. In any case the years of growth came to an end in the 1970s: structure plans, ideal documents perhaps for broad-brush indication of options in spatial development, became less and less suitable to cope with a 'no change' situation. This is an over-statement, but combined with an increasing preference by Government to curtail the content of structure plans, and recently by a Government less disposed to plan making by the public sector anyway, to withdraw structure plans all together, the heady days of 1960s optimism were lost.

More than 40 years' experience of the planning system has established a powerful plan-making bureaucracy in central and local government. The basic ingredients were provided by the painstaking but imaginative experimentation in the 1940s based on Abercrombie's grand strategy, Pepler's attention to procedures and Holford's team's introduction of new techniques. The consistency of application since then has been remarkable, the benefits being seen in a lengthy, unbroken period during which time there has been a sustained management of urban change: plan making under constant review covering the whole of urban Britain, and control of development by public and private bodies in the community interest. But that sounds rather grand, and the reality is rather different. Planning policies tend to run behind developments and trends, and all too often the planning machine has given the impression of existing more for the benefit of those who run it (professionals and politicians) than those who are served by it. However, the fact is that for approaching half a century British cities have been publicly regulated by a system designed to guide, shape and control the form and appearance of the urban environment.

Housing

The circumstances of war-time Britain had the effect of giving weight to policy resolutions by the State as to where and how people should live. It was a culmination of measures going back to the middle of the nineteenth century, but more particularly government experience since the 1890s, and above all, a shift in attitudes towards State-provided housing. The housing of post-war Britain represented a major aspect of planned development after 1945.

As we have seen, the ideals of private suburbia were deeply rooted, particularly in England, and in design terms the Unwinesque tradition of vernacular cottage architecture and the predeliction for low-density layouts had been articulated in the inter-war council estate. Meanwhile private inter-war suburbia had its distinctive style where the semi-detached house was dominant. Rather grander still was the villadom of the well-to-do. The then editor of *The Architectural Review*, J.M. Richards, offered an affectionate description of the English suburb in *The castles on the ground* (1946), which instead of pouring scorn on suburban taste, took more seriously the needs it fulfilled and the impulses that created it. It confirmed an underlying tension between public and private housing interests. 'Ewbank'd inside and Atco'd out, the English suburban residence and the garden which is an integral part of it stand trim and lovingly cared for' (Richards, 1946; 1973 edn, p. 13). The private suburb gave to its inhabitants two important things: a sense of belonging to a fairly sympathetic world and an outlet for idealistic and creative instincts. It meant that the keynote had to be informality and so the idea of a planned suburbia was almost a contradiction in terms.

But there were very different opinions being canvassed at the end of the war. At the extreme from Richards stood Sir Charles Reilly, Professor of Architecture at Liverpool. In 1944 he was appointed planning consultant to Birkenhead and that year sketched out an estate plan 'of houses round greens, as in pre-Industrial Revolution England, and the greens themselves arranged like the petals of a flower round a community building, the modern equivalent of the village inn' (Wolfe, 1945, p. 10). This scheme became known as the Reilly Plan and attracted considerable political comment. For the Labour and Communist Parties this approach to community planning as against ordinary suburban planning held much appeal; the plan created a physical setting in which neighbourly cooperation was likely to develop, in distinction to the perceived isolationism of the normal suburb.

In the event, post-war council-house architecture and estate layout has been much more pragmatic and the course of their evolving styles not without its many surprises. Britain ended the war with 475,000 houses either destroyed, or so badly damaged that they were made permanently uninhabitable. During the six years of war 2 million marriages had taken place and there was a severe housing shortage. A public-sector housing drive was quickly mounted, based on a continuation of rent control and subsidized council housing that was no longer restricted to slum clearance but extended to meet general needs. The production of prefabricated, temporary houses was begun. The general understanding was that to all intents and purposes the State would now be responsible for the nation's housing stock – its quality, quantity and distribution. As Aneurin Bevan, Minister of Health (responsible for housing) remarked:

> If we are to plan, we have to plan with plannable instruments, and the speculative builder, by his very nature, is not a plannable instrument . . . We rest the full weight of the housing programme upon the local authorities, because their programmes can be planned, and because in fact we can check them if we desire to   (Bevan, cited in Donnison and Ungerson, 1982, p. 142)

The design, layout, methods and materials were tightly controlled in a flow of instruction and exhortation to local authorities. The *Housing manual* of 1944 laid primary emphasis on the provision of three-bedroom, two-storey houses. The *Housing manual 1949* gave advice on a wider range of dwelling types; prepared with the assistance of a sub-committee of the Central Housing Advisory Committee and a panel of architects appointed by the Associations of Local Authorities, this Ministry of Health publication, lavishly illustrated, offered a variety of designs based on the standard of 900–950 square feet for three-bedroomed houses, an advance on the 1944 standard. It contained advice on site selection, layout, landscape, roads, architectural treatment, standards of accommodation, house planning, services, equipment and construction. The manual was a complete guide to the building of six types of dwellings: the kitchen–living room house, the working kitchen house, the dining kitchen house, old people's dwellings, three-storey terrace houses and flats and maisonettes. There was no suggestion that local authorities should slavishly copy standard designs, but council-house architecture nevertheless received a considerable stamp of uniformity.

By 1951 the Labour government had built 900,000 houses, falling short of its target of 240,000 dwellings a year. The Housing (Financial and Miscellaneous Provisions) Act, 1946, increased the Exchequer subsidy to £16 10s per house for 60 years; a rate contribution of £5 10s was also required. This trebled the money value of subsidies compared with 1939. Local authority house building was suitably stimulated and in 1948 more than 190,000 council houses were completed (compared with the previous highest total of 121,000 in 1939). The Conservatives (returned in 1951) promised 300,000 houses a year and in 1953 319,000 were in fact built, followed by 348,000 the next year. These higher totals were obtained through more generous subsidies and a stimulus to private building. This success suggested that the general housing shortage was now considerably eased, and attention returned to slum clearance. The Housing Repairs and Rents Act, 1954, reduced subsidies for general needs, but retained them for clearance of slums; two years later subsidies for general needs were totally abolished, leaving the general housing need to be met by private enterprise. Subsidies were resumed in 1961 and thereafter had a chequered history with changing problems in housing supply and differing political judgements (Burnett, 1978).

The attack on the slums proved a very significant event in post-war urban planning. The Census of 1951 showed that many houses lacked amenities with which the council house since 1919 had been equipped. One third of the dwelling stock of England and Wales was then more than 80 years old, and 37 per cent of all households lacked a fixed bath, 8 per cent a wc (another 13 per cent were required to share), 6 per cent piped water (another 14 per cent sharing) and 6 per cent a kitchen sink. A huge backlog of unfit dwellings was apparent, and in the event the period between the mid-1950s and mid-1970s wrought a major transformation. In England and Wales 1,165,000 houses were demolished or closed in the period 1955–74, in a massive programme of compulsory purchase whereby local authorities considerably extended their council-land holdings. Between 1945 and 1954 just 90,000 in total had been cleared, an average of 9,000 per year, but from 1961 onwards the annual total demolished was never less than 61,000 (with the exception of 1974, when the number fell to 41,000); the years of greatest activity were 1966–72. In Scotland, a further 296,000 houses were demolished or closed in the period 1955–74, making nearly 1.5 million in total for Great Britain (Cherry, 1976).

Community disturbance was considerable, with very high annual transference rates of people from slum housing to alternative accommodation of very different style, quality, location and community setting. Sociologists' strictures about loss of familiarity due to the disruption to social life, as in the study of Bethnal Green (Young and Wilmott, 1957), at first went largely unheeded, though their conclusions were unmistakable:

> The physical size of reconstruction is so great that the authorities have been understandably intent upon bricks and mortar. Their negative task is to demolish slums which fall below the most elementary standards of hygiene, their positive one to build new houses and new towns cleaner and more spacious than the old. Yet even when the town planners have set themselves to create communities anew as well as houses, they have still put their faith in buildings, sometimes speaking as though all that was necessary for neighbourliness was a neighbourhood unit, for community spirit a community centre. If this were so, then there would be no harm in shifting people about the country, for what is lost could soon be regained by skilful architecture and design. But there is surely more to a community than that.
>
> (Young and Wilmott, 1962, p. 198)

Abercrombie's *Greater London Plan* had now to be looked at in rather a different light, and much more was to be heard of the Bethnal Green survey and its implications. First-hand experience suggested that something was wrong: in Birmingham, for example, the Vicar of redeveloped Ladywood concluded that 'we had forgotten the people' (Power, 1965). But for the record, in England and Wales in the period 1955–74, 3,116,000 persons were moved as a result of clearances; in 1968, the record year for demolition, nearly 189,000 were rehoused.

This was a phenomenal period of renewal, embarked upon by the Conservatives and maintained with vigour by Labour. All major urban areas participated with enthusiasm, with political support to professional interests to engage in this activity: not only local authority housing, architecture and planning departments, which bolstered political pride in identification with a popular value of sweeping away the past and building anew, but also the construction industry which had the windfall of long-term contracts.

The pace of slum clearance slackened in the early 1970s, local authority programmes having survived for some years through their own momentum. National economic problems led to restrictions on capital expenditure, and in any case the sustained attack on the number of unfit dwellings had significantly reduced the scale of the problem. But the end of slum clearance came more with a change in values: away from demolition, to conservation and rehabilitation. A Ministry of Housing and Local Government enquiry into the Deeplish district of Rochdale (1966) indicated a surprising level of satisfaction with even the poorest houses. The insensitivity of the local authority machine encouraged the build-up of community resistance to, and a political rethink about, wholesale clearance. In Liverpool, it was held that the politics of redevelopment showed the insensitivity of the urban renewal process (Muchnick, 1970). Norman Dennis (1970) showed how in Sunderland a change in attitude led to a hardening resistance to slum clearance; another study charted the conflict between a local community and a city planning department, Newcastle (Davies, 1972). One local politician in London (Taylor, 1973) was driven to reflect on the need to preserve identity and to design to an intimate human scale. One London community, centred on Tolmer's Square, battled against property developers (Wates, 1976).

Clearance switched to a policy of improvement. Powers for house improvement had long been available, local authorities being enabled to improve council housing and give discretionary grants to private owners for improvement of individual properties. In the 1960s the tactic of improvement switched from individual properties to whole areas (Thomas, 1986). The Housing Act, 1969, overcame the previous cumbersome procedures and introduced the idea of General Improvement Areas; the Housing Act, 1974, introduced Housing Action Areas. The number of improvement grants approved in England and Wales rose sharply from 156,000 in 1970 to a record 360,000 in 1973, to fall again to 231,000 in 1974 and decline thereafter. The comparable figures for Scotland showed a similar pattern: 23,000 (1970), 92,000 (1973) and 68,000 (1974). But no sooner had this new approach been introduced than criticisms were mounted: not only the costs and slowness of improvement schemes, but also the social conflicts inherent in gentrification when improvement benefited not the original occupant but an incomer where areas of working-class housing (particularly in London) were transformed into desirable enclaves for higher-income households.

Post-war housing policy has also had a major visual impact through different approaches to the architectural style of dwellings provided in the public sector. In particular, the mixed development of multi-storey and tower blocks came to dominate large areas of British towns and cities (Horsey, 1988). Post-war architects, amongst whom Frederick Gibberd was soon prominent, popularized a style which drew on many influences. Mixed development met the sociological dictates of urbanity and community; it met the planning critics of inter-war sprawl; and it met architectural requirements of variety in materials (concrete, brick, wood, pebbles and strong colours). One inspiration came from Scandinavia, as reflected in early work which included the LCC Alton East Estate, Gibberd's work at Harlow and Gibson's Tile Hill Estate at Coventry. Another came from Le Corbusier and pre-war German and Dutch architecture, which gave us the LCC's Roehampton Lane (Alton West) Estate; this latter style tended to predominate in the 1950s.

Mixed development implied an increased variety of house types, with a breakaway from the traditional semi-detached, as suggested in the Ministry's *Flats and houses*, (1958). With an emphasis on design and economy the Ministry advised on the density of residential areas, showing how schemes of varying densities could be fitted to the same unit area of land. There was a consequential revival of terraced housing, with maisonettes in four-storey blocks and flats in a variety of shapes: T, Y and cruciform. Mean-while the idea of traffic-free residential areas, as on Radburn lines (see p. 103) was also encouraged. But the most significant development was the increase in the number of flats built by local authorities. Tall blocks (five or more storeys) accounted for 26 per cent of all local authority buildings in 1966, though by 1970 the figure had fallen to 10 per cent in the aftermath of the Ronan Point disaster in 1968, in the London Borough of Newham when, following a gas explosion, a structural failure resulted in partial collapse. The actual reasons for the popularity (albeit relatively short-lived) of the high-rise phase are many: it was architecturally fashionable; it may have suited municipal prestige; it answered immediate problems of increasing density as the big cities ran out of building land within their own boundaries; and it met the spurious argument about saving agricultural land (mounted by the farming lobby and the Conservative-dominated shire counties). New subsidy arrangements increased the grant payable to blocks over six storeys. But a reaction against high rise was quickly mounted and the additional subsidy was withdrawn in 1967.

Of all British cities Glasgow has the largest number of council flats in high blocks: 33,600 in blocks of five or more storeys (almost twice the total of its nearest challenger, Birmingham), the majority resulting from a com-pressed 'burst' of construction in the 1960s. The origins of this boom, in contrast to London's espousal of mixed development, have been traced by Horsey (1988). All cities have different records in this respect and they all merit individual research if we are to piece together the various aspects of post-war urban development (Manchester's Moss-side development was different from Sheffield's Park Hill estate of 'streets in the sky', and differ-ent again from Newcastle's development at Byker, with its famous 'wall'). In Glasgow a fortuitous coalition of interests between a new Convenor of Housing Committee, a principal housing officer and a flamboyant local designer produced a remarkable decade of high-rise building, which included the highest blocks in Europe at Red Road, Baldornock.

The nature and extent of housing programmes in the post-war years has therefore been of great significance for urban form, community life and degrees of individual happiness. Both the design and location of public authority houses have been very considerably affected, while the private sector has been responsive to market demands. (The Parker Morris Report, *Homes for today and tomorrow* (1961), recommended standards for all new houses, whether public or private, more space and better heating being the overriding considerations: the recommendations were mandatory for New Town housing in 1967 and for local authorities in 1969, but not for the private sector.)

But after 40 years of post-war public sector housing there is now evi-dence of widespread rejection, and some community groups are looking to the promise of community architecture (Wates and Knevitt, 1987). The origin of this new movement lay in the protestations of community-based voluntary groups concerned with their perceptions of the anti-social effects of conventional architecture and planning. Calls for citizen partici-pation in planning encouraged groups to undertake practical work, and in

1974 the first self-help General Improvement Area was completed, at Black Road, Macclesfield. In recent years, of particular importance has been the professional conversion of the Royal Institute of British Architects, through their president, Rod Hackney, who has been able to persuade the Prince of Wales to his cause.

In the late 1980s we now see town planning and architecture – shapers of the housing environment – charged with professional disrepute: once the great hope of being effective providers of an environment of social purpose, the two professions have been derided for giving the public the wrong thing, and in the wrong manner. They have been savaged by Alice Coleman et al. (1985) who, terming post-war public housing rather satirically as 'Utopia', asks:

> Why should Utopia have been such an all-pervading failure, when it was envisaged as a form of national salvation? It was conceived in compassion but has been born and bred in authoritarianism, profligacy and frustration. It aimed to liberate people from the slums but has come to represent an even worse form of bondage. It aspired to beautify the urban environment, but has been transmogrified into the epitome of ugliness. Its redemption, after 40 years, is not only a matter of improving the buildings, but also of winning the hearts and minds of those who create and control them.
>
> (Coleman et al., 1985, p. 180)

Warning shots in this attack had been fired earlier; for example, by Pearl Jephcott and Hilary Robinson (1971), following their research into the extent of resident satisfaction with high-rise blocks in Glasgow; and by Oscar Newman (1972), who studied the relationship between design and crime and vandalism in New York. Coleman's work was a logical extension, aiming to see which forms of design and layout were most associated with 'lapses in civilised behaviour'.

Over a period of five years, between 1979 and 1984, Coleman and her team studied over 4,000 blocks of flats and a slightly larger number of houses in two areas of London (Southwark and Tower Hamlets) and, for comparison, a council estate on the south-east side of Oxford, all in the context of a regard for flats and houses in many settings elsewhere. Her findings have attracted considerable attention, which cannot be summarized here. But consider one aspect: fifteen design variables were identified which affected the behaviour of residents, especially children and users of blocks of flats. Litter, graffiti, vandal damage, the numbers of children in care, urine and excrement pollution all became more common as the design values worsened within each variable. Coleman bluntly blames features of Utopian design as the chief factor in many aspects of social decline in new or redeveloped areas. Although her wide-ranging attacks on the public housing-building 'industry' go further than her data alone would justify, the story of post-war public housing seems to have come full circle.

New Towns, Expanded Towns and Green Belts

The idea of New Towns has a long pedigree, but it received its twentieth-century fillip through the garden city movement (Osborn and Whittick,

1963). The propagandists for New Towns had powerful voices during the war and Abercrombie's *Greater London Plan 1944* embraced the principle in the strategy of decentralization. But the fact remains that the Labour Party manifesto of 1945 contained nothing about New Towns. Yet within nine months of taking office the Government had introduced a New Towns Bill, which took precedence over the promised measure on compensation and betterment (Cullingworth, 1979).

In response to Abercrombie's plan, Stevenage was identified by an inter-departmental committee as a potential first experiment; W.S. Morrison, Minister of Town and Country Planning, appeared sympathetic, but the fall of the Caretaker Government intervened. Lewis Silkin succeeded as Minister and it is largely through his influence that New Towns in Britain gained their significant role in post-war planning. In part to by-pass probable reluctance by his Government colleagues to any priority for New Towns, he appointed a departmental committee, chaired by Lord Reith, with the following terms of reference:

> to consider the general questions of the establishment, development, organisation and administration that will arise in the promotion of new towns in furtherence of a policy of planned decentralisation from congested urban areas; and in accordance therewith to suggest guiding principles on which such towns should be established and developed as self contained and balanced communities for work and living.

Appointed in October 1945 the committee worked quickly, producing three Reports. An *Interim report* (Cmd. 6759, March 1946) emphasized that a New Towns programme should be a matter for central Government: the location of a New Town should be a Government decision and that a new agency should be set up to plan and develop the town (it was not to be a matter for local authorities). The agency should have powers of compulsory purchase and therefore the site of the town should be publicly owned. Finance for development should come from the central Government. Central coordination would keep the location of industry in step with development. Finally, the case being so clear, a recommendation was made to proceed immediately with Stevenage. The die was cast. A *Second interim report* (Cmd. 6794), published in April 1946 spelled out the points in greater detail, but additionally referred to the community aspects of settlement. The *Final report* (Cmd. 6876) was published in July, dealing with various planning principles, including the question of size: a population of between 30,000 and 50,000 was thought desirable. Moreover the towns were to be of diverse and balanced social composition:

> if the community is to be truly balanced, so long as social classes exist, all must be represented in it. A contribution is needed from every type and class of person; the community will be poorer if all are not there, able and willing to make it.   (para.22)

Silkin's Bill received an unopposed second reading in May; for the Conservatives W.S. Morrison gave it general support. It was unopposed at the third reading in July, though Lord Hinchingbrooke thought it 'a State experiment in the life and happiness of our people and in my opinion like all

State experiments, it will work havoc, bitterness and grave social damage'
(Cullingworth, 1979, p. 25). Royal assent was given to the Bill in August.
The New Towns Act, 1946, provided for the designation of sites for New
Towns; the setting up of development corporations for their development;
and it gave them the range of powers they would use.

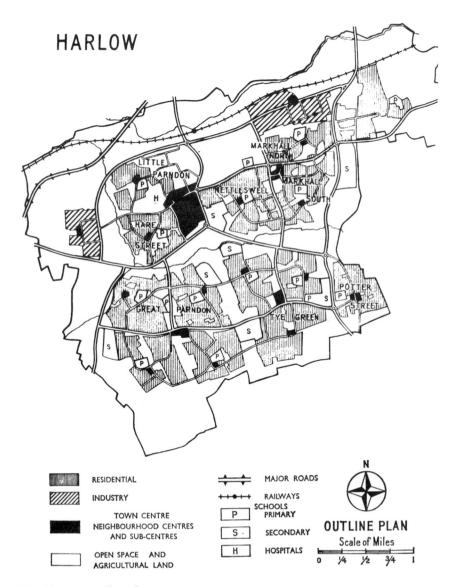

6.1   Harlow: outline plan

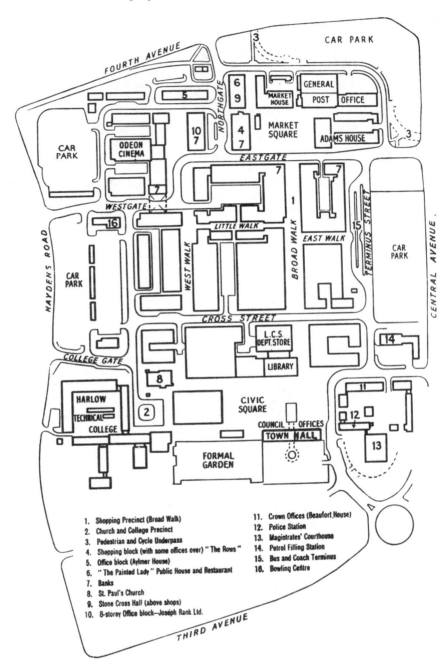

1. Shopping Precinct (Broad Walk)
2. Church and College Precinct
3. Pedestrian and Cycle Underpass
4. Shopping block (with some offices over) " The Rows "
5. Office block (Aylmer House)
6. " The Painted Lady " Public House and Restaurant
7. Banks
8. St. Paul's Church
9. Stone Cross Hall (above shops)
10. 8-storey Office block—Joseph Rank Ltd.

11. Crown Offices (Beaufort House)
12. Police Station
13. Magistrates' Courthouse
14. Petrol Filling Station
15. Bus and Coach Terminus
16. Bowling Centre

6.2   Harlow Town Centre

The New Towns programme quickly unfolded, not only for London but for other parts of the country. Projects for London began with Stevenage, designated in November 1946 under the provisions of the Town and Country Planning Act, 1932. This designation was not without its local hostility; the validity of the designation order was challenged by a residents' protection society and the High Court held in favour of the objectors. The Court of Appeal reversed this judgement and the reversal was upheld by the House of Lords in July 1947.

Then in chronological order came the following: Hemel Hempstead (1947) replacing Redbourn as proposed in the Abercrombie plan, was designed to fill in the area between Harpenden, St Albans and Hemel Hempstead itself; Harlow (1947), 23 miles north-east of London, expanded a small settlement of 4,500 people; Crawley (1947), a town of 9,500 population, lay astride the Brighton Road, 30 miles south of London; Hatfield and Welwyn Garden City (both 1948) lay very close to each other 18–20 miles north of London (Welwyn was already a sizable town of 18,500 inhabitants); Basildon (1949) met rather different objectives, planned not only to accommodate overspill but to tidy up an untidy area of shack development between London and Southend; Bracknell (1949) replaced Abercrombie's proposal for White Waltham, three miles south-west of Maidenhead, west of London.

The New Town device for planned urban development was utilized for other purposes elsewhere. Aycliffe (1947), north of Darlington, adjacent to a major trading estate was designated to act as a regional growth magnet for South Durham. Peterlee (1948), near Hartlepool, aimed to provide a central node for dispersed mining settlements in East Durham. In Scotland, East Kilbride (1947) was a New Town on the London model, as an overspill centre for Glasgow, but Glenrothes (1948) had a function akin to Peterlee, as a collector point for the East Fife coalfield, on the lines advocated in the Regional Plan for Central and South-east Scotland (Mears, 1948). Cwmbran (1949), adjoining Newport, was seen as a focus for new development in South Wales. Corby (1950) was different again, designed for substantial housing development for the expanding steel works there.

The precise factors which weighed in Silkin's mind in this programme of designations are reviewed by Cullingworth (1979); also the factors in the rejection of some proposals which finally did not feature in the list. The fact is that the New Towns were quickly seen as jewels in planning's crown. This, after all, was the age of centralist planning; the State was the wise, beneficent steersman to a nobler future. New Towns would be civilized, attractive, agreeable places in which to live, with all the richness of community life which the new social order would bring. They answered three insistent demands in the early post-war years. First, they were a rational answer to the unplanned metropolis of the inter-war period; we had long since passed the time of asking *whether* the State should build houses, now it was a question of determining precisely *where* the nation should locate its dwelling stock. Second, it was a logical way, as indicated in the scientifically precise plans of war-time Britain, of organizing the huge scale of building development that demand dictated would occur anyway. Third, New Towns consituted experiments in social engineering – well in tune with the psychological requirements for post-war reconstruction.

The first phase of New Town building survived early tribulations, particularly the economic crisis of 1947 and the cutback on public expenditure. There was Treasury alarm at mounting financial commitments and Silkin received no consistent enthusiasm from his colleagues for his proposals. In any case the number of dwellings actually completed by 1950 was pathetically small, and housing shortages were felt acutely elsewhere.

Alternative proposals for town development reflect these concerns. Dalton succeeded Silkin as Minister in February 1950 and initiated another method of organizing arrangements for overspill from the big cities, without quite the extravagant implications of new corporations which Silkin's schemes had required. Dalton proposed to introduce a Bill to give financial help to local authorities to carry out major town expansion in their own areas to relieve overcrowding in the areas of other authorities. But the Labour government fell in October 1951 and the Conservatives took up office. Macmillan became Minister of Housing and Local Government (the term 'Town and Country Planning' having now been dropped) and soon introduced a Bill in very similar terms. The Town Development Act received the royal assent in August 1952.

Progress on arrangements for the voluntary transfer of those in housing need from the big cities to the smaller surrounding townships was at first very slow. But in due time the contribution to population redistribution was significant enough, particularly dispersal from London, with a total of 55,000 dwellings built in no less than 32 towns including Basingstoke, Swindon, Huntingdon, Thetford, Haverhill, Wellingborough, Andover, Witham, Aylesbury and Houghton Regis (listed in order of number of dwellings built under the Act). Birmingham had its reception areas at Tamworth (pre-eminently), but also Daventry, Droitwich, Lichfield and elsewhere, with a total of 13,500 dwellings constructed. Manchester had modest arrangements with Macclesfield and Winsford; Liverpool had major schemes at Winsford (again) and Ellesmere Port; Wolverhampton built at Wednesfield and Seisdon; Salford had a major involvement with Worsley; Newcastle upon Tyne expanded at Killingworth and Cramlington; Bristol utilized Warmley; and Walsall also took up the provisions of the Act. In Scotland there were 42 reception areas, for Glasgow, where about 38,000 people were housed, the major schemes being at Linwood, Johnstone, Erskine and Kirkintilloch. The history of these various expansions has occasionally been recorded, none showing better than that by Harloe (1975), in his study of Swindon, how local personalities (in that case, Murray John, the dynamic Town Clerk) could do so much to determine particular courses of action.

The Town Development Act, 1952, did not apply to Scotland and it became necessary to cope with Glasgow's housing problem by means of a second New Town. This was at Cumbernauld (1956), 15 miles to the northeast of the city on the Stirling Road, another addition to the heart of the industrial belt between Forth and Clyde. After this, a Town Development Act for Scotland was enacted in 1957, and the schemes noted above were prepared.

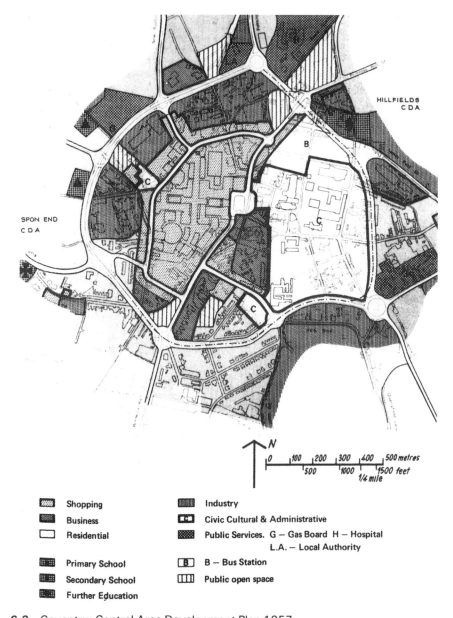

HILLFIELDS
CDA

SPON END
CDA

N
0   100   200   300   400   500 metres
    500   1000   1500 feet
                        1/4 mile

	Shopping		Industry
	Business		Civic Cultural & Administrative
	Residential		Public Services. G — Gas Board H — Hospital
			L.A. — Local Authority
	Primary School		B — Bus Station
	Secondary School		Public open space
	Further Education		

6.3 Coventry: Central Area Development Plan 1957

But the housing problems of the big cities would not go away. The pressure on local councils to obtain building land to cope with housing demand, and the force of demographic forecasts which by the end of the 1950s were being revised upwards, resulted in a series of dog-fights between the large urban authorities and the shire counties, in which the Ministry inevitably became involved. Lymm in Cheshire was refused as an overspill site for Manchester; Birmingham's proposal to develop at Wythall in Worcestershire was similarly rejected. Ultimately another wave of New Towns was designated, first by the Conservative government and then by Labour, until a halt was called in the early 1970s.

The London County Council (1961) had wanted a New Town at Hook, in Hampshire, planning a compact settlement designated for universal car ownership and complete pedestrian segregation, but Hampshire County Council preferred major town-expansion schemes at Andover and Basingstoke, and the proposal failed to come to fruition. The new generation therefore began at Skelmersdale (1961), inland from Liverpool and

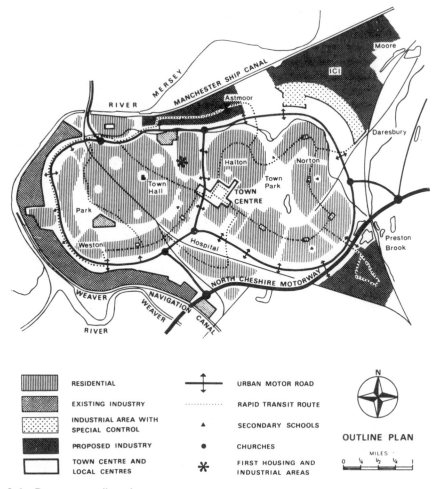

	RESIDENTIAL		URBAN MOTOR ROAD
	EXISTING INDUSTRY		RAPID TRANSIT ROUTE
	INDUSTRIAL AREA WITH SPECIAL CONTROL	▲	SECONDARY SCHOOLS
	PROPOSED INDUSTRY	●	CHURCHES
	TOWN CENTRE AND LOCAL CENTRES	✳	FIRST HOUSING AND INDUSTRIAL AREAS

OUTLINE PLAN

MILES

6.4 Runcorn: outline plan

Southport, already with a population of 10,000, designated for the relief of North Merseyside. Dawley (1963), later expanded and renamed Telford, situated between Wolverhampton and Shrewsbury, was to accommodate pressure from the West Midlands, but it also served the purpose of tidying up the old mining and industrial area of Oakengates and Wellington. Redditch (1964), a flourishing old town in its own right, became the second and last New Town for the Midlands. Runcorn (1964), another sizeable township of 28,000 population, followed for Merseyside and in the same year Washington largely filled in the gap between South Tyneside and Sunderland.

A further phase of New Town designation ensued, with designations for substantially increased target population figures to a quarter of a million or more. Milton Keynes (1967) embraced the existing settlements of Bletchley, Stony Stratford, Wolverton and New Bradwell, in addition to 13 villages; the constellation neatly filled in the North Buckinghamshire area between London and Birmingham. Peterborough (1967), where three townships each of 20,000–30,000 population have been developed to the west of the cathedral city, and Northampton (1968) also thicken up this previously relatively empty part of England. Warrington (1968) was another addition for Merseyside where three areas of publicly owned, derelict land were available: an RAF recruiting station (Padgate), an American Air Base (Burtonwood) and a Royal Ordinance factory (Risley). Finally for England, a proposal for Ipswich being withdrawn, Central Lancashire New Town (1970) had a designated area of 55 square miles, embracing Preston, Chorley and Leyland.

In Wales, Newtown (1967) was a small proposal situated between Birmingham and Aberystwyth, intended to revitalize mid-Wales. For South Wales, Llantrisant had already received the Royal Mint, but its New Town designation was withdrawn. In Northern Ireland, Craigavon, Antrim, Ballymena and Londonderry were all designated between 1965 and 1969, following the Belfast Regional Survey and Plan carried out for Stormont by Professor Robert Matthew (Murie, 1973).

In Scotland, Livingstone (1962), 15 miles west of Edinburgh, but basically for Glasgow overspill, was intended to create a new focus of industrial activity in the East Central belt. Irvine (1966), located in the west between Ayr and Glasgow, offered hopes of industrial expansion based on the old town. Stonehouse, also for Glasgow, was designated in 1972, but after the building of the first houses, was aborted in 1976: a vivid illustration of a change in priorities, for resources were to be channelled into the renewal of inner Glasgow (the Glasgow Eastern Area Renewal – GEAR – scheme). The advent of the inner city debate meant the end of New Town designations for the foreseeable future.

Britain has 28 New Towns, therefore, created for a variety of different purposes, of varying population sizes and environmental design. Their distinctive features have been chronicled (with evident pride) by Schaffer (1970) and Evans (1972); the first because, as a civil servant, he had been much associated with the programme, the second because it was written for the Town and Country Planning Association, long the champions of planned dispersal. When first designated, the areas already had a population of 945,000; now they contain rather more than 2 millions. Hence they have only contributed in a limited way to post-war housing, but they have been a major feature of a commitment to planned decentralization, even though, as Aldridge (1979) concludes, by the end it was a programme without a policy. Various factors conspired to maintain the momentum of the New Towns, once launched by Silkin; they became significant contributors to housing programmes and then effective instruments in promoting regional development.

We cannot leave this section on New Towns and town development without reference to green belts, which give shape to redistribution policies and concepts of 'containing' urban Britain. The green belt has been a popular subject for academic observers (Mandelker, 1962; Thomas, 1970; Munton, 1983; and Elson, 1986) and there is little new to be said. Promoted nationally by ministerial circular in 1955, approved belts now cover nearly 11 per cent of England, an area similar to that devoted to urban development, and greater than is covered by either National Parks or Areas of Outstanding Natural Beauty. This is the legacy of Howard's Social City, other similar advocacy at the turn of the century, and Unwin's and Abercrombie's Plans for London.

Green belts were made feasible by the land use planning system established by the Town and Country Planning Act, 1947: local authorities were obliged to prepare development plans showing land use allocations and, because of the compensation provisions, green belts could be included at no direct cost to local authorities. The threat of peripheral urban development on a huge scale persuaded Duncan Sandys (Minister of Housing and Local Government) to issue Circular 42 in August 1955 asking planning authorities outside London to consider establishing clearly defined green belts – issued apparently against the advice of senior civil servants, who took the view that while the designation of green belts was easy, the real problem was where development *should* be located. Thirty years on, this remains a pertinent question, but in the meantime the limits of urban development have been rigorously held in check by this planning device. By 1963 the first round of green belt submissions had been vetted by the Ministry and controls were in operation around most of our major cities. Over the next six years green belts fell out of ministerial favour, but rehabilitation followed in 1970. Today, major green belts surround the main conurbations of Birmingham–Coventry, West Yorkshire and South Yorkshire, Greater Manchester, Merseyside, Cheshire and South-east Lancashire and, of course, London; elsewhere sizeable green belts have been approved for North-east Lancashire, South-east Dorset, Bristol–Bath, Tyneside, Nottingham–Derby, Oxford, Stoke, Luton–Dunstable, Cambridge and Cheltenham–Gloucester.

Aesthetic control

As with legislation in 1909 and 1932, the Town and Country Planning Act, 1947, gave powers to local authorities to control development in terms of its appearance, and its siting in relation to its surroundings. There was little elaboration as to how this was to be achieved, save occasional guidance notes; otherwise there was reliance on the all-embracing, but rather vague idea of protecting 'amenity' (Punter, 1987). But development in post-war Britain would be on a rather firmer footing.

The redevelopment of central areas (1946) gave to the new planning authorities a fresh kit of tools, including use-classes, plot ratios, daylight factors, sight lines and parking standards. The *Housing manual 1944* was one of a series giving guidance on new housing followed by the *Manual* of 1949 and *Houses* (1952). They helped to popularize, particularly in the first generation New Towns, a brick-and-tile vernacular architecture which evolved from a Scandinavian style, eminently suitable for standard components and standard layouts set by cost targets. A compendium design guide came with *Design in town and village* (1953): Thomas Sharp wrote on the English village, Frederick Gibberd on the design of residential areas and William Holford on design in city centres.

'Design' meant the arrangement of the various parts of a developed area – buildings, roads, spaces – so that they functioned properly, could be built economically and gave pleasure to look at and be in. In other words, it was appreciated that the appearance of an area develops from its function and the way it is built; it is not something which is applied afterwards. Civic design was as much concerned with the spaces between buildings as with the appearance of the buildings themselves, and the same held for the design of residential areas. To quote Holford in *Design in town and village*:

> The designer's task is to seek out the local or regional or metropolitan character of a place and show how it can be extended and intensified by means of new buildings and landscape, street furniture and pavings, town planning and civic decoration.   MHLG (p. 120)

Holford saw design as a social art, a view which encouraged the impression that the designer within the town planning profession, if not the profession as a whole, was really the grand integrator of the fashioning of the built environment.

The prototype and test-bed for the new approach was to been seen first in some of the New Towns, particularly Harlow, where the design of the neighbourhood units provided a classic model to follow. A little later it appeared in city-scale work, as at Coventry where the axial shopping mall, exploiting its fall in levels to provide two tiers of shops, made a striking feature. Elsewhere, local authority treatment could descend to little more than fashionable mediocrity. As Esher (1981) reminds us: 'the monuments of that era, Plymouth and Exeter, Bristol and Hull, with their shopping boulevards and bowls of flowers and shrubby roundabouts and patterned paving and utility brick or Portland stone facades, dated very rapidly' (p. 45).

Evidence of design capability was limited. The special issue of the *Architectural Review* in 1955, entitled 'Outrage', written by Ian Nairn, strongly attacked the visual products of planning. He was particularly severe on the fragmentation of planning control as exercised by a variety of planning authorities, their insensitive reliance on planning standards and by-law regulation, and also the failures of advertisement control. The theme continued in the issue of the *Architectural Review* entitled 'Counter Attack', published in 1957, this time highlighting those agents and elements exempted from aesthetic control. At the same time it gave encouragement to local amenity groups to press for improvements.

The Ministry of Housing and Local Government responded to architectural pressure by setting up an Urban Planning Group within the Ministry, which proceeded to produce a series of planning bulletins in the early 1960s to update advice on town-centre redevelopment. Meanwhile, Gordon Cullen in a popular book, *The concise townscape* (1961), showed the fun and drama to be had from the way towns and cities actually looked, popularizing the word 'townscape' as the art of giving visual coherence and organization to the jumble of buildings, streets and spaces that make up the urban environment.

If public regulation and control could not achieve success, then perhaps the lobby and pressure of special interest groups might. The founding of the Victorian Society in 1959 reflected the growing anxiety about the destruction of nineteenth-century buildings, but the earlier founding of the Civic Trust in 1957 as an independent charity to promote the development of public taste and awareness for better design suggested an even broader concern, that of urban conservation. Duncan Sandys' initiative in creating this body (not without some alarm expressed by his senior officials in the Ministry of Housing and Local Government) was soon to pay dividends, because it directly fostered the subsequent founding of a large number of local societies (1,200, ultimately by the mid-1980s). Many of these became directly involved in local conservation or planning issues: promotional as in the Magdalene Street 'face-lift' at Norwich in 1959, or confrontational in many battles connected with redevelopment schemes.

Duncan Sandys was to figure again, this time in promoting a Private Members' Bill, which came to the statute book as the Civic Amenities Act, 1967. This advocated the idea of the conservation of coherent areas of townscape, rather than simply the preservation of individual buildings: from negative control to creative promotion. The Act provided for the designation of conservation areas, and this proved a popular initiative by those many local authorities which contained areas of special architectural or historic interest. A higher standard of planning control could be applied to these designated areas, with special consideration given to the height and bulk of buildings, materials, colours, vertical or horizontal emphasis and the grain of design.

But outside these specially protected areas concern mounted at the architectural ravages of commercial development, particularly in association with new highway requirements. The redevelopment of Piccadilly Circus became a major *cause célèbre* in the 1950s and 1960s (Cherry and Penny, 1986). In 1952 Jack Cotton, a Birmingham property developer, bought the Cafe Monico on the north side of the Circus; the LCC owned the adjacent site of Piccadilly Mansions. A deal was struck whereby the LCC obtained part of the Monico site for road improvements; Cotton would have permission to redevelop. He was persuaded to buy up the remaining freeholds of the Monico block in order to promote an acceptable redevelopment scheme; this took shape as a podium, a tall block and a large advertisement panel. At Cotton's press conference in October 1959 the drawings exhibited showed an advertisment 100 ft in height for an imaginary soft drink, reading 'Snap Plom for Vigour'. To many this brashness spoke volumes about the form which urban redevelopment was taking. A public inquiry lasted 18 days; the Inspector (Colin Buchanan) recommended against and in May 1960 the Minister issued his decision rejecting the application. The Piccadilly Inquiry in many ways was a turning point in confirming the frailty of the planning system in dealing with the aesthetics of a major proposal of this kind. But perhaps worse was to come, because for many years the redevelopment of the Circus dragged on indecisively through revised traffic calculations, and scheme after scheme was prepared afresh.

Throughout the country the property boom (Marriott, 1967) of the fifties and sixties, posed a set of new challenges for aesthetic control, and has continued to do so since. In effect, it spelled the demise, short-lived though it was, of the practice of comprehensive civic design by local authorities. In principle, a working system for the effective regulation of the new build-ings and environments in schemes of planned redevelopment had promised so much, but the cultured hand of the architect planners, working in a consensus situation where good manners and taste would prevail, proved unequal to the task; commercial brashness and greed proved too strong. London became a 'paper metropolis' as office construction changed the skyline of the City; and all major towns experienced a demand for shops, offices, hotels and entertainment complexes in a central area investment scramble. Office building, in fact, became a feature of strategic location policy. The Location of Offices Bureau, set up in 1963, was a public agency given the task of persuading the business community that office dispersal from London was to its advantage. Briefly, office development permits were required for new offices in London. The Bureau was closed down in 1979 and an interesting experiment in State control over the geography of office location came to an end (Manners and Morris, 1986).

Perhaps it was with a sense of relief that local authorities turned to a more manageable problem in the 1970s: a new approach to the control of residential areas. This was highlighted by Essex County Council's *Design guide for residential areas* (1973), with a format that was followed, if not exactly copied, by a host of other authorities throughout the country.

To conclude this section, it is clear that the approaches to aesthetic control in post-war urban Britain began well, though they soon attracted the hostility first of architects and then of the lay public. The new scale of architecture has since posed insuperable problems; and the earlier view that town planning could provide a protective shield of refinement over new development and so avoid the brash, the banal and the ugly, was not to be. Esher (1981) has suggested that Britain has experienced three 'Rebuilds': the Enlightenment, the Industrial Revolution and the Welfare State: 'fashioned by wartime social democrats in England, which would for the first time in history build cities that were not dramatizations of privi-lege and poverty' (p. 278). He goes on:

the Third Rebuild turns out to have been as essential, as submissive to politi-cal and financial circumstances, as its predecessors. And like them it has no end, dissolving into a new period, taken over by a new generation . . . which

welcomes the unemphatic, the intimate and the affectionate as the creative
product of our limitations.   (p. 297)

Transport

From the point of view of highway planning the post-war period began with
the Ministry of War Transport's Report *Design and layout of roads in
built-up areas* (1946). The general principles of the road patterns, earlier
enunciated by Alker Tripp, and demonstrated in strategic form by
Abercrombie for Greater London as a gigantic cartwheel of spokes and
ring roads, with several rims, were accepted. Holden and Holford's City of
London Plan put the seal on the principles of precinct planning and the
canalization of traffic, crucial aspects of redevelopment which were soon
to be seen in Coventry, Plymouth and elsewhere.

But the simple mix of ring roads, precincts and a general improvement in
the design of road junctions, and an adherence to standard highway
widths, building lines and sight-lines did not prove adequate for long,
although it was not until the 1960s that the opportunities for a radical
revision of policy and method were presented. Traffic volumes soon rose
after the war, and in 1949 the number of motor cars in use once more
exceeded 2 million, the 1939 figure. By 1957 this figure had doubled to 4
million and by 1961 had trebled to 6 million. The motor age had arrived and
by the end of the 1950s one and a quarter million new vehicles were being
registered every year. A planner, Colin Buchanan, who during the 1950s
had had somewhat of a chequered career as an inspector in the Ministry of
Town and Country Planning (Bruton, 1981), argued that a new situation
had arisen which called for a fresh approach.

> A single invention, in the course of a few years' development, has placed
> within the grasp of every man and woman a means of rapid *personal* move-
> ment ten to twenty times faster than walking. Suddenly, at a stroke, the
> familiar arrangements of buildings, streets and footways that have endured
> so long as to seem unchangeable, are jerked out of date as people race and
> jostle in the streets in their newfound mobility. It is not a matter of building a
> few new roads, it is a matter of dealing with a new social situation.
>
> (Buchanan, 1958, p. 207)

Buchanan saw that new urban arrangements were needed unless the new
mobility were surrendered or drastically restrained.

But it took some time before any clear view emerged as to what these new
arrangements should be. In the meantime there was no great political
thrust for change, and in any case public expenditure restraints were
tight. The ten-year road plan announced in 1946 by Alfred Barnes, Minister of Transport, which sought a comprehensive reconstruction of principal national routes, with 800 miles of motorways, was soon abandoned
with enforced financial cutbacks. During the 1950s pressure for road
improvements mounted; the British Roads Federation, which represented
road construction interests, joined forces with professional lobbies, motor
manufacturers and traders, while the TUC aligned with the employers'

associations for more spending. The culmination was that in 1957 the then Minister of Transport, Harold Watkinson, announced a programme of large projects: the motorway age had arrived. In the first batch, the Preston by-pass (1958) and the Lancaster and Maidstone by-passes (1960) formed not only part of the national motorway pattern but also constituted important local features in the urban environment. Over the next few years the planning of urban motorways had considerable impact on the metropolitan areas of the West Midlands, Greater Manchester, Merseyside and Greater Glasgow, and the M4, snaking across West London, was the longest road viaduct in Europe. Later, with the construction of the M25 as an orbital route around London, Abercrombie's outer ring had come to fruition.

Basically, however, British cities 'got by' for a surprisingly long time. The conventional wisdom about 'ring and spoke' road patterns survived, as indicated by the commencement of Birmingham's inner ring road (Smallbrook Ringway) in 1957. Traffic flows generally speeded up as highway improvements were carried out and congestion spots, often alleged to be caused by fixed-track trams, were removed. During the 1950s British urban roads managed to carry heavy and patently increasing traffic volumes through a variety of incremental schemes. The Road Traffic Act, 1956, permitted the installation of parking meters in spite of vigorous opposition from the roads lobby. (The then Minister, Boyd Carpenter, only secured his Bill because he promised to use the proceeds from the meters for the provision of new off-street car parks.) The Roads and Road Improvement Act, 1960, introduced the traffic warden, with new penalties for parking offences, in the context of an unresolved debate about road pricing: payment for road space in the interests of rationalizing the use of roads. New traffic management schemes were introduced, including an extension of one-way systems, restrictions over right-hand turns, and the no-entry box junction. Additionally, through development control powers, the granting of planning permission for buildings was made conditional upon provision of parking spaces, particularly significant for central area commercial development.

Buchanan's call for a new approach was timely, when a new political opportunity opened up. Ernest Marples became Minister of Transport and succeeded in establishing a new level of priority for road and transport matters. In 1961 he set up a working group, in the Ministry, 'to study the long term development of roads and traffic in urban areas and their influence on the urban environment'; the leader was Colin Buchanan. A steering group, chaired by Sir Geoffrey Crowther (and including among its members Sir William Holford), was appointed to act alongside it and to give an independent opinion on the recommendations of the study group, as they emerged.

The Buchanan Report, *Traffic in towns* was published in 1963, attended by extensive publicity; it proved to be one of the major planning documents of the decade. The general principle was established in terms of societal choice:

> The broad message of our report in that there are absolute limits to the amount of traffic that can be accepted in towns, depending on their size and

density, but up to those limits, provided a civilised environment is to be retained or created, the level of vehicular accessibility a town can have depends on its readiness to accept and pay for the physical changes required. The choice is society's. But it will not be sensible, nor indeed for long be possible, for society to go on investing apparently unlimited sums in the purchase and running of motor vehicles without investing equivalent sums in the proper accommodation of the traffic that results.   (para. 44)

Buchanan's study group recommended two kinds of roads: distributors designed for movement and access roads to serve buildings. Overall, there would be a hierarchical network of primary, district and local distributors, linked, in urban areas, by an urban motorway system. This network permitted the concept of environmental areas, seen not as homogeneous precincts (as in Tripp's model of 20 years earlier) but as 'rooms', of mixed use if necessary, in a town where it was important to maintain the quality of environment. In these areas there would be little vehicle penetration, allowing primacy of movement to the pedestrian. Case studies of alternative schemes were prepared for settlements of different sizes and conditions: Newbury, Norwich, Leeds and Central London. The term 'traffic architecture' was coined to capture the idea of building and circulation systems designed together as a single, comprehensive process, albeit with huge cost implications. In order to implement the recommendations, it was suggested that development plans in urban areas should be supplemented by transportation plans, which would assess the main movement needs in the future and show how these would be shared by various forms of transport, including the car. Public transport policies were required; there should be a comprehensive parking policy; and urban traffic flows should be regulated in a scheme of total traffic management.

The Buchanan Report showed what sort of cities were needed and how to get them. It outlined a set of principles and indicated how they would work in particular instances. A new approach to central area redevelopment was implied if the argument was accepted, that if we were to have any chance of living with the car, then a different type of city was needed. The steering committee urged that the traffic problem should be met 'without confusion over purpose, without timidity over means, and above all without delay' (para 55).

In fact, wholesale reconstruction on the lines advocated by Buchanan's comprehensive approach has not been followed. Costs proved horrendous and design implications frightening; plans for Piccadilly Circus foundered in the 1960s with continuing uncertainty about estimates of anticipated traffic flows. The major cities engaged in a series of land use transportation studies, but pragmatism prevailed, with interest shown in opportunities offered by new transport technology such as new fixed-track systems. There was a general recognition that different cities could tackle the competing needs of cars and public transport in a variety of different ways. World-wide differences in approach could be seen, but British cities (notably London) came to reply on a strategy of traffic limitations. This implied vigorous control of parking in the centre, high-capacity rail links to the suburbs, an efficient rail-based distribution system within the centre, bus-priority measures for short-distance distribution, and a general strategy of decentralization to sub-centres. The link between urban form and transport was never clearer, but realizable solutions seemed as far away as ever. Glasgow, Liverpool, Newcastle and Leeds pressed on with their extensive highway systems, but other cities abandoned them and by the mid-1970s an urban road policy in the context of an explicit town planning framework was stood on its head. Urban road construction took a back seat as new interest was shown in restrictions on existing road usage, possibilities of upgrading public transport (as suggested by the introduction of the metro for Tyne–Wear), and policies on subsidized fares.

In a sense, however, the problem identified by Buchanan may have passed. The working group forecast 19 million cars (27 million vehicles) on British roads by 1980 and 30 million cars (40 million vehicles) by 2010. In 1963 there had been 10.5 million vehicles, so what was involved was a doubling within 10 years and nearly a trebling within 20 years. This forecast rate of increase simply did not materialize, and once again British cities got by with incremental adjustments, while an accelerated process of decentralization helped to transfer traffic flows from the centre to a series of nodes within the city region.

The other factor was public opinion, and pressure from opposition groups began to mount. Concrete flyovers, wholesale clearance for new routes, and concern over noise and lead pollution, were seen as affronts to living conditions; in the environmentally conscious 1970s new highway planning became politically beleaguered. There were furious debates in respect of schemes for Oxford and Bath, but the biggest single reversal of policy concerned London, where for many years three ringways had been in mind. Ringway One was an inner ring road running largely through working-class areas of housing stress. Ringways Two and Three threatened the middle-class outer suburbs. Ringway Two fell from favour and Ringway Three was replaced by the Orbital M25. Ringway One remained; dubbed as the 'London Motorway Box', it attracted hostility from the anti-roads lobby and the Inner London Boroughs. The Heath government fell in 1974 and the Box largely fell at the same time. High inflation rates in the early period of the Wilson government settled it: new primary roads for London could not be afforded. Radical urban restructuring involving major highway schemes was at an end.

Regional strategies

Britain's pursuit of regional economic policies since the war, which by 'stick and carrot' incentives have steered or, more likely, encouraged forms of economic development to the disadvantaged regions, have had an indirect effect of the physical environment of many towns and cities. Trading estates have been laid out, factories built and resources in unspecified ways recirculated as investment for related development. Other policies too have had significance for towns in regions which have benefited, as, for example, from New Town and town-expansion programmes, motorway building and aid to particular industries such as coal, textiles and shipbuilding.

Regional strategies in a direct land use planning sense have contributed to urban change in selected areas. The spirit of decentralization policies, first outlined as a national principle in the Barlow Report (1940) and then made explicit in Abercrombie's *Greater London Plan 1944*, has been maintained. For some time the advisory plans for London, the West Midlands and the Clyde Valley sufficed, the belief being that the development plans would fill in the detail and provide working arrangements to secure the intended redistributive objectives. But the regional thrust lost ground, symbolically with the closure of the Ministry's regional offices after 1954.

A new awareness of regional questions emerged in the early 1960s as land use pressures mounted: a substantial rise in numbers of both population and households was forecast; the numbers of vehicles on the roads was rising fast; countryside pressures on recreation sites was being felt; and (as an immediate problem) the cities ran out of housing land within their boundaries. New strategies for regional distribution were called for, and a fresh interest in the regions was shown by Whitehall. A Northern Housing Office of the Ministry was opened in 1962 and a year later a Newcastle regional office was set up, with both housing and planning functions.

A stream of regional studies followed throughout the 1960s and into the 1970s. The first was *The south-east study* (1964) which put forward broad-based regional proposals covering the period to 1981 of a kind not seen since the end of the war. The White Paper, *London-Employment: Housing: Land* (Cmnd 1952, 1963) had explained:

> The Government recognize that the need to match jobs, land, transport and housing over the next 20 years in London and South East England calls for a regional plan . . . The regional study is examining the growth and movement of population in the South East, including overspill from London, and related employment and transport questions. It will examine the need for a second generation of new and expanded towns which would provide both houses and work for Londoners, well away from London itself, and draw off some of the pressure on the capital.

The scene was set. Whereas Barlow and Abercrombie had assumed that the problem was *distribution* of population and employment; the issue for the 1960s was also *growth*.

The south east study, 20 years after Abercrombie, proved a major restatement. A population increase of about 3.5 million was forecast in the South-east in the period 1961–81, just over 1 million of which would be from net inward migration, the remainder in the form of natural increase. The heart of the strong population growth lay in London itself and an over-spill of about 1 million people was expected. Since London was not able to accommodate its own natural increase, it meant that the whole of the 3.5 million population growth had to be found elsewhere – a population increase of well over a third for the area outside London.

The problem was compounded by employment growth in London. Over the seven years 1955–62 the average annual increase in jobs in the London conurbation was 42,000; over the next three years, 1959–62, the average increase amounted to over 63,000. The 300,000 extra jobs created over the seven-year period was in proportional terms close to the rate of employment growth in England and Wales, but for the South-east as a whole the rate was much higher. The region was booming, particularly in service employment, where 80 per cent of the additional jobs had been found.

Housing, transport and locational problems were clearly of great magnitude, the greatest pressures of land shortage being felt on the periphery, where encroachments into the green belt were likely to be strongly resisted. A strategy of developing centres of growth, alternative to and well clear of London was selected, to be achieved in two ways. Local planning authorities would have to allocate much more land in their development plans in order to accommodate well over 2 million additional population by 1981. For the remainder, between 1 million and 1.25 million, a second generation of new and expanded towns was advocated, on a much bigger scale than those then being built (see page 165). Major cities might develop in the Southampton–Portsmouth area, around Bletchley and around Newbury. New Towns might be built at Ashford and Stansted. Large-scale town-expansion schemes could be based on Ipswich, Northampton, Peterborough and Swindon. Additions could be made to existing New Towns around London, particularly Stevenage and Harlow, but also at Basildon, Crawley and Hemel Hempstead, and also to a dozen other towns in the South-east, all of which offered scope for an expansion of at least 30,000 population: Aylesbury, Banbury, Bedford, Chelmsford, Colchester, Hastings, Maidstone, Medway Towns, Norwich, Poole, Reading and Southend.

This major statement concerning the regional distribution of urban growth was followed by two other studies, published by the newly formed, but short-lived Department of Economic Affairs: *The West Midlands* (1965) and *The North West* (1965), the latter accompanied by an appendix, *The problems of Merseyside*. They were largely concerned with population and household predictions over the period to 1981 and the possibilities that existed for redistribution.

In England and Wales the regional initiative passed partly to the newly established Regional Economic Planning Councils. They proceeded with great energy to produce their own regional reports, though long before their demise in 1979 they had lost their force, located in no-man's land between central and local government. Nonetheless between 1966 and 1974, 16 reports of regional significance were published, covering whole regions (sometimes twice) and parts of regions. But, in addition, the Central Unit for Environmental Planning (within the Ministry) published feasibility studies for Humberside (1969) and Severnside (1971) and there were various reports by consultants, for example Buchanan's *South Hampshire study* (1966). The minister, Richard Crossman, set up sub-regional studies, conducted by joint teams from local authorities, as in the *Coventry–Solihull–Warwickshire study* (1971). The South-east Joint Planning Team published reports in 1970, (*Strategic plan for the South East*), and 1976, (*Strategy for the South East*), and elsewhere in the country regional strategy teams worked in particular areas.

In Scotland, a survey and plan for the Lothians (1966) was followed by a similar study for Grangemouth–Falkirk (1968); expansion plans for the Central Borders (1968) and Tayside (1970) were followed by a strategy for South-west Scotland (also 1970) and a West-central Scotland Plan (1974). In Wales, Deeside (1970) and Mid-Wales (1973) were the subject of regional reports. In Northern Ireland, the Belfast Regional Survey and Plan (1963), prepared by consultant Robert Matthew, adopted the general redistributive policies over a city-region scale for overspill population to satellite centres; it was updated and revised by Stormont's own *Regional physical development strategy* (1975).

The growth phase came to an end, though population and employment dispersal continued, and the period of the regional planning reports was concluded. In areas of extreme pressure, notably outer metropolitan London, housebuilders' associations continue to complain that insufficient land has been allocated to meet housing demands. The London and South East Regional Planning Conference (SERPLAN) regularly monitor trends and it seems likely that an adequate supply of building land is available, but only on the basis of five-year forecasts. In the meantime proposals have been submitted for private-sector mini New Towns in the green belt around London and beyond. The regional question has degenerated into *ad hoc* regional study – on-going analysis of the demand–supply equation for land release. The time seems ripe to move again from regional study to regional plan: analysis to prescription, particularly in view of the impact of the Channel Tunnel.

The inner city question

For one reason or another the inner city has always been a target for public regulation and control. In the nineteenth century the problem was ill-health, sanitation, poor housing, overcrowding and social disorder; between the wars it was diet, hygiene and the slums; in the mid 1960s it had become deprivation; a current thread throughout was an unfit dwelling stock and environmental disadvantage. After the war, city plans promised reform through housing programmes and a coordinated approach to land-use planning. It was believed that continued high rates of building construction and enlightened social welfarism would produce a trickle-down effect to gradually remove all residual problems.

The 1961 Census presented small-area statistics for the first time, repeated at a 10 per cent sample for 1966. By 1971 the facts of central area deprivation were clear enough and a set of disjointed and somewhat tentative initiatives in the older, inner parts of our big cities unfolded (Home, 1982). The Local Government Act, 1966, gave grants to local authorities with substantial numbers of Commonwealth immigrants, to be spent on such matters as education and child care. In 1967–8 Education Priority Areas programmes were specifically area-based and targetted on the inner city and other deprived areas. In 1968 an urban programme was established under the Home Office, and over the years several thousand small-scale projects, put up by local authorities and voluntary organizations, were approved for capital expenditure. The Community

Development Programme (CDP) followed in the period 1969–76, with 12 local projects established in deprived neighbourhoods aimed at new ways of meeting peoples' needs in local communities.

After 1970 the newly created Department of the Environment, under Secretary of State Peter Walker, began to take more of a lead on urban problems, and in 1972 three inner area studies were commissioned: Small Heath, Birmingham; Stockwell, South London; and Liverpool. Consultants' findings were published in one summary form, *Inner area studies: Liverpool, Birmingham and Lambeth* (1977). It emphasized the problem of housing and jobs, but beyond looking at forms of area management and pleas for much financial help, the reports did not give all that clear a lead on policy. In 1972–3 three pilot projects covering Sunderland, Oldham and Rotherham had earlier looked at the issues concerned with a 'total approach' to urban management.

In retrospect, this was a highly creative period, when the politics of urban changes were very much in flux (McKay and Cox, 1979); the initiatives were largely ineffective except in as much that the period paved the way for the legislation, and the further, more focused action, that followed. The resolution of economic and social problems in the context of housing policy and land planning failed to materialize in any comprehensive sense. A search was in progress for new forms of intervention in the environment, the objectives being social, economic and institutional, and the traditional armoury of statutory town planning seemed weak, if not irrelevant. However, in practice, local authority planning staffs were increasingly involved in inner city planning, particularly with housing schemes, renewal projects and the chairing and coordination of multi-departmental teams.

The reasons for Government initiative in this area, however disjointed during this period 1966–77, are rather obscure. Prime Minister Wilson may have borrowed the idea of President Johnson's Poverty Programme in the USA; the Wilson government may have also found it both easy and necessary to respond to an admittedly wayward Conservative politician, Enoch Powell, and his inflammatory exclamations on the prospect of racial conflict. There was certainly the influence of pressure groups such as Shelter (representing the homeless and badly housed) and Child Poverty Action Group. But it seems more likely that on this occasion a handful of key politicians and civil servants actually took the lead; Peter Walker at the Department of the Environment (DOE) and Robert Carr, Home Secretary (the Home Office set up the Urban Deprivation Unit in 1972), were clearly influential, and Derek Morrell was a key official over CDP in the Home Office.

The Government White Paper, *Policy for the inner cities* (1977, Cmnd 6845) proposed to revamp existing inner city programmes, transfer Home Office initiatives to the DOE and expand the programme brief to include not only social projects but also industrial, environmental and recreational matters. Funding for the urban programme was to be significantly increased. Special local/central government 'partnerships' were to be set up in the larger cities to supervise the implementation of programmes. In Scotland special help was proposed, including further support for the

Glasgow Eastern Area Renewal project. The White Paper represented an important policy shift; dispersal policies, pre-eminent for 30 years were now secondary to a switch of resources to inner areas.

The White Paper was followed by the Inner Urban Areas Act, 1978. It gave additional powers to local authorities with severe inner area problems and the provisions only applied to three types of designated districts. First, there were districts containing special areas: these were the partnership areas in Birmingham, London (seven Boroughs: Greenwich, Hackney, Islington, Lambeth, Lewisham, Newham, Southwark and Tower Hamlets), Liverpool, Manchester, Salford, Newcastle upon Tyne and Gateshead. Second, there were the districts containing Inner Area Programmes: the Programme Authority Areas in a further 15 authorities in England. A third category simply covered other districts in 14 authorities in England and five in Wales. (The Act did not apply to Scotland, which followed its own procedures for extensive housing renewal and had the show-piece of the Glasgow Eastern Area Renewal (GEAR) project to show for it). But in England and Wales a total of 48 designated areas had new powers to make loans and grants for industrial building (economic regeneration soon became the most important feature) and to declare improvement areas. The partnership areas soon attracted most attention because of the joint administrative arrangements which were required between central and local government. No such partnership arrangements extended to the second category of districts, though they were invited to draw up programmes; in the case of the third category, local authorities simply made use of the powers of the Act.

The years since the 1978 Act have seen a succession of inner city initiatives. New programme authorities and designated districts have been announced. The machinery of the partnerships has been simplified. There is greater emphasis on the role of the private sector in schemes for inner-city revival, as reflected in the setting up of two Urban Development Corporations in 1981 (London Docklands and Merseyside) and the introduction of the Urban Development Grant in 1982 as a lever to private investment. Four more Urban Development Corporations have been announced: at Trafford Park (Greater Manchester), Teesside, the West Midlands and Tyne and Wear. Successful garden festivals have been held in Liverpool (1984), Stoke (1986) and Glasgow (1988). Tourism potential is being realized and a variety of local economic initiatives have been established.

Enterprise Zones were introduced in two rounds (1981 and 1983), enabling legislation being provided by the Local Government, Planning and Land Act, 1980. A planning agreement is prepared by the local authority concerned, with aims to simplify statutory planning controls; this agreement is then complemented by a number of financial aid provisions with a primary emphasis on tax relief. The general idea behind them was that they would provide a setting for vigorous entrepreneurs, capable of generating an industrial renaissance. The sites selected were largely vacant and under-used; the lower Swansea Valley was formerly heavily polluted by mineral-processing industries, and elsewhere the closure of major manufacturing plants created large and unoccupied sites. Now with 27 designated sites, with representation in all the countries of the United

Kingdom, but none bigger than 900 acres in size, they were unlikely to do that, but derelict land and buildings have been brought back to productive use and new jobs have been created.

Returning specifically to inner city matters, the urban programme now constitutes the major thrust of planning policy for environmental recovery, but it has long since over-ridden traditional procedures in schemes for housing and redevelopment. The inner city partnerships prepare annual inner area programmes, on a rolling three-year basis which is agreed by a partnership committee, chaired by a Department of the Environment Minister. The committee includes representatives of local authorities, health authorities, Government departments and the voluntary and private sector. Considerable resources are now channelled to the partnerships each year. The programme authorities and the designated districts receive smaller allocations. Each partnership authority has a different spending pattern, but overall expenditure on social projects such as recreation and personal social services accounts for rather more than two-fifths of the total; that on economic projects, such as site works, accounts for about a third; and that on environmental projects, such as restoration of derelict land and housing, for a quarter.

Recent approaches to inner city renewal have relied very heavily on institutional innovations and tighter targeting of expenditure patterns. Some of the work carried out is directly related to housing and the appearance of the physical environment, and therefore very much in the traditional planning scope. But much of the activity is now broadly economic and social; just where town planning, in the sense established during the post-war years, now actually begins and ends is questionable. The search for comprehensive solutions to complex urban problems has once again defied disciplinary and professional boundaries. Town planning as we know it today was created out of the initiatives taken to tackle the problems of the late Victorian city, particularly its housing and environmental inequalities; the late twentieth-century urban crisis is once again calling for a re-assembly of skills and methods of approach which cut across established ways of doing things. In this situation 'making plans' becomes a very different exercise.

7 Reflections

On the past

In reviewing the planned changes introduced into the urban environment in Britain, as a consequence of successive measures of urban regulation over a period of 150 years, we have trodden ground frequently tilled by other workers. Available texts are plentiful and naturally varied. Some have presented developments over two centuries as essentially one story (Cherry, 1972; Lawless and Brown, 1986), unfolding chronologically and content to highlight processes of change; Hohenberg and Lees (1985) provide a European context. More usually, however, partial selectivity has prevailed, to permit greater detail in a thematic approach: Ashworth (1954) focused on the nineteenth-century origins of town planning, while Hall (1974) and Ravetz (1986) have considered twentieth-century developments in general, and Whitehand (1987) the relationship between planning and processes of development. More specifically, the turn of the century was the concern of Sutcliffe (1981). Post-1945 developments have occasioned several reviews: for example, a general commentary on town planning in modern society (Ravetz, 1980), a critique of city rebuilding (Esher, 1983), and a study of public policy (McKay and Cox, 1979). More general works have considered particular subjects: changes in architecture, design and townscape (for example Burke, 1976); also housing (notably Burnett, 1978), and transport (Dyos and Aldcroft, 1969; Kellett, 1969). Certain cities have been explored, including London (Olsen, 1976; Young and Garside, 1982), Glasgow (Checkland, 1981), Edinburgh (Hague, 1984), and Cardiff (Daunton, 1977). Twentieth-century topics have included the development of regional cities (Gordon, 1986); the story of New Towns (Osborn and Whittick, 1963; Cullingworth, 1979); the history of the town-planning profession (Cherry, 1974); and the history of ideas (Hall, 1988).

Against this work, our aim, as pursued throughout the previous chapters, has been twofold. First, it has been to construct a synoptic canvas, both to describe and to explain events and developments across the two centuries. The thread of continuity appears in an acknowledgement of the fact that the nature of public intervention in urban affairs, specifically from the point of view of the urban environment, can only be understood in the context of societal change. From this perspective, therefore, our story is in effect the study of the design, spatial structure and use of urban artefacts and space in the British industrial city; this is set against the processes of social and economic change, political and institutional development and technological innovation. This consistent weave throughout the breadth of the canvas offers some explanatory capability for the developments which have occurred. It suggests at least a compass, rather than a series of individual maps, for the traveller in planning history.

The second aim has been to chart the events of the last 150 years from the point of view of State intervention in urban affairs. There is selectivity, therefore, in the story. Our review is not one simply of processes of change, wherever the origins of those processes might be; rather it is an account of how the State (local and central government and public agencies) came to take measures and become involved in the regulation of the environment, giving support to national or community interests against those of the private individual, or property and business considerations. Of course, the State's actions only make sense when seen in context, and background situations are sketched in wherever considered appropriate, but the account is written essentially from this point of view: why, with what objectives, and with what consequences has the State taken progressive measures to determine how and where we should live, what our cities should look like, and how they should function socially and economically.

The result is an exercise in planning history. It is neither urban history, nor art history, nor historical geography, nor political history, nor history of public policy, though it derives much from all these approaches. It is a history of how the State over the last two centuries has come to prescribe standards for urban living conditions, prepare plans and take steps to determine or influence, as far as it is able, the unfolding course of town development, through day to day control and guidance.

Our theme, then, has been the conscious regulation of the environment from the 1830s to the 1980s, and the perspective that of initiatives and responses in public sector intervention, against or on behalf of a range of private and community interests. The chronology which we have presented can be quickly summarized. Beginning with the urban health crisis of the 1830s and 1840s, sanitary improvements through Private Acts and statutory by-laws ensured quality of water, and effective drains and sewers. Later in the century invasion of private property rights brought measures for the demolition and replacement of unfit dwellings. A highly innovative 25 years at the end of the century brought about a new approach to the solution of the problems of the late Victorian city; the question of working-class housing could be answered by new approaches in housing design and spatial distribution. The issue was changed from houses to city form. A statutory planning system was built up from 1909 onwards, based on the practice of plan preparation and the control of private development by local authorities. In the 1940s a vigorous expansion took place with a battery of reconstruction plans; the 1947 Town and Country Planning Act established the statutory basis for dealing with post-war development. Since then, years marked by measured achievement have been followed by a period of uncertainty induced by various factors: public hostility to certain forms of local authority housing practice; a general intellectual apathy or indifference to solutions about urban problems; and, recently, an ideological reversal of sympathies away from the notion of State planning.

Such an over-concise chronology suggests a 'seamless web' of history, neat transitions from one phase to another, and an internal coherence throughout. Far from it; there has been no irreversible line of progress, no inevitable step forward to an enlightened future. There is only one thread of coherence, and that is one which we demonstrate: the public sector hand on the tiller of city development. The State, public agencies and local government have all taken successive steps to intervene in addressing problems of the built environment. It is not possible to detect any conscious long-term strategy for urban affairs, or community interests; only rarely has there been any articulated notion that spatial form might somehow have a relationship with social structures. The State has become a conscious builder, it is true, but its role has been to reflect the interests of others, rather than actually take much of a lead in these matters.

The lessons learned, then, are that the State has, from time to time, slipped into taking powers of public regulation rather than striven to assume them. For much of the time it has been almost an unwilling promoter of public authority; but the steps once taken may soon have seemed irreversible, and a series of events has unfolded, with remarkably little conscious purpose. Bodies interacting with the State, notably the professions or the special-interest groups may have exhibited greater long-term coherence in their work, but that is another matter.

The whole scene of plan making for cities, in which the State has assumed (until recently) an ever-widening frame of reference, has been constantly in flux. The objectives of one set of policies may have won ground, but in a period of subsequent consolidation the ground may have changed and policy taken on quite different objectives. For example, we have seen that in the years following the 1830s Government responded to pressure from medical opinion that housing and related environmental problems were best met by effecting sanitary improvements in towns. Consequently the early motor behind environmental regulation was public health. But by the end of the century the arguments had changed. It was now reasoned that housing and social betterment would best be achieved through environmental improvement. Sanitarianism was taken for granted; environmentalism was then the banner for progress. Attention therefore turned to housing standards which lay beyond the simple criterion of physical fitness: instead, to questions of space, air, orientation and to general facilities. The environment in which the house was situated was now held to be of singular importance: hence the passion for low density, concern over the appearance of dwellings and the setting of open space. The environment would provide conditions conducive to a happier way of life; the social degradation of the slums could be tackled in this way.

Environmentalism held the central argument of the new activity of town planning for nearly half a century, and has re-appeared from time to time since. But the ground changed even before the Second World War. Medical evidence suggested in the 1930s that perhaps the quality of the environment by itself did not necessarily achieve all that much. The real nature of the problem was poverty and low wages which led to dietary deficiency in working-class households wherever they were located; and if the cost of new accommodation in low-density housing estates had the effect of imposing greater pressure on weekly income to the extent that diet was adversely affected, and ill health resulted, then the problem was not really environment but inequality. After 1945, in the context of advances in State welfarism, housing and planning had a more explicit relationship with national policies relating to the redistribution of resources.

The point to stress is that the cautious experiments in the public regulation of the British city in the middle of the nineteenth century, the take-up of municipal socialism and city developments associated with it towards the end of the century, and the broadly welfarist traditions of twentieth-century planning have all mirrored the changing socio-political conditions of the time. Government, after the setting up of the first batch of municipal corporations in 1835, did not unquestioningly embark on measures of health and sanitary reform out of high-minded, abstract philanthropy. Forms of late Victorian urban management did not loftily follow an ordained path from Coketown to Garden City. Twentieth-century town planning was no sole shaft of enlightenment from an apolitical profession. Instead, we do well to acknowledge that public regulation was extended in various forms because a variety of people (largely outside Government, in the first instance) wanted to share the consequences that would flow from it. This is not to deny, and certainly not to disparage, some of the motives: philanthropy, public service, distributive justice, welfare for the disadvantaged and the notion of beautiful cities, but it is to say that we have to place these sources of change in context. Conscious public regulation does not just happen; it is made to happen, by and large by interests that will benefit from them. Our model of explanation therefore might be one of 'reform and response', whereby policies are determined and action taken as a result of pressure, negotiation, bargaining and the formation of alliances. In consequence, the planning of cities has been an uncertain and open-ended affair, bound up with an interplay between competing forces.

The British governmental system is characterized by a capacity to provide periodic responses to demand for reform and innovation, in which there are three interactive elements (Cherry, 1982). First there is the bureaucracy (local government and the civil service), in part unionized and professionalized; overall it is well established and inherently conservative in outlook. Second, there are the active pressure groups who are reformist in nature and therefore challenge and seek to exert leverage on particular issues. Third, there are the elected politicians whose duty it is in a representative democracy to frame policy, take decisions and implement programmes of development.

In this scenario of governance, environmental regulation is unmistakably a political act. It represents the outcome of conflict between competing views. It is in this context that we have seen in earlier chapters the interplay of forces which consecutively has led to measures for urban health reform and sanitary improvements, for housing fitness and standards of accommodation, for low-density suburbs, council estates, New Towns, urban renewal, parks, roads, civic spaces and all the changing ingredients in our urban environment. As a consequence, any particular policy may have demonstrated not so much its own intrinsic merit, but rather the strength of the protagonists in whose interests it was promoted. Over time the protagonists have ranged from individual people of outstanding influence and persuasion (Chadwick, Octavia Hill, Henrietta Barnett, Unwin, Beatrice Webb, Abercrombie, Duncan Sandys and Holford, to name but a few); those representing political power (John Burns and Lewis Silkin, for example); professionals (including doctors, statisticians, architects and planners); those working on behalf of capital and property interests; and community lobbies of many kinds.

It follows that what has been done in the name of environmental regulation (ranging from by-laws, housing projects and planning schemes, to statutory town planning) rests neither on abstract theory, nor on the application of scientific criteria (though scientific norms may be called into play), nor on apolitical, rational grounds (though objectivity may be claimed). Rather, it has rested on value judgements and a sense of political balance as to what people in positions of power consider certain desired objectives to be, and what the chances of attaining those objectives actually are. Plan making is therefore not just a technical activity, it is deeply political in the sense that it derives fundamental legitimacy from values expressed in the community. It also means that plan making is not scientifically fixed to matters which are right or wrong; in matters of broad consideration there are no technically correct solutions, only culturally preferred options, in which fickle changes of fashion can be so important. Plan making has therefore become a highly sophisticated process of checks and balances, and complex bargaining and negotiation over time, in which powerful interests, such as the professions, both mediate and promote their own preferences.

However, we should not dismiss the plan-making system which has become institutionalized in the twentieth century as too shallow-rooted to be taken seriously. It is remarkable that during the century certain consistant views have been articulated, notably the view of the importance of the idea of the 'good environment' – healthy, attractive and convenient to its users. A persistent claim has been that the public regulation of the environment is important because the operation of the free market fails to provide those environmental conditions except in relatively rare circumstances. It is held that preferences such as family living at low-to-medium densities, the prevention of urban sprawl, the protection of the countryside, and provision for community identity in settlement planning, none of which would result from the operation of an unfettered market, may yet be derived from a sympathetic planning system.

Take the planned provision of open space – a typical example of a culturally derived environmental requirement, where public sector intervention to provide it seems so important. Open space standards have received a kind of technical blessing for over half a century, from the National Playing Fields Association's figure of 6 acres per thousand population, suggested in 1924, to Abercrombie's 10 acres per thousand for satellite towns in his *Greater London Plan*. The fact is that open space standards of this relative generosity only make sense in the context of broadly supported demands to reject the overcrowding and ill-health of the Victorian city. Societal preferences came first, articulated by professional and community interest groups, and in the nineteenth century, at least, met by individual philanthropists; scientific validation of a kind came second, which those responsible for plan making adopted.

The political context of town planning is particularly well shown in post-war Britain when there was a wholesale adoption of welfare and economic policies. There may have been totalitarianism in Central Europe, but the concept of a benevolent State prevailed in Britain, buttressed by a touching faith in institutions of local democracy and a cadre of enlightened, expert and neutral administrators. The harnessing of the professions to the work of local government was particularly significant. In this setting town plans for cities came into their own with a new found vigour. The redistributive policies inherent in decentralist land use strategies and the potential for public control over individual actions fitted the mood and political will for reconstruction. As Deakin (1987) describes, by the mid-1960s this conventional wisdom was crumbling; confidence in organs of the State weakened and unsolved problems lingered or even got worse, as with disparities in housing. Doubts about the welfare state brought no comfort to those who would still pin faith in the ability to prepare simple, easily understood plans for complex urban phenomena. The notion of town planning was reviled by both Left and Right (the Left because it was alleged that town planning was simply the handmaiden of capitalism and the Right because town planning was associated with an overblown, wasteful bureaucracy which weakened the capacity for individual enterprise). Keynesian economic orthodoxy proved an inadequate tool to deal with the recession of the 1970s and beyond; and social science, with which town planning was increasingly associated, failed to realize its former promise of explanatory power and a predictive capacity for future policy. By the 1980s an attitudinal revolution was virtually complete: belief had been lost in any positive role in government with regard to either long-term, strategic shaping of the urban environment or in shorter-term environmental management, while concern about the negative functions of plan making persisted. Planning relapsed into a lip service to policy often without much purpose.

It may seem surprising that with such a ready acknowledgement of the political context of plan making, a more explicit interpretation of urban change from the point of view of political economy has not been made. That analysis has been reflected in urban sociology, radical geography and elsewhere and vigorous intellectual speculation has characterized the last 20 years. It would not now be disputed that the changing spatial arrangements of the capitalist city have to be seen against the unfolding logic of the need to maximize its productive capabilities. The nineteenth-century manufacturing town concentrated the processes of accumulation, while in the twentieth century a changed urban infrastructure, leading first to suburbanization and then to metropolitanization, facilitated the greater circulation of capital. In other words cities, in their form and shape, concentrated or decentralized, and with internal land use patterns which reflect class divisions in society, mirror the capitalist system at various stages in its evolution. In the 1970s this analysis was accompanied by an argument which held that urban processes inherent in the capitalist city had a capacity to frustrate the redistributive aims of social policy, with the result that inequalities may actually be increased rather than reduced. Allocation decisions concerning housing, industrial zoning, provision of public facilities, and decisions as to transport networks came under scrutiny, and the agents or agencies of resource allocation were held to be main instruments of building and maintaining the capitalist city.

The argument does not die down as Harvey, one of the earliest (and most readable) proponents of this analysis continues to develop his particular perspective (1985a; 1985b). We can readily conclude: that the British city can only be understood in the context of the dynamics of capitalism; that the city is the centre for a set of cultural, political and consumer-based innovations; and that power groups command the utilization of space, so that cities are built up as a mosaic of dissimilar communities. This leaves us with a very powerful tool for understanding the processes of urban and metropolitan change in accordance with the nature of the economic system which underpins it.

There is no need to rehearse the chronology of urban history from earlier chapters to endorse that conclusion. Suffice to say by way of example that if we analyse our own contemporary situation we see a focus on an entrepreneurial culture which emphasizes competitive individualism and results in competition between localities and regions. In this way planning for the inner city becomes a question of dealing with the sharp disparities between the swathes of deprivation in particular neighbourhoods and the architecture of spectacle in the commerical, leisure and entertainment complexes in city-centre redevelopment schemes – the very result of the competition which is today held in such high favour.

On the future

Earlier chapters have chosen to work within this framework, though without subscribing to any analysis dependent on a 'political economy' point of view. It is for others to demonstrate the grand scenarios as they see them from this perspective. Our aim has been more modest, but there have often been some surprising illustrations to reveal. The research field is still wide open, with an agenda to penetrate history and discover just *why* certain interventionist and regulatory policies were formulated, and why others were not. *Who* were the beneficiaries? *What* were the reformist drives? There is still a corpus of knowledge to accumulate; this is the promise of planning history. The potential is rich because in detail the research is fine-tuned, compared with the preference for abstract theoretical analysis by the political economists, where a predictive capacity (in the sense of informed guidance to particular courses of action) is relatively weak. The empiricist, case-study approach (within a broad conceptual framework) is more likely to have an immediate applicability to other situations, because of the light which is shed on actual events and the personal and institutional relationships which govern them.

So what about the future? What are the next phases in plan making for cities? There seem to be three choices in the run-down to the end of the century and beyond. First, there is the continuation of present interventionist practices as the operative basis of plan making: *ad hoc*, piecemeal and no more than responsive to particular pressures, exemplified in the setting up of Urban Development Corporations, the designation of Enterprise Zones, and a maintenance of statutory forms of town planning – though with further limitations on local government practice in terms of its strategic role and comprehensive oversight of environmental change. This pragmatic approach would leave the institutional framework of town planning in place, though relatively toothless; it would maintain the possibility for lobbies and residential groups to use the system for local amenity protection, and give a measure of local control to district councils who rather like the powers accorded to them. The weakness of this option is that the system is unclear as to its ultimate effect or purpose.

The second choice is to return to the dirigiste spatial strategies of the 1940s and 1960s. The comprehensive plans of the war years were particularly compelling because they also offered a vision of urban form which was understood and to which support was given. There is a good deal of merit in this option because it can be readily argued that metropolitan change over the next quarter of a century does require broad strategic direction: how is wasted effort to be eliminated, unless the private sector is guided in matters such as housebuilding, and on new proposals for retail centres, business parks and the like in areas of pressured development on the urban fringes? Assuming that there could be some sort of consensus as to what sort of spatial strategies were to be put forward, there would still be real difficulties in being confident about the consistency of public and political support that would be forthcoming. Plan making in Britain is hamstrung by its dependent socio-political culture in which certain developments may be highly desirable, but power is rarely granted to agencies to realize them. Criticism is directed to planning for its non-achievement: one answer to that is to have more planning – of a certain focused, purposive kind. But this scarcely seems attainable. Christopher Wren's plan for London was not implemented; Victorian London was not the subject of Parisian-style urban surgery; Colin Buchanan's proposals for radical reconstruction to accommodate the motor vehicle were shelved; and Abercrombie's decentralist strategy has only succeeded because the operation of private markets dictated its success. Britain rather distrusts the grand plan.

A third choice is somewhere between the two. Plan making may shed some of its more institutionally based characteristics and statutory procedures (the first option) and become more a matter for pragmatic solutions, the difference being that it would adhere to a set of well-argued principles which would be seen as part of social and economic policy for our metropolitan, regional cities. Plan making would assume more the nature of a movement (as town planning did at the beginning of the century) and less that of a system kept in place by statute and formal practices in local government. One general aim would be the creation of socially acceptable, economically efficient and harmonious and environmentally pleasing cities. We might argue that in our present day the decentralist tradition of Howard, put into effect by Unwin and confirmed by

Abercrombie, still commands much support and while this remains the case the practice of plan making would be a matter of seizing those opportunities, wherever they are to be found, of creating the twenty-first-century Social City as a successor to Howard's vision. Fixed models would go; free-ranging innovation would replace them. Perhaps Marx was right when he wrote of the 'urbanisation of the countryside'. Further bouts of planned decentralization do seem in order, with the collar of the green belt removed in favour of a broadly green setting.

This advocacy would seem to accord with the facts of late-twentieth-century urban change. There is an increasingly outmoded urban form inherited from the industrial city, with squalid older environments, an over-generous provision of industrial land as a legacy of 'smoke-stack' cities, and an infrastructure of centrality in the heart of cities which is unsuited to forms of development in the future. Trends are already quite clear: city centres will be given over to entertainment, leisure and new retail magnets – a world of affluence and privilege adjoining the inner areas, with characteristics more akin to third-world deprivation. The outer city represents the other side of the coin, with its economic buoyancy and attractive residential areas.

Cities have become polymorphous and regionally dispersed, the various districts loosely held together around particular nodes of attraction. To plan for cities of this kind, planning becomes project-based around development schemes, both new and decentralist, and those aiming to redevelop older, outworn areas, though there will be a requirement for some coordinating overview. This is a very different approach to that which Holford's team in the Ministry of Town and Country Planning adopted as a comprehensive planning system in the mid-1940s. At that time, in common with their professional peers, they were vitally interested in what cities would actually be like, as a whole, as well as in their individual parts. Forty years later, and for the foreseeable future, that concerted design imperative has been lost from the agenda. Again, 40 years ago there was enough confidence about the future that it made sense to plan for it definitively; not so today, where rapidity of change and uncertainty as to the future weakens the resolve to plan for the longer term. Today a concern for urban appearance has been overtaken by others: for example, as a residual link with the social sciences, there is a fashionable interest in how cities function economically and socially, rather than in the visual stimuli they afford.

So we look again at the promise of further decanting of population and the establishment of new communities. We ask, as Marshall asked a hundred years ago: does it make sense for the poor and the unemployed to be concentrated so markedly in their present areas of deprivation? Does it not make sense for some, at least, of the urban underclass to have the opportunity of a new start in different surroundings? This is no more than what William Booth and Ebenezer Howard advocated in response to the challenge of the late Victorian city. This will not be done in forms of public-sector development; Reith's socially balanced, mixed communities in the New Towns may have offered a fleeting opportunity, but not now. The private market will not do it either.

Capitalism does need a helping hand and so we return to planning: moral purpose *can* be harnessed to social and economic objectives and the physical shaping of space. This could be a crucial component of plan making over the next quarter century: an overall purposive strategy and the release of skills to assemble land, inject infrastructure, design space, provide shelter and facilities, and create the conditions for the good life. This demands no great dreams for the future ideal city; it is more limited, but still a worthy and attainable role. The days of ideal cities and perfect communities have gone; so too have the assumptions which lay behind the post-war planning machine and the statutory functions discharged by local government. But the legitimacy of the activity of plan making has not gone with them; the mechanics of delivery may have to be changed.

All this accords rather well with the emergence of different styles of planning in recent years, a multi-faceted feature which might well be accentuated. There is, of course, the bedrock system of statutory development plan preparation and control by local authorities, changed but little since 1947. This has been accompanied by public investment planning where a major initiative is undertaken by local authorities or a public agency, as in New Towns, and forms of urban redevelopment. Both these approaches to plan making are dominantly public sector-led. But other styles of planning are not. Popular planning by community groups is one example, as typified in the work of community action and community architecture. Then there is private sector planning (always in evidence but probably more so in the future), where major private development projects are concerned with retail centres, science parks, high-technology developments, trade centres and the like – all with limited local authority imprint. Another style might be described as leverage planning, where the private sector has an enabling role to play: a private–public combination as in enterprise zones and the entrepreneural work of urban development corporations. Finally, we see another style of planning altogether: planning by private management, whereby the private sector actually takes over former public sector enterprises, as in the management of council houses by housing corporations. In short, we can see a multiplicity of styles of planning, with a weakening reliance on the unitary system of statutory planning undertaken by local authorities which has dominated plan making since the war.

As the variety of ways in which the planning function is discharged increases, so the relationships between professional roles will change. The planning profession was formally established in 1914 but for some little time the new activity of town planning had dwelt uncertainly in professional circles. The design tradition of architecture, and the fact that architects were active in the early development of town planning schemes (none more so than Unwin at Earswick, Letchworth and Hampstead), gave the Royal Institute of British Architects an early involvement, and its 1910 Town Planning Conference must have given it the edge over the other professions. But the municipal engineers who staffed local government offices claimed that the 1909 Act largely placed responsibility for schemes on them; they were holding conferences too, and the emergent town planning field was contested. The surveyors also had a stake through engaging in land assembly, layout and land management; practitioners were active in early scheme preparation, and Thomas Adams was the first president of the Town Planning Institute. Additionally the lawyers were prominent in the early movement, clerks to councils being important promoters of local authority schemes.

So town planning as a new profession emerged uncertainly around the competing claims of four professions which argued for, if not primacy, then a major stake. Professional responsibility for plan making took time to be resolved (Cherry, 1974); it was not until 1932 that the examinations of the Town Planning Institute could be taken without prior success in the examinations of one of the other sister professions; and it was not until 1959 that the Royal Charter gave the Institute symbolic parity. In the meantime the Schuster Report on the *Qualifications of planners* (Cmd 8059, 1950) emphasized the need to widen the membership of the Institute and suggested that chief planning officers need not possess technical skill in design. Planning was recognized as something different from the produce of engineering, architecture and surveying – though just what it was has defied definition for a very long time. Meanwhile, landscape architects had set up their own profession, their first president (1930) being a town planner, Thomas Mawson, and in post-war Britain the ground covered by town planning has fragmented further. The strength of the social sciences (geography in particular) usurped the previous dominance particularly of architecture and engineering, and special interests in planning, particularly in transportation and regional planning, followed by a late revival of urban design, demanded special recognition. Throughout this complex period the synoptic view that because town planning was an overarching profession, all its members should be educated to a competence in all its fields, has been hard to maintain.

All this is important for the ways in which plan making and the operation of the town planning system is actually regarded. It affects the whole business of preparing plans for cities: what sort of plans, for whom, and who is the author. We have seen in earlier chapters just how, over 150 years, very different approaches to plan making and forms of environmental control have been effected. Early town planning schemes were very different from the 1947-style development plan, and different again from structure plans. It is not to be expected that the two-dimensional plan has reached any final form.

It is unlikely, too, that we have established any firm and conclusive pattern for professional hegemony over plan making. Just as 80 years ago expertise in existing professions was reassembled to deal with the requirements of the new activity of town planning, and just as there have been adjustments subsequently, there is now a need to have inter-professional working of a more fluid kind than has been the case. But this is not just a matter for the four original professions; there are many other employment associations (social workers, housing experts and the like) who also impinge on town planning and they may find that it can broaden their own interests. Plan making is a composite exercise; plans reflect a wide constituency of interests, as we have seen throughout the history of the industrial city.

References

Aalen, F.H.A. 1987: Public housing in Ireland, 1880–1921. *Planning Perspectives*, 2, 2, 175–93.

Abercrombie, Patrick 1933: *Town and country planning*. Oxford: Oxford University Press.

— 1945: *Greater London plan 1944*. HMSO.

— and Jackson, H. 1948: *West Midlands plan*. Ministry of Town and Country planning, mimeo.

— and Matthew, R.H. 1949: *The Clyde Valley regional plan 1946*. Edinburgh: HMSO.

Adams, Ian H. 1978: *The making of modern Scotland*. London: Croom Helm.

Addison, Paul 1977: *The road to 1945: British politics and the second world war*. London: Quartet Books.

Adshead, S.D. 1923: *Town planning and town development*. London: Methuen.

Aldcroft, Derek H. 1986: *The British economy, vol. I, The years of turmoil 1920–1951*. Brighton: Wheatsheaf Books.

Aldridge, Henry R. 1915: *The case for town planning*. London: The National Housing and Town Planning Council.

Aldridge, Meryl, 1979: *The British new towns*. London: Routledge and Kegan Paul.

Ashworth, William 1954: *The genesis of modern British town planning*. London: Routledge and Kegan Paul.

Ball, Michael 1983: *Housing policy and economic power*. London: Methuen.

Bannon, M.J. (ed.) 1985: *The emergence of Irish planning 1880–1920*. Dublin: Turoe Press.

Barnett, Jonathan 1987: *The Elusive City : five centuries of design, ambition and miscalculation*. London: The Herbert Press.

Beattie, Susan 1980: *A revolution in London housing: LCC architects and their work 1893–1914*. London: The Greater London Council/The Architectural Press.

Beevers, Robert 1988: *The garden city Utopia: a critical biography of Ebenezer Howard*. London: Macmillan.

Bell, Colin and Rose 1969: *City fathers : the early history of town planning in Britain*. London: The Cresset Press.

Bolsterli, Margaret Jones 1977: *The early community at Bedford Park.* London: Routledge and Kegan Paul.

Booth, General William 1890: *In darkest England and the way out.* 1970 edn. London: Charles Knight.

Boumphrey, Geoffrey 1940: *Town and country tomorrow.* London: Thomas Nelson.

Bournville Village Trust 1941: *When we build again.* London: George Allen and Unwin.

Branson, Noreen and Heinemann, Margot 1971: *Britain in the nineteen thirties.* London: Weidenfeld and Nicholson.

Briggs, Asa 1959: *The age of improvement 1783–1867.* London: Longman.

— 1963: *Victorian cities.* London: Oldhams 1968 edn. Harmondworth: Pelican Books.

Bruton, Michael 1981: Colin Buchanan. In Cherry, Gordon E. (ed.), *Pioneers in British planning* London: The Architectural Press, 203–23.

Buchanan, C.D. 1958: *Mixed blessing : the motor in Britain,* London: Leonard Hill.

Buckingham, James Silk 1849: *National evils and practical remedies.*

Bullock, N. 1987: Plans for post-war housing in the U.K.: the case for mixed development and the flat. *Planning Perspectives* 2, 1, 71–98.

— and Read, James 1985: *The movement for housing reform in Germany and France 1840–1914.* Cambridge: Cambridge University Press.

Burke, Gerald 1976: *Townscapes.* Harmondsworth: Pelican Books.

Burnett, John 1978: *A social history of housing.* Newton Abbott: David and Charles.

Carter, Harold 1983: *An introduction to urban historical geography.* London: Edward Arnold.

Central Housing Advisory Committee (Parker Morris Report) 1961: *Homes for today and tomorrow.* London: HMSO.

Chadwick, George F. 1966: *The park and the town: public landscape in the 19th and 20th centuries.* London: The Architectural Press.

Champion, A.G. 1983: Population trends in the 1970s. In Goddard, J.B. and Champion A.G., (eds), *The urban and regional transformation of Britain.* London: Methuen, 187–214.

Checkland, S.G. 1981: *The upas tree.* Glasgow: University of Glasgow Press.

— 1983: *British public policy 1776–1939 : an economic, social and political perspective.* Cambridge: Cambridge University Press.

Cherry, Gordon E. 1970: *Town planning in its social context.* London: Leonard Hill.

— 1972: *Urban change and planning.* Henley on Thames: G.T. Foulis.

— 1974: *The evolution of British town planning.* Leighton Buzzard: Leonard Hill.

— 1976, Aspects of urban renewal. In Hancock, Tom (ed.), *Growth and change in the future city region.* London: Leonard Hill.

— 1979, The town planning movement and the late Victorian city. *Trans. IBG,* 4, 2, new series, 306–19.

— 1980: The place of Neville Chamberlain in British town planning. In Cherry, Gordon E. (ed.), *Shaping an urban world.* London: Mansell, 161–79.

— 1981: George Pepler 1882–1959. In Cherry, Gordon E. (ed.), *Pioneers in British planning*. London: The Architectural Press, 131–49.

— (ed.) 1981: *Pioneers in British planning*. London: The Architectural Press.

— 1982: *The politics of town planning*. Harlow: Longman.

— and Penny, Leith, 1986: *Holford: a study in architecture, planning and civic design*. London: Mansell.

— 1987: Review article. *Planning Perspectives*, 2, 1, 99–104.

— 1988: The urban crisis: explanations and the future. *The Planner*, 74, 1, 20–4.

Chisholm, Michael 1983: City, region and – what kind of problem? in Patten, J. (ed.), *The expanding city: essays in honour of Professor Jean Gottman*. London: Academic Press, 39–76.

Cole, G.D.H. and Cole, M.I. 1937: *The condition of Britain*. London: Victor Gollancz.

— 1945 *Building and planning*. London: Cassell.

Coleman, Alice *et al*. 1985: *Utopia on trial*. London: Hilary Shipman.

Commissioners for the Special Areas (England and Wales) 1936: *Third report*. London: HMSO.

Committee on Public Participation in Planning (The Skeffington Report) 1969: *People and planning*. London: HMSO.

Coones, Paul and Patten, John 1986: *The Penguin guide to the landscape of England and Wales*. Harmondsworth: Penguin Books.

Crawford, Alan 1985: *C.R. Ashbee: architect, designer and romantic socialist*. Yale University Press.

Creese, W.L. 1966: *The search for environment: the garden city before and after*, Yale University Press.

Cronin, James E. 1984: *Labour and society in Britain 1918–1979*. London: Batsford.

Cullen, Gordon 1961: *The concise townscape*. London: The Architectural Press.

Cullingworth, J.B. 1975: *Environmental planning, 1939–1969, Vol I, Reconstruction and land use planning 1939–1947*. London: HMSO.

— 1979: *Environmental planning, Vol. III, New towns policy*. London: HMSO.

— 1988: *Town and country planning in Britain*. Tenth edition. London: George Allen and Unwin.

Daunton, M.J. 1977: *Coal metropolis Cardiff 1870–1914*. Leicester: Leicester University Press.

— 1983: *House and home in the Victorian city: working class housing 1850–1914*. London: Edward Arnold.

— 1987: *A property-owning democracy?* London: Faber and Faber.

Davies, J.G. 1972: *The evangelistic bureaucrat: a study of a planning exercise in Newcastle upon Tyne*. London: Tavistock.

Day, Michael G. 1981: The contribution of Sir Raymond Unwin and R. Barry Parker to the development of site planning theory and practice c. 1890–1918. In Sutcliffe, Anthony, (ed.) *British town planning: the formative years*. Leicester: Leicester University Press, 156–99.

Deakin, Nicholas 1987: *The politics of welfare*. London: Methuen.

Dennis, Norman 1970: *People and Planning*. London: Faber.

Dennis, Richard 1984: *English industrial cities of the 19th century: a social geography.* Cambridge: Cambridge University Press.

Departmental committee set up by the Minister of War Transport, 1946: *Design and layout of roads in built-up areas.* London: HMSO.

Design of dwellings sub committee of the Ministry of Health Central Housing Advisory Committee (The Dudley Report) 1944: *The design of dwellings.* London: HMSO.

Dickens, Charles 1854: *Hard times,* London. 1969 edn. Harmondsworth: Penguin.

Dolman, Frederick 1895: *Municipalities at work: the municipal policy of six great towns and its influence on their social welfare.* London: Methuen. 1985 edn. New York: Garland Publishing.

Donnison, David and Ungerson, Clare 1982: *Housing policy.* Harmondsworth: Penguin.

Durant, R. 1939: *Watling: a survey of social life on a new estate.* London: S. King.

Dyos, H.J. 1961: *Victorian suburb: a study of the growth of Camberwell.* Leicester: Leicester University Press.

— and Aldcroft, D.H. 1969: *British transport: an economic survey from the seventeenth century to the twentieth.* Leicester: Leicester University Press. 1974 edn. Harmondsworth: Pelican Books.

— and Wolff, Michael (eds.) 1973: *The Victorian city: images and realities.* 2 vols. London: Routledge and Kegan Paul.

Edwards, Arthur M. 1981: *The design of suburbia: a critical study in environmental history.* London: Pembridge Press.

Elson, Martin J. 1986: *Green belts: conflict and mediation in the urban fringe.* London: Heinemann.

Engels, Frederick 1845: *The condition of the working class in England.* 1969 edn. London: Panther Books.

Esher, Lionel 1981: *A broken wave: the rebuilding of England 1940–1980.* Allen Lane. 1983 edn. Harmondsworth: Pelican.

Evans, Hazel 1972: *New towns: the British experience.* London: Charles Knight.

Expert Committee on compensation and betterment 1942: *Final Report.* Cmd 6386. London: HMSO.

Faulkner, Tom and Greg, Andrew 1987: *John Dobson, Newcastle architect 1787–1865.* Tyne and Wear Museums.

Fishman, Robert 1977: *Urban utopias in the twentieth century.* New York: Basic Books.

Flinn, M.W. 1965: Introduction to Edwin Chadwick, *Report on the sanitary condition of the labouring population of Great Britain.* Edinburgh: Edinburgh University Press.

Forshaw, J.H. and Abercrombie, Patrick 1943: *County of London plan,* London: Macmillan.

Frazer, W.M. 1950: *A history of English public health.* London: Ballière, Tindall and Cox.

Fried, Albert and Elman, Richard M. (eds) 1969: *Charles Booth's London,* London: Hutchinson. 1971 edn. Harmondsworth: Pelican.

Garside, Pat L. 1988: 'Unhealthy areas': town planning, eugenics and the slums 1890–1945. *Planning Perspectives*, 3, 1, 24–46.

Gaskell, S. Martin 1983: *Building control: national legislation and the introduction of local bye-laws in Victorian England*. London: Bedford Square Press.

— 1986: *Model housing: from the Great Exhibition to the Festival of Britain*. London: Mansell.

Gauldie, Enid 1974: *Cruel habitations: a history of working class housing*. London: Allen and Unwin.

Gavin, Hector 1847: *Unhealthiness of London and the necessity of remedial measures*. London: John Churchill. 1985 edn. New York: Garland Publishing.

Geddes, Patrick 1915: *Cities in evolution: an introduction to the town planning movement and to the study of civics*. Williams and Norgate. 1968 edn. London: Ernest Benn.

George, Henry 1880: *Progress and poverty*. New York. 1911 edn. London: Dent.

— 1884: *Social problems*. London: Kegan Paul, Trench, Trubner. 1931 edn.

Gibberd, Sir Frederick 1972: 'The master design; landscape; housing; the town centres' in Evans, Hazel: *The new towns: The British experience*. London: Charles Knight, pp. 88–101.

Gibbon, Sir Gwilym 1942: *Reconstruction and town and country planning*. London: The Architect and Building News.

Goddard, J.B. and Champion, A.G. (eds), 1983: *The urban and regional transformation of Britain*. London: Methuen.

Gordon, George (ed.) 1986: *Regional cities in the U.K., 1890–1980*. London: Harper and Row.

Grant, James 1837: *The great metropolis*. Two vols. London: Saunders and Otley. 1985 edn. New York: Garland Publishing.

Green, Brigid Grafton 1977: *Hampstead Garden Suburb 1907–1977: a history*. London: Hampstead Garden Suburb Residents Association.

Gregory, Terence 1973: 'Coventry' in Holliday, John (ed.): *City centre redevelopment: A study of British city centre planning and case studies of five English city centres*. London: Charles Knight.

Hague, Cliff 1984: *The development of planning thought*. London: Hutchinson.

Hall, Peter *et al.* 1973: *The containment of urban England*. Two vols. London: George Allen and Unwin.

— 1974: *Urban and regional planning*. Harmondsworth: Pelican Books.

— and Hay, Dennis 1980: *Growth centres in the European urban system*. London: Heinemann.

— (ed.) 1981: *The inner city in context*. London: Heinemann.

— Breheny, Michael, Mcquaid, Ronald and Hart, Douglas 1987: *Western sunrise: the genesis and growth of Britain's major high tech corridor*. London: Allen and Unwin.

— 1988: *Cities of tomorrow: an intellectual history of urban planning and design in the twentieth century*. Oxford: Basil Blackwell.

Hambleton, Robin 1986: *Rethinking policy planning*. Bristol: School for Advanced Urban Studies, University of Bristol.

Hardy, Dennis 1979: *Alternative communities in nineteenth century England*. London: Longman.

— and Ward, Colin 1984: *Arcadia for all: the legacy of a makeshift landscape*. London: Mansell.

Harley, J.B. 1973: England *circa* 1850. In Darby, H.C. (ed.) *A new historical geography of England*. Cambridge: Cambridge University Press, 527–94.

Harloe, Michael 1975: *Swindon: A Town in Transition*. London: Heinemann.

Harrison, Michael 1981: Housing and town planning in Manchester before 1914. In Sutcliffe, Anthony, *British town planning: the formative years*. Leicester: Leicester University Press, 106–53.

Harvey, D. 1985a: *Consciousness and the urban experience*. Baltimore: Johns Hopkins University Press.

— 1985b: *The urbanization of capital*. Baltimore: Johns Hopkins University Press.

Haverfield, F. 1913: *Ancient town planning*. Oxford: Clarendon Press.

Hawtree, Martin 1981: The emergence of the town planning profession. In Sutcliffe, Anthony, (ed.), *British town planning: the formative years*. Leicester: Leicester University Press, 64–104.

Hayek, Friedrich A. 1944: *The road to serfdom*. Chicago: University of Chicago Press.

Henderson, Philip 1967: *William Morris: his life, work and friends*. London: Thames and Hudson. 1986 edn. London: Andre Deutch.

Hennock, E.P. 1982: Central/local government relations in England: an outline 1800–1950. *Urban History Yearbook*. Leicester: Leicester University Press, 38–49.

Henslowe, Philip 1984: *Ninety years on: an account of the Bournville Village Trust*. BVT.

Herington, John 1984: *The outer city*. London: Harper and Row.

Hill, Octavia 1883: *Homes of the London poor*. London: Macmillan. 1970 edn. London: Frank Cass.

Hiorns, Frederick R. 1956: *Town building in history*. London: George G. Harrap.

Hohenberg, Paul M. and Lees Lynn Hollen 1985: *The making of urban Europe*. Harvard: Harvard University Press.

Holden, C.H. and Holford, W.G. 1951: *The city of London: a record of destruction and survival*. London: The Architectural Press.

Hole, James 1866: *The homes of the working classes with suggestions for their improvement*. London: Longmans, Green. 1985 edn. New York: Garland Publishing.

Hollingshead, John 1861: *Ragged London in 1861*. London: Smith, Elder. 1985 edn. New York: Garland Publishing.

Home, Robert K. 1982: *Inner city regeneration*. London: E. & F.N. Spon.

Hopkins, Eric 1986: Working-class housing in Birmingham during the Industrial Revolution. *International Review of Social History*, XXXI, I, 80–94.

Horsey, Miles 1988: Multi-storey council housing in Britain. *Planning Perspectives*, 3, 2, pp. 167–196.

Horsfall, T.C. 1904: *The improvement of the dwellings and surroundings of the people: the example of Germany*. Manchester: Manchester University Press.

Howard, Ebenezer 1902: *Garden cities of tomorrow*. London: Faber. 1965 edn.

Hughes, Michael R. (ed.) 1971: *The letters of Lewis Mumford and Frederic J. Osborn*. Bath: Adams and Dart.

Hygiene Committee of the Women's Group on Public Welfare 1943: *Our towns: a close-up*. Oxford: Oxford University Press.

Jackson, Alan A. 1973: *Semi detached London: suburban development, life and transport, 1900–39*. London: George Allen and Unwin.

Jackson, Frank 1985: *Sir Raymond Unwin: architect, planner and visionary*. London: Zwemmer.

Jacobs, Jane 1961: *The death and life of great American cities*. New York: Random House.

Jephcott, Pearl and Robinson, Hilary 1971: *Homes in high flats*. Edinburgh: Oliver and Boyd.

Jewkes, John 1948: *Ordeal by planning*. London: Macmillan.

Jones, Gareth Stedman 1971: *Outcast London: a study in the relationship between classes in Victorian Society*. Oxford: Oxford University Press. 1976 edn. Harmondsworth: Peregrine.

Kellett, John R. 1969: *Railways and Victorian cities*. London: Routledge and Kegan Paul.

Kropotkin, Peter 1899: *Fields, factories and workshops tomorrow*. 1974 edn. London: George Allen and Unwin.

Lawless, Paul and Brown, Frank 1986: *Urban growth and change in Britain*. London: Harper and Row.

Lees, Andrew 1985: *Cities perceived: urban society in European and American thought, 1820–1940*. Manchester: Manchester University Press.

London, Jack 1903: *The people and the abyss*. New York: Macmillan. 1978 edn. London: Journeyman Press.

London County Council 1961: *The planning of a new town*. Alec Tiranti.

Macfadyen, Dugald 1933: *Sir Ebenezer Howard and the town planning movement*. Manchester: Manchester University Press.

Mandelker, D.R. 1962: *Green belts and urban growth: English town and country planning in action*. Madison: University of Wisconsin Press.

Manners, Gerald and Morris, Diana 1986: *Office policy in Britain: a review*. Norwich: Geo Books.

Manzoni, Herbert J. 1941: Problems of decentralization: central redevelopment and satellite towns. Statement II. In Towndrow, F.E. (ed.) *Replanning Britain*. London: Faber and Faber, 91–9.

Marriott, Oliver 1967: *The property boom*. London: Hamish Hamilton.

Marshall, Alfred 1884: The housing of the London poor, I. Where to house them. *Contemporary Review*, 45.

Marwick, Arthur 1968: *Britain in the century of total war*. London: The Bodley Head. 1970 edn. Harmondsworth: Pelican.

Mass-observation 1943: *People's homes*. London: John Murray.

Masterman, C.F.G. 1909: *The condition of England*. London: Methuen.

McAllister, Gilbert and Glen Elizabeth, (eds) 1945: *Homes, towns and countryside: a practical plan for Britain*. London: B.T. Batsford.

McKay, David H. and Cox, Andrew W. 1979: *The politics of urban change*. London: Croom Helm.

Mears, Sir Frank 1948: *A regional survey and plan for central south east*

Scotland. Edinburgh: Central and South East Scotland Regional Planning Advisory Committee, HMSO.

Meller, Helen 1980: 'Cities and evolution: Patrick Geddes as an international prophet of town planning before 1914' in Sutcliffe, Anthony (ed.): *The rise of modern urban planning 1800–1914*. London: Mansell, pp. 199–223.

— 1981: Patrick Geddes 1854–1932. In Cherry, Gordon E., *Pioneers in British planning*. London: The Architectural Press, 46–71.

Melling, Joseph 1983: *Rent strikes: people's struggle for housing in West Scotland 1890–1916*. Edinburgh: Polygon Books.

M'Gonigle, G.C.M. and Kirby, J. 1936: *Poverty and public health*. London: Victor Gollancz.

Miller, Mervyn 1981: Raymond Unwin 1863–1940. In Cherry, Gordon E., *Pioneers in British planning*. London: The Architectural Press, 72–102.

Mingay, G.E. 1986: *The transformation of Britain 1830–1939*. London: Routledge and Kegan Paul. 1987 edn. London: Paladin.

Ministry of Health 1935: *Town and country planning in England and Wales*. London: HMSO.

Ministry of Health, Ministry of Works 1944: *Housing manual 1944*. London: HMSO.

Ministry of Health 1949: *Housing manual 1949*. London: HMSO.

Ministry of Housing and Local Government 1952: *The density of residential areas*. London: HMSO.

Ministry of Housing and Local Government 1953: *Design in town and village*. London: HMSO.

Ministry of Housing and Local Government 1964: *The south east study 1961–1981*. London: HMSO.

Ministry of Housing and Local Government 1966: *The Deeplish study: improvement possibilities in an area of Rochdale*. London: HMSO.

Ministry of Town and Country Planning 1947: *The redevelopment of central areas*. London: HMSO.

More, Thomas 1518: *Utopia*. 1965 translation. Harmondsworth: Penguin Books.

Morris, A.E.J. 1972: *History of urban form: prehistory to the Renaissance*. London: George Godwin.

Morris, R.J. 1986: Urbanization. In Langton John, and Morris, R.J. (eds), *Atlas of industrializing Britain*. London: Methuen, 164–79.

Morrison, Bill 1982: London: current trends and future policies. *Built Environment*, 8, 1, 71–6.

Muchnick, David H. 1970: *Urban renewal in Liverpool: a study of the politics of redevelopment*. Occasional Papers on Social Administration no. 33. London: G. Bell & Sons.

Mumford, Lewis 1938: *The Culture of cities*. London: Secker and Warburg.

— 1961: *The city in history*. London: Secker and Warburg.

Munton, Richard 1983: *London's green belt: containment in practice*. London: George Allen and Unwin.

Murie, Alan 1973: Planning in Northern Ireland: a survey. *Town Planning Review*. 44, 4, 337–58.

Muthesius, Stefan 1982: *The English terraced house.* Yale University Press.

Newman, Oscar 1972: *Defensible space.* New York: Macmillan.

Oliver, Paul, Davis, Ian and Bentley, Ian 1981: *Dunroamin: the suburban semi and its enemies.* London: Barrie and Jenkins.

Olsen, Donald J. 1976: *The growth of Victorian London.* London: B.T. Batsford. 1979 edn. Harmondsworth: Peregrine Books.

Orbach, L.F. 1977: *Homes for heroes: a study of the evolution of British public housing, 1915–21.* London: Seeley, Service.

Orwell, George 1937: *The road to Wigan Pier.* London: Victor Gollancz. 1962 edn. Harmondsworth: Penguin.

— 1939: *Coming up for Air,* London: Victor Gollancz. 1962 edn. Harmondsworth: Penguin.

Osborn, F.J. 1918: *New towns after the war.* London: J.M. Dent, 1942 (revised).

— and Whittick, Arnold 1963: *The new towns: the answer to megalopolis.* London: Leonard Hill.

Ostrowski, Waclaw 1970: *Contemporary town planning: from the origins to the Athens Charter.* The Hague: International Federation for Housing and Town Planning.

Owen, Robert 1813–14: *A new view of society.* 1970 edn. Harmondsworth: Penguin Books.

— 1821: *Report to the County of Lanark.* 1970 edn. Harmondsworth: Penguin Books.

Pearson, Lynn F. 1988: *The architectural and social history of cooperative living.* London: Macmillan.

Pilgrim Trust 1938: *Men without work.* London: Pilgrim Trust.

Planning Advisory Group 1965: *The future of development plans.* London: HMSO.

Plowden, William 1973: *The motor car and politics in Britain.* Harmondsworth: Pelican.

Pooley, Colin G. and Irish, Sandra 1987: Access to housing on Merseyside, 1919–39. *Trans. IBG,* 12, 2, new series, 177–90.

Powell, C.G. 1980: *An economic history of the British building industry 1815–1979.* London: The Architectural Press. 1982 edn. London: Methuen.

Power, N.S. 1965: *The forgotten people.* Evesham: Arthur James.

Preston, W.C. 1883: *The bitter cry of outcast London.* London. 1969 edn. Bath: Cedric Chivers.

Priestley, J.B. 1934: *English journey.* London: William Heinemann.

Punter, John 1987: A history of aesthetic control, part 2, 1953–1985. *Town Planning Review.* 58, 1, 29–62.

Purdom, C.B. 1925: *The building of satellite towns.* London: J.M. Dent.

Rasmussen, Steen Eiler 1934: *London: the unique city.* 1974 edn, 2 vols. Massachusetts Institute of Technology.

Ravetz, Alison 1974a: From working class tenement to modern flat: local authorities and multi-storey housing between the wars. In Sutcliffe, Anthony (ed.) *Multi-storey living: the British working class experience.* London: Croom Helm.

— 1974b: *Modern estate: planned housing at Quarry Hill.* London: Croom Helm.

— 1980: *Remaking cities.* London: Croom Helm.

— 1986: *The government of space: town planning in modern society.* London: Faber and Faber.

Richards, J.M. 1946: *The castles on the ground: the anatomy of suburbia.* London: The Architectural Press. 1973 edn. London: John Murray.

Richardson, Benjamin Ward 1876: *Hygeia, a city of health.* London: Macmillan. 1985 edn. New York: Garland Publishing.

Rosenau, Helen 1959: *The ideal city: its architectural evolution in Europe.* London: Methuen, 1983 edn.

Royal Commission on the distribution of the industrial population (the Barlow Commission) 1940: *Report.* Cmd 6153, London: HMSO.

Schaffer, Frank 1970: *The new town story.* London: MacGibbon and Kee. 1972 edn. London: Granada.

Self, Peter 1957: *Cities in flood: the problems of urban growth.* London: Faber and Faber.

Sharp, Elizabeth 1986: The acquisition of the London green belt estates: a study of inter-war relations. Ph.D. thesis, University of London.

Sharp, Thomas 1932: *Town and countryside: some aspects of urban and rural development.* Oxford: Oxford University Press.

— 1940: *Town planning.* Harmondsworth: Penguin.

Sheail, John 1981: *Rural conservation in inter-war Britain.* Oxford: Clarendon Press.

Simon, E.D. 1929: *How to abolish the slums.* London: Longmans, Green.

— 1945: *Rebuilding Britain – a twenty year plan.* London: Victor Gollancz.

Simpson, Michael 1985: *Thomas Adams and the modern planning movement.* London: Mansell.

Sitte, Camillo 1889: *City building according to artistic principles.* Vienna.

Smailes, A.E. 1953: *The geography of towns.* London: Hutchinson.

Struther, Jan 1939: *Mrs Miniver.* London: Chatto and Windus. 1980 edn. London: Futura Publications.

Sutcliffe, Anthony 1980: The growth of public intervention in the British urban environment during the nineteenth century: a structural approach. *Papers on Planning and Design.* 24, Toronto: Department of Urban and Regional Planning, University of Toronto.

— 1981: *Towards the planned city: Germany, Britain, the United States and France 1780–1914.* Oxford: Basil Blackwell.

Swenarton, M. 1981: *Homes fit for heroes: the politics and architecture of early state housing in Britain.* London:

Tarn, John Nelson 1973: *Five per cent philanthropy: an account of housing in urban areas between 1840 and 1914.* Cambridge: Cambridge University Press.

Taylor, Nicholas 1973: *The village in the city.* London: Temple Smith.

The Control of Land Use. 1944. Cmd 6537. London: HMSO.

Thomas, Andrew D. 1986: *Housing and urban renewal.* London: George Allen and Unwin.

Thomas, David 1970: *London's green belt.* London: Faber and Faber.

Thompson, E.P. and Yeo, Eileen 1973: *The unknown Mayhew: selections from the Morning Chronicle 1849–50.* Merlin Press. 1973 edn. Harmondsworth: Pelican Books.

Timms, Edward and Kelley, David 1985: *Unreal city: urban experience in modern European literature and art.* Manchester: Manchester University Press.

Traffic in Towns. 1963. Reports of the Steering Group and Working Group appointed by the Minister of Transport. London: HMSO.

Trevelyan, G.M. 1942: *English social history.* New York: Longmans. 1944 edn. London: Longmans.

Tripp, H. Alker 1942: *Town planning and road traffic.* London: Edward Arnold.

Tudor Walters Report 1918: of the Committee appointed by the President of the Local Government Board and the Secretary for Scotland to consider questions of Building Construction in connection with the provision of dwellings for the working classes in England and Wales and Scotland and to report upon the methods for securing economy and despatch in the provision of such dwellings, Cmd 9191.

Unwin, Raymond 1909: *Town planning in practice: An introduction to the art of designing cities and suburbs.* London: Fisher Unwin.

Vine, J.R. Somers 1879: *English municipal institutions: their growth and development 1835–1879 statistically illustrated.* London: Waterlow. 1985 edn. New York: Garland Publishing.

Waller, P.J. 1983: *Town, city and nation: England 1850–1914.* Oxford: Oxford University Press.

Wannop, Urlan 1986: Regional fulfilment: planning into administration in the Clyde Valley. *Planning Perspectives,* 1, 3, 207–29.

Ward, Stephen V. 1988: *The geography of interwar Britain: the state and uneven development.* London: Routledge.

Warren, Herbert and Davidge, W.R. 1930: *Decentralisation of Population and Industry.* London: P.S. King.

Wates, Nick 1976: *The battle for Tolmers Square.* London: Routledge and Kegan Paul.

— and Knevitt, Charles 1987: *Community architecture.* Harmondsworth: Penguin.

Watson, J. Paton and Abercrombie, Patrick 1943: *A plan for Plymouth.* Plymouth: Underhill.

Webb, Sir Aston (ed.) 1921: *London of the future.* London: T. Fisher Unwin.

Weber, Adna Ferin 1899: *The growth of cities in the nineteenth century: a study in statistics.* New York: Macmillan. 1963 edn. Cornel University Press.

West, John 1983: *Town records.* Chichester: Phillimore.

West Midlands Group 1948: *Conurbation, a planning survey of Birmingham and the Black Country.* London: The Architectural Press.

White, Arnold 1886: *The problem of a great city.* London: Remington. 1985 edn. New York: Garland Publishing.

White, Morton and White, Lucia 1962: *The intellectual versus the city.* 1977 ed. Oxford: Oxford University Press.

Whitehand, J.W.R. 1987: *The changing face of cities.* Oxford: Basil Blackwell.

Wilkes, Lyall and Dodds, Gordon 1964: *Tuneside classical: the Newcastle of Grainger, Dobson and Clayton.* London: John Murray.

Wilkinson, Ellen 1939: *The town that was murdered.* London: Victor Gollancz.

Williams-Ellis, Clough 1928: *England and the octopus.* Portmeirion:

— (ed.) 1938: *Britain and the beast.* London: J.M. Dent.

Wohl, Anthony S. 1974: *The eternal slum: housing and social policy in Victorian London.* London: Edward Arnold.

— 1983 *Endangered lives: public health in Victorian Britain.* London: Dent: 1984 edn. London: Methuen.

Wolfe, Lawrence 1945: *The Reilly plan: a new way of life.* London: Nicholson and Watson.

Wright, Myles 1982: *Lord Leverhulme's unknown venture.* London: Hutchinson Benham.

Yelling, J.A. 1986: *Slums and slum clearance in Victorian London.* London: Allen and Unwin.

Young, Ken 1985: Re-reading the municipal progress: a crisis revisited. In Loughlin, Martin, Gelfand, M. David, Young Ken, (eds). *Half a century of municipal decline 1935–1985.* London: George Allen and Unwin.

— and Garside, Patricia L. 1982: *Metropolitan London: politics and urban change 1837–1981.* London: Edward Arnold.

— and Mills, Liz 1983: *Managing the post-industrial city.* London: Heinemann.

Young, Michael and Willmott, Peter 1957: *Family and kinship in east London.* London: Routledge and Kegan Paul. Harmondswoth: 1962 edn. Pelican.

Young, T. 1934: *Becontree and Dagenham.* Pilgrim Trust and Becontree Social Survey Committee.

Index